Going the Distance

The Making of a World-Class
Endurance Cyclist

Joe Barr

with Robin Sheeran

Gill Books

Gill Books
Hume Avenue
Park West
Dublin 12
www.gillbooks.ie

Gill Books is an imprint of M.H. Gill and Co.

978 07171 9060 7

Design and print origination by O'K Graphic Design, Dublin
Edited by Jane Rogers
Proofread by Ruairí Ó Brógáin
Maps by Derry Dillon

Printed by CPI Group (UK) Ltd, Croydon, CR0 4YY.
This book is typeset in 11.5/17 pt Sabon.

A CIP catalogue record for this book is available from the British Library.

5 4 3 2 1

MIX
Paper from
responsible sources
FSC
www.fsc.org   FSC® C020471

This book is dedicated to four people.

First and foremost to my mum, Elizabeth, who taught me that kindness is an easy thing to give.

To Jillian, my one true compass. Thank you for taking my hand again and for making the greatest leap of faith. I will never let go.

And to my boys, Reuben and Ross; you teach me everything about unconditional love. I love you both to the moon and back.

For all those in the dark: keep the bike moving forward, the light will find you again.

Acknowledgements

A heartfelt thank-you to Robin Sheeran, who saw the potential in this story and who helped me wrestle it from the past. It's been a challenging but forgiving process, and I am grateful to have done it with you.

To Sarah Liddy from Gill Books, who believed in the story and paved the way for action.

To my family for all the support they provided along the bumpy way.

To Tommy Pyper and his wife, Dorothy: everyone needs someone to encourage their potential. I probably wouldn't be here today had you not picked me up and brought me home from my first crash.

To Brendan Clarke and Maria Radtke, who gave me my first professional opportunity.

To Micky Kerr – your treatment room provided a refuge and a springboard for my body and mind.

To Tony Culley-Foster, who walked the walk before me and who taught me that 'there always needs to be a story'. Some things endure, and you are one of them!

To my US brothers: Len Forkas, Marc Poland and Bob Gentile. You have opened your homes and your hearts to me, and it's a privilege to call you my friends.

A special mention to Gary Fryett, who was instrumental in creating some of my greatest mainstream and cyclo-cross memories.

Another special mention to Alan Hamilton, who has contributed so much to the team and who walked with me during dark and difficult times, both on and off the bike.

There have been team members who have travelled hundreds of miles – and members who have travelled thousands. If you have helped, crewed, fed, watered, filmed, listened and been part of Team Joe Barr in any way: thank you, I owe you every mile.

To the global ultra-cycling community – you have given me a place to call home. Thank you for being my tribe. I'll see you on the start line.

Contents

Prologue

I can still remember exactly how it felt.

The road ramped up out of the forest and onto the high bogland. Leaning hard on the pedals, I pushed ahead to the top of the climb, then pulled away over the crest. My heart was thumping fast and I reached down for my bottle, eased my aching legs and glanced behind me. Not a soul to be seen. I was off the front of the race in the dead silence of an Irish country road.

Over my shoulder, twenty hardmen were still toiling up through the forest, their bikes swinging from side to side. I shifted through the gears and swooped almost silently past stone walls and thorn bushes. A blackface sheep skittered across the way and over a ditch. In a mile or so the road swept steeply down to the left.

I relaxed my hands on the bars and slipped back a little on the saddle to shift the weight off my arms. These heart-stopping descents are payback time for the grinding climbs. Bum up, head down – body tensed for the pothole or the farmyard dog. My fingers twitched over the brakes, picking the exact line through the left-hand bend, leaning steeply through the apex. The tick, tick, tick, whirr of the freewheel and then powering on, down into the village.

It was the first time I'd broken away from a pack of experienced riders. The prize was almost within my grasp. At 16 years old I already knew this had to be my life, straining my heart, soul and sinew to throw myself head first across a finish line. I had to be away from the monotony of home and school, away from closed minds and a humdrum life to a place where the multicoloured peloton flashed across town squares and crowds filled the air with shouts of 'Allez! Allez! Allez!'

Now, forty years later, I found myself slumped in the front seat of a crew car in the Arizona desert spooning oatmeal into my mouth from a plastic bowl. I glanced at my hands, swollen and calloused. Every part of my body hurt. I was at the rough end of a 3,000-mile race across the North American continent. That fleeting memory of my first win came at me out of nowhere. My fresh-faced, childish joy as I threw my arms high in the air and the bike spun across the finish line next to a lemonade warehouse.

Was I even the same person? My body laughed at the idea. Thousands upon thousands of miles pushing myself to the limit and beyond had left me with the usual cyclists' unwanted tattoos. The scar tissue on my knees and elbows from countless crashes that left me surfing the tarmac. Broken bones – so many broken bones. My face held traces of reconstructive surgery, one smashed cheekbone still sitting higher than the other.

I wiped the salty sweat from my face and cast my eyes across the desert horizon.

'I'm still that kid,' I whispered. 'I'm still that kid.'

CHAPTER I

Nurse Duffy and the Green Sunbeam

I can't remember the first time I rode a bike. I'm told I was just three years old. It was a Sunbeam, a little metallic green thing with chunky tyres. I learned my handling skills between the ridges in the vegetable patch in our back garden. We lived in a place called Newtowncunningham, a small village that straggles along the main Derry to Letterkenny road, just a few miles from the border with Northern Ireland. It's in County Donegal, not the mountainous, Irish-speaking west Donegal of the tourist brochures but a calmer, flatter, more everyday sort of a place.

We lived down a little road that ran from the village towards the sea and finally lost interest in itself and petered out into Lough Swilly. No one ever came down there apart from our neighbours and the birdwatchers going to the wildlife sanctuary by the coast. We had our own close little community, and many of the families still live in the same houses. The disused track of the old Lough Swilly Railway ran by our house and there was a railway bridge at the bottom of the garden.

I was born in June 1959. My mother's family were local people and my grandparents lived a mile or so up the road. They were by no means wealthy and my grandfather had spent much of his life away in England working on construction sites. They were caring people who loved me a lot and I spent a big part of my childhood with them. My father's family were from Derry. They had a wholesale grocery business, but they were also egg and tea merchants. My dad, his brothers and his sister worked in the Donegal side of the business, Barr Bros and North Western Tea Co., which had a tea-blending warehouse in Newtowncunningham.

My mum went out to earn money from an early age, living and working in big farmhouses over the border in County Antrim. She kept house, cooked dinner for the farmworkers and so on, making trips home every few weeks on the train. It must have seemed a pretty good decision at the time for her to marry into my father's business.

The warehouse was a fascinating place for me as a kid. Big wooden tea chests arrived from all corners of the world with the names of exotic places stamped on them. There was a huge pine floor and they'd tip the tea out of the packing cases into little piles. Then the blenders would use their flat wooden shovels to mix the tea in precise quantities. They knew just the right amount to use without having to measure it. It was incredibly dusty work. There were days when you'd open the door and you couldn't see my dad for the dust. The company provided work for some of the locals and it was well respected in the area. It produced a blend of tea called Moyle that came in a red pack and was sold all over Donegal. It was very popular.

My dad's family would always have been seen as outsiders in the village. Even though it was only 12 miles from Derry there was a big cultural difference between the country people and the city folk. The business had a good reputation but my dad didn't dress in pinstripe suits. A big old woolly jumper and tracksuit bottoms were more his style. He spent a lot of time in the village pub, and the people there were wary of him – he was known to be aggressive when the drink was on him.

If there was any money being made in the business it never seemed to make its way back to our house. I was the eldest of eight children and we had to squeeze into a two-bedroom semi. I can't speak for my brothers and sisters, but I had a terrible relationship with my dad. He was abusive towards me; violently abusive. He used to beat me regularly and I never understood why. Here's an example. We used to play football in the fields near the house. They were marshy and full of reeds. I developed a terrible cough that never really went away and the sound of that cough really riled my dad. If I coughed at night he'd come into my room and beat me. It got so bad that he came in one night and put a pillow over my face to stop me coughing, holding it there for so long that I was fighting to breathe. This kind of behaviour, controlling and angry, used to happen in a lot of Irish families and was never spoken about; it was all brushed under the carpet for decades. But before she died my mum spoke to me and my partner, Jill, about those beatings. It was a relief to me that she finally acknowledged it and spoke about it to someone outside the family. The situation was never resolved during my father's lifetime.

The only solution I had to my dad's violence was to run away to my granny's. My mum did her best, but she wasn't in a position to protect me in the family home. From the age of six I spent more and more time at the house along the road. I loved being there and my grandparents were awfully good to me. It was just such a sharp contrast with home, where I'd been living in terror of the next beating. Soon I was staying away from my parents' for weeks on end and by the time I was ten or eleven, by which time my grandfather had passed away, I was living permanently at my granny's. Mum used to walk up every night to help Granny before bed. Granny had chickens out the back of the house and I could play about on my bike. I felt free and happy.

That's how I took this turn towards my mum and her family, I suppose. My mum was everything my dad wasn't. She was loving and supportive. As a teenager she'd been a beautiful raven-haired young woman. When I began bike racing, she'd make sure I had my entrance fee, and my freshly washed kit would always be blowing on the line at the back of the house. I remember her sitting with me washing down the wheels of the bike at eleven o'clock at night. When I wanted to live with my grandparents, she gave me her blessing because she knew how things were with my dad. Sometimes, when she saw the coast was clear, she'd come up and walk me down to our house and I'd spend time with my brothers and sisters. I kind of blanked my dad and his family out of my thinking.

The thing with my dad, his outright hatred and anger towards me, festered for years until I was in my early twenties. I was living in Belfast at the time and came up home for the weekend. I'd never really fought back with him, but things came to a head that day and the two of us came to blows. I'm not proud of what happened, but he was being really nasty to my mum and sisters and I wasn't having that. I'd always felt very protective of them. I'd arrived in the car and walked into this family row. 'That's it. You're not doing this any more!' I shouted. I finally stood up to him – somebody needed to. It got out of hand and someone called the Gardaí. The local policeman from the village showed up. He could tell I wasn't the one to blame and advised me to head back to Belfast and let things blow over.

I put my father out of the house that day and he only returned once, to pick up his clothes. He moved back to Derry and I never spoke to him again. Looking back, it doesn't give me any satisfaction – more a sense of sadness and pain that this had happened in my own family. When I became a dad myself I felt that lack of a father figure. Through my career there were always more experienced cyclists who took me under their wing, and some of them even took me into their family home. There's definitely a link there with that failure of my relationship with my dad.

Back in those early days, though, when I'd first moved out of the family home, the district nurse would often drop by to see my granny. They did their rounds by bike back then. I wasn't really allowed to go on the road by myself, but we came to an agreement that I could ride the mile to our house with Nurse Duffy on her old black roadster and me on the little Sunbeam. As soon as I saw the gates, I would open up and race to the finish line. It was my first taste of that feeling of independence you can get from being out on a country road on your bicycle. After I'd outgrown it, that bike kicked around my mum's house for years. I've lost count of the times it was repainted when it was passed on to different kids in the family.

The Troubles in Northern Ireland kicked off in 1969, when I was ten, and despite being so close to the border we really wouldn't have known the terrible things that were unfolding just a few miles down the road. Then one day in 1971, my dad announced that we were all moving to Derry. He'd always wanted to get back to the city. This was a shock to us all, particularly my mum, who'd only ever lived a sheltered life in a quiet village. We couldn't have moved at a worse time. Derry was where the Troubles really began. It started out with rioting but by then the IRA and the British Army were fighting a war with lead bullets and bombs. My mum just freaked out – she hated every minute of it. We all did. It was so alien for us; we just didn't fit in. There was this whole Protestant versus Catholic thing going on that had never existed for us in Newtowncunningham. Despite being in the Republic the village was a mixed community where people got along just fine.

Then my dad made the crazy decision to send me to Templemore, a completely Protestant secondary school. To put a little Catholic boy from Donegal into a school like that was asking for trouble and it felt like my dad did it to spite me. My mum pleaded with him not to do it but he ignored her. I went to Templemore for about a year and I was regularly beaten to a pulp. I managed to keep my background hidden for a while but when I was rumbled the bullying started up. They'd drag me behind the bike sheds for a kicking or beat me up in the corridors.

We lived in a house on Marlborough Street. It had three storeys and from the top you could look across the city over the Bogside to the famous city walls. There was a shirt factory at one end of the street and the British Army had a sort of pillbox there. So you had this weird situation where there would be factory women coming out of work and at the same time there would be rubber bullets flying around. Bloody Sunday in January 1972 was what finished Derry for us. The house looked out over Rossville Flats, where the worst of the day's events took place. I saw it happening from the top of the house. As a 12-year-old boy I didn't know what was going on, but I could tell there was crazy stuff happening a few streets away. You could see the smoke going up and hear the cracks of the rifles in the Bogside. Fourteen people were killed by the British Army.

And that was when my mum put the foot down. Living in the city was bad enough for a country woman like her, but living in the city with this war going on around us was on a completely different level. She gave my dad an ultimatum: 'We're going back home. You can stay here if you want but me and the kids are going.' Luckily, they hadn't sold the house in Donegal so we were straight back to Newtowncunningham. I was glad to see the back of Derry. I'd hated every minute of it.

One of the few good memories I do have of Derry was a trip to McClean's shop in Great James Street in the city centre. My dad was attempting to convince us all that living in the city wasn't such a bad thing and he agreed to buy me a bike. The shop was a proper Aladdin's cave, full of bikes on a polished wooden floor. I stood open-mouthed staring at the bike in the window, a bright yellow Raleigh Chopper. The Chopper was an icon for kids of the seventies, with its 'ape hanger' handlebars, banana seat and gear lever that looked like it belonged in a sports car. Everyone wanted a Chopper. And if you rode a Chopper you were automatically cool. Buying the Chopper was the greatest the thing my dad ever did for me, and I don't think he ever realised it.

As soon as I finished at Templemore on a Friday afternoon I got straight onto the Chopper and rode it to County Donegal to spend the weekend with my granny. It's probably not much more than 15 miles, but when you're on a Raleigh Chopper and you've never been more than two miles down the road, all of a sudden 14 or 15 miles is a long way. Because I was riding at the same time every week, I started seeing two guys on racing bikes who rode out from Derry towards County Donegal at the same. They were pretty nifty riders. One of them, I later discovered, was a fairly successful competitive racer. They used to fly past me as I struggled along the main road, but I eventually got a bit fed up with being passed so easily and tried to keep up with them. Each Friday I managed to keep up for a bit longer. Then one week I somehow managed to slipstream behind them all the way up the road and over the border. They couldn't drop me and I could sense that they were pushing hard. In the end I was overcome by the excitement and rode straight past the turn-off for home. We headed right on in the direction of Letterkenny, the better part of 30 miles from Derry. The ego in me took over and just before we reached the town I exploded. This was my first experience of what cyclists call the 'knock' or the 'bonk'. I ground to a halt. Every single ounce of energy in me was used up. I was like a shrivelled rag and I must have been a pitiful sight struggling back down the road. My granny gave me a packet of sticky Jacob's Mikado biscuits when I staggered through the door and I ate every single one of them.

Once we'd moved back to County Donegal, I started school in Letterkenny and it seemed perfectly natural to ride there and back every day. It was a round trip of about 25 miles and I never bothered with the bus. Then one morning at the breakfast table I discovered something that was to change my life. It was a promotional gimmick on the back of a cereal packet, Rice Krispies or Sugar Puffs or whatever. You had to colour in pictures of cyclists taking part in something called the Tour de France. I'd never seen anything like this before. All these guys in exotic-sounding teams racing though the mountains on bikes. It was totally beyond my experience – so colourful and exciting. When the pack was only three-quarters eaten I took it and hid it so we could get another one.

I was desperate to know more about this new world of bike racing, but there was no Channel 4 or Eurosport back in those days, no internet. There was one glossy cycling magazine, *Cycle Sport International*; I used to flick though it in the newsagents in Letterkenny, but I couldn't afford to actually buy it. The results they printed were probably weeks out of date by the time I saw them, but the magazine introduced me to some seriously cool cyclists. There was Eddy Merckx, the Cannibal, the greatest bike racer ever, although he was nearing the end of his career then.

Luis Ocaña, a tragic hero who won the 1973 Tour. Then there was my inspiration – the tiny Belgian climber Lucien Van Impe. He won the Tour overall in 1976, but he won the King of the Mountains classification six times. I was the same size as little Lucien and climbing hills seemed to suit me.

I started really getting to grips with the Chopper then, taking it to bits on Granny's kitchen floor and putting it together again. Raleigh kept making alterations to the design to make it more comfortable or cooler looking, but I was making my own alterations to make my bike faster and slicker. That's how I took my first steps in learning to be a mechanic. The kitchen is still my favourite place for working on my bikes, not a fancy workshop. I have a couple of bikes sitting there now; they're a bit more expensive than the Chopper but definitely not as cool.

Bike racers were quite thin on the ground in Donegal, although I did see some guys out on the road from time to time, like the ones I'd chased up the road from Derry. I was aware there was some sort of racing scene going on and I became determined to have a go at it myself. I persuaded my mum and dad to let me trade in the Chopper for a racing bike. We made the trip back to McClean's in Derry and I came home with a very nice purple Falcon. It wasn't a flying machine, but it was the right shape, with the drop handlebars and ten-speed gears, and I was soon out on the roads doing my best Van Impe impersonation.

I discovered that local cycling clubs held circuit races on weeknights during the summer. There was a circuit called Ballyholey about five miles from Newtowncunningham. It was basically a route around the country roads used for racing on a regular basis. There were lots of circuits across Donegal and if you said to a cyclist there was a race on the Ballyholey circuit next Thursday they'd know what you meant. Ballyholey is sort of nestled between Letterkenny and the little town of Raphoe.

It's still used for racing, and the main attraction is a long, steep hill.

I must have been all of 15 years old when I rocked up to Ballyholey on the Falcon ready for my very first race. I didn't have a clue what I was letting myself in for. I didn't realise it at the time but three or four of the very best riders in Donegal were taking part. It finished up a bit of a disaster, to be frank, but a disaster with a happy outcome. Part way round the course you came to a sort of island in the road with a Yield sign, the same as a Give Way sign in the UK. You had to ride around the sign and go back the way you came. This being Donegal, no one had actually decreed which way you were supposed to go around. I had somehow managed to get myself to the front of the race with two of the best riders. I went around the island in one direction and Tommy Burns, who would have been Donegal's top racer at the time, went the other. There was an almighty crash. I wrote off my beloved but cheap Falcon and absolutely trashed Tommy's top-end thoroughbred race bike.

I'd ridden up to the race but the forks on the bike were now so badly bent I had no way of getting home. I couldn't even get back to the start area. Then a guy a appeared in a car, a little green Vauxhall Viva, and he offered to give me a lift home. His name was Tommy Pyper and he was a cyclist himself. 'Throw the bike in the back,' he said. This was easier said than done. Tommy was a plumber at Letterkenny General Hospital and the boot of the car was crammed full of copper piping and all sorts of plumber's tools. We had to shove them all over to one side to fit the knackered Falcon in. I noticed he had this funny way of driving the Viva. Once he worked up a head of steam, he'd switch off the engine and let the car coast for a bit. I can only think that he had just enough petrol to take me home and get back to Letterkenny. It must have been a way of saving money at a time when a lot of people in Donegal wouldn't have been able to afford extra journeys in a car. I knew I'd be in for a beating from my dad if he saw the bike, and the first day of my racing career would also be my last. So when Tommy asked where I lived, I carefully directed him to my granny's house.

I propped the bike against the hedge and went in to tell her what had happened. 'Son, you're going to get killed,' she said. I just nodded. My mum was sympathetic when she found out, but my dad predictably went ballistic: 'This bike racing nonsense is stopping now!' And given the state of the bike, it probably would have stopped there and then, but my experience of fettling the Chopper meant I now knew my bottom bracket from my rear mech. I managed to straighten the forks and the bike was soon back on the road again. After the embarrassment of my first race, I was now eager to prove myself against the big boys.

Meeting Tommy Pyper was my first step on the pathway to real racing. I spent a lot of time with him in his tiny kitchen working on bikes. At one stage I pretty much moved in with the Pyper household. We had no proper tools so we improvised with his plumbing equipment. Tommy kept his bike collection hanging on racks in his coal shed. We used to make up one bike out of two knackered ones. Looking back at it now it was all so agricultural it was hilarious.

It was from Tommy that I learned the difference between the mass-market street racing bike I'd been riding and the hand-built lightweight frames used by professionals and serious amateurs. Tommy Burns' bike, the one I'd knackered in the Ballholey crash, was handcrafted by the master frame builder Dave Moulton. It was worth eight or nine thousand euros in today's money.

13

Thankfully, he never demanded the money for repairs or I'd have been seriously screwed.

I somehow managed to get hold of a scruffy second-hand lightweight frame that I was sure would be the key to my cycling success. It must have been three sizes too big for me but I got a can of paint stripper from the shed and cleaned it back to the bare steel. I then lovingly applied a few coats of the most disgusting yellow aerosol paint. As far as I was concerned it looked the dogs. Tommy wasn't sure. He went off and came back with a marker pen. 'What name do you want on it?' I thought for a minute. 'Ken Bird,' I said, naming one of the top frame-builders who regularly graced the pages of *Cycling Weekly*. Tommy carefully faked up the name on the crossbar with the pen. We stood back to examine his handiwork and almost pissed ourselves laughing. The next day we went out over the hills on a test run. Inevitably, the rain started to lash and the Ken Bird logo dribbled down the frame like wet mascara. It was the sort of fun I should have been having with my dad, and Tommy came to replace that relationship a little bit.

Tommy was busy with his own young family and his work but he still managed to find time for me. He was kind and supportive, could see some sort of potential in me and started coaching me about how to ride the local circuits – where you had to take care and where you needed to be sure you were in the right gear. Above all, I shared a lot of my crazy dreams of future cycling success with him and he never burst that bubble.

Even as a young teenager I was on a steep learning curve. I was training very hard, out on the roads getting the miles in every day. Apart from the weeknight club events, the main races in the Donegal cycling calendar were held in towns and villages across the county during the summer fair weeks. These festivals were advertised in the local papers, the *Derry Journal* or the *Donegal*

Democrat. There would be a parade, music, maybe a funfair and a bike race. The very best of the Donegal riders came to those races. There would be maybe 15 or 20 cyclists taking part.

Tommy was originally from the pretty little town of Ramelton and when the local festival race was advertised, he was able to brief me precisely on the ins and outs of a course he knew better than any other. I was maybe 16 years old but I was constantly out on the roads getting the miles in and, like my hero Van Impe, I was becoming a great little hill climber. I was ready for my first race win.

I'll never forget that night in Ramelton. I don't know why, but I decided to go flat out from the start until I couldn't go flat out any more. The more experienced guys must have thought this young lad would blow up well before the finish. But my plan, if you could call it a plan, worked to perfection. I wasn't 500m down the road before I was out on my own and I just rolled away from the entire bunch. Coming into Ramelton you cross a lovely old bridge on the River Lennon. To add to the excitement the route included a few circuits around the town before the finish. The streets were full of people there for the festival and they cheered me on. The finish line was by the bridge next to a local landmark, the crumbling old warehouse belonging to the McDaid's soft drinks company whose fizzy Football Special is still famous throughout Donegal. I coasted to victory with my arms in the air, light years ahead of everyone else. For a young kid it was exactly like winning a stage in the Tour de France. I closed my eyes and thought: 'This is it; I've arrived!'

The local papers used to do a write-up of all the races. Obviously, some journalist was just making most of it up back at the newspaper office but suddenly my name was all over the back pages. I wouldn't say I got a big head over it but people started to take notice, even the little group of teenagers who met at the Orange Hall in Newtowncunningham on a Friday night. It would be: 'I saw your name in the paper, Joe. When are you racing again?'

It was a real confidence booster and I'd have to admit I used that to my advantage. I had more than a few girlfriends in my teenage years and I suppose I did play the local sports star card from time to time. The problem was that I couldn't put all my effort into cycling and expect to have a normal life outside school or work. If I was going to be successful, cycling would have to take all my energy.

I wasn't particularly aware of local cycling clubs at that stage. When you looked at the Tour de France guys on the cereal packets, they were all in teams, but the club thing was different. When I started to look into it more seriously, I found there were two. The local Donegal club was just starting up, but the City of Derry Wheelers was a really well-established old club. I was introduced to a guy called Ivan Dunne at City of Derry, who impressed me with his connections to cycling in Belfast, and that's how my connection with the club began.

Tommy Pyper was showing me the ropes around those Donegal races, but it was Tommy Burns, whose bike I'd wrecked that time in Ballyholey, who introduced me to cycling beyond the local festival circuit. He had a big reputation and took part in races all over the country. Tommy was able to show me stuff I'd never heard of before, like federations and licensing. In Donegal no one ever bothered with racing licences. It was hard enough just to get hold of kit, even a pair of shorts. You were usually given them by someone who had a couple of spares lying in a cupboard somewhere. I was racing in trade jerseys, what you'd call replica kit these days, but you couldn't ride in proper national races in a trade jersey. It turned out there were all sorts of rules to this cycling game.

The first big ride I remember with City of Derry was out around the coast to the town of Limavady in Northern Ireland. Tommy Pyper was with me and we had to ride all the way back to Letterkenny at the end of it. It was something like seven hours in the saddle. This was a longer distance than I'd ever been on my bike before. I didn't know the other cyclists and I didn't know the roads, so it was all a bit intimidating.

I rode in the blue-and-yellow jersey of City of Derry Wheelers for a couple of years and I was able to get my racing licence. It wasn't, as I'd once naively thought, a golden ticket to the Tour de France but it did open the door to the whole new world of cycling. With my licence I could enter the ranks of open racing. This was run on an all-Ireland basis with proper officials under the control of the national body. I was now a genuine athlete competing against serious, experienced bike racers.

As my cycling career blossomed, my school career was going nowhere. I passed my secondary level exams but I didn't do any work for them. I'd already worked out that I wanted to build a career in bike racing, even though I hadn't a clue how to set about it. One of the teachers, a geography teacher called Mr Dowds, got so frustrated with me: 'You have to realise that this nonsense with riding bicycles is going to be absolutely no use to you. You're never going to be able to get anywhere with it!' I just dug my heels in and resolved to prove to all the doubters they were wrong. I suppose my one regret now is that I didn't get the chance to go to university, but that wasn't even on my radar at the time. Once I'd met Tommy Pyper the books were left in his house every day after school and I was off on the bike training.

I left school at 18 but you couldn't exactly sign up to be a professional rider in Letterkenny. Training and racing were my top priorities and I found myself working in a big potato-processing factory in Newtowncunningham to earn money to go racing in the summer. The farmers from all around brought their spuds to the depot to be graded and put into bags. It was pretty grim work. I did everything in that factory from filling the bags to driving forklifts. I also worked as a farm labourer. Back-breaking badly paid stuff like potato picking. I never went back to my father's business; that would have been asking for trouble. The casual work went on for five or six years, but somehow I held on to the dream that someday I would turn professional.

CHAPTER 2

A Golden Era

I should have known better when Tommy Burns told me to sign my race entry with the name 'Joe Brown'. In my late teens I'd started travelling what seemed like the length and breadth of the island with Tommy. He knew the racing scene inside out and I learned a lot from him. This particular race was in the County Leitrim village of Glenfarne, about five miles from the border with Northern Ireland. It's best known as the site of the Rainbow Ballroom of Romance, where youngsters used to flock to dance to the showbands back in the sixties – they even made a movie about the place. I asked Tommy what the craic was with the false name and he said, 'Look, it's just a licence thing. You don't give your right name. You just make one up and pay your fee. No harm done.'

The one thing Tommy had overlooked was what would happen if I won and it wound up on the back pages of the *Belfast Telegraph*. Which, of course, is precisely what happened. I'd not only won the race; I'd won the wrong sort of race as far as my Northern licence was concerned: a National Cycling Association race. My fake ID was soon rumbled and all hell broke loose.

You may like to take notes here as I'll be setting an acronym test at the end of this paragraph. There were three cycling federations in Ireland at the time: the NCA, the ICF and the NICF. The NCA was a purely Irish organisation, a bit like the GAA, and it wasn't recognised by the world cycling authority, the UCI (Union Cycliste Internationale), for international competition. The ICF, or Irish Cycling Federation, was the internationally recognised body. It sent teams to the Olympics, the world championships and that kind of thing. The NICF was a sort of Northern Ireland counterpart to the ICF. The NICF and the ICF took part in each other's races, but woe betide any cyclist who was caught competing with the wrong sort. The rivalry between the federations reached fever pitch in 1972 when members of the NCA infiltrated the Olympic road race in Munich in protest – one of them even hid in a wood with his bike until the race approached and then joined in. The NCA had some great riders, particularly from down in Munster, Kerry especially, and from around Dublin. There were also pockets of NCA membership in the North but, without putting a political slant on it, they would have been mainly in areas like west Belfast. Thankfully, the squabbling has since been brought to an end and cycling underwent its own kind of Good Friday Agreement.

The official line from the old federations was 'ne'er the twain shall meet', but up in far-flung Donegal the riders kind of made up their own rules as they went along. There was no malice in it – mostly it was due to the cost. But I was a member of the City of Derry Wheelers in Northern Ireland and the next thing I heard after my Glenfarne victory was that I'd been called to a tribunal in Belfast. If I was found guilty the penalty was a year's ban from racing. That would have been a real punch in the kidneys. In the end I didn't have to go to Belfast. Ivan Dunne from the Derry club managed to smooth things over with the NICF executive for me, but it was an early introduction to the small 'p' politics that dogs the sport of cycling.

I had a lot to learn. The races were held on a Saturday in Northern Ireland and Sunday down South. It took so long to progress up through the ranks and that became a problem later in my career because I was too late turning professional. Nowadays if you're over 23 a professional team wouldn't look at you. Back in my day there was still a sliver of hope for 28- or 29-year-olds to get a professional contract.

A lot of the Northern racing was based around Belfast and in the early eighties if I was riding on Saturdays and Sundays I'd sometimes stay over with a friend, Geordie Wilkes, in Dundonald, a loyalist area in the east of the city. I struck lucky in Dundonald, for it was there that Geordie introduced me to the Kane family. Ask anyone who's been in the Irish pushbike racing scene since the 1960s and they'll have heard of Dave Kane. He's done so much for the sport all over the island and there's immense respect for him. Dave raced all over the world for Ireland and Northern Ireland and took part in numerous world championships and Commonwealth games. He also owns one of the best bike shops in the country. As well as being a phenomenal bike racer, Dave had worked in the city's famous Harland and Wolff shipyards.

The Kanes were a cycling family but Dave couldn't drive so Geordie used to chauffeur them all around the country to the races. The sons Mark and Paul became very successful cyclists, but I could see immediately that their sister, Deborah, had something special about her. She was an incredibly talented rider at a time when women's racing wasn't taken as seriously as it is today. I got to know her better through hanging out together at the races and it wasn't long until I'd asked her out. We were an unusual couple at the time for, although we had a shared passion for bikes and racing, she was Protestant and I was Catholic and that mattered in eighties Belfast, where some young couples struggled against the disapproval of their parents or local community.

I always looked up to Dave as a mentor. He was concerned by the long trek I was constantly making back and forth to County

Donegal, so he and his wife, Maggie, started to let me stay over at their house. Here was another family who took me into their home – a pattern that was to be repeated several times in my life as a young rider. It started out with the occasional overnighter but eventually I was spending longer periods there and Dave took a real interest in my development as a racing cyclist. I'm the first person to admit that I'm not the greatest rider there has ever been, but I think he recognised the effort I was making and the work ethic I had. You don't get ahead in the endurance cycling world I now inhabit without a shedload of drive and stubbornness.

I learned a huge amount from Dave and that learning proved to be the key to my future development. He took the raw, unformed talent that I had and knocked it into some sort of shape. I don't mean in an aggressive way – Dave wasn't that sort of guy; he'd just give you advice and patiently point out your mistakes.

I was forever straining at the leash, wanting to do things that were beyond my capability, but Dave would take me to one side and explain that I had to take things one step at a time. His methods were incredibly basic by today's standards. There was no fancy sports science involved. He told me to leave the shop in Ballyhackamore and ride around the Ards Peninsula. When I could do that in three hours we could move on to the next thing. The peninsula circuit is a beautiful ride through the fishing villages by the Irish Sea, looping around Portaferry and back up along the Strangford Lough shore towards Belfast. Not that I noticed the stunning views – I was too busy knocking my pan in trying to hit Dave's target. It was a bloody hard job and it took months, but I finally cracked it. I reckon I still know every bump in those roads. Dave's method allowed me to gradually build up and maintain the speed that I needed to be competitive at a higher level of racing. I know for a fact he did the same for many other cyclists, including his son Mark, who raced for Ireland at the Olympics.

The other thing Dave had was an incredible race brain. He knew how to win a race even if he wasn't the strongest rider. As a matter of fact, the chances of him being the strongest were slim to nil because he just wasn't built the right way. He was lanky and an excellent climber but he didn't have the power to be able to sprint to the finish line. What he did have was an uncanny ability to read the race in such a way that he'd won it before the sprinters stood a chance. I was no different from Dave in my physical capabilities – great in the hills, but when I started to sprint for the line it was like I'd hit reverse gear. It seemed hopeless. I desperately needed some of Dave's tactical racing intelligence. He sat me down at the back of the shop over a cup of coffee and taught me precisely how to win a race – the Tour of Ards. I'd entered that race so many times and kept finishing fourth, or seventh, or ninth. I had the capability but kept getting blown away by the sprinters. The course ran around my old peninsula stomping ground with a pan-flat, very fast run in, finishing outside the football ground in Newtownards. This time I followed Dave's instructions to the letter, conserving my energy in the pack until just the right moment. Then I opened up full gas far enough out on the Portaferry Road to leave the big sprinters for dead.

Dave was like an encyclopaedia of racing knowledge and knew his way around most of the big races in Ireland. With his help I was able to put that knowledge to good effect.

As racing began to take over my life, the amount of driving I was doing at the weekends was crazy. I'd pack up the car in Donegal, drive to a race in Northern Ireland on a Saturday, drive home again, up early on the Sunday and drive to a race in the South. It might be at the other end of the island. That's the way it worked in those days. The Southern guys really only bothered with the Sunday racing. Some of them travelled, but not many. But the Northern lads tried to cram in as much as possible. So effectively we were having a double hit every week. At times I barely had money for the fuel and was driving home on fumes. I had four hours more driving to do than the Belfast guys and I sometimes had to sleep in the car.

Back then most of the northern races were run from Orange halls. There would be tea and home-made cakes for the cyclists after the races and we'd stand around socialising surrounded by Orange banners and portraits of Queen Elizabeth. I made a lot of great friendships in Orange halls down the years. There were no restrictions on the numbers, so some of the races had over a hundred riders depending on the importance of the race, the weather and whether some of the top riders were away on international duty. And they were long races too: 100 miles or more on open roads with traffic roaring past. Even juniors were riding 100-mile races.

The races were officially amateur so there was no appearance money. There'd be a big silver cup for the winner and brown envelopes for the first, second and third. It never amounted to much. A massive pay day – and I mean massive – would have been a hundred quid. Was it strictly legal? It's hard to tell. Put it this way: the races were always hosted by a local club so the entry fees were divided up into so much for the club and so much for the prizes. There was no big commercial sponsorship so the sport just about paid for itself. Those brown envelopes still exist in amateur cycling today but the prize money hasn't increased to match inflation – it's hardly enough to keep you in inner tubes.

My first big win in open racing came in 1982 at the Tommy Givan Memorial event at Hillsborough in County Down.

Hillsborough is a tidy little village that looks more like something from the English home counties than a typical Irish settlement. It has some classy pubs, an oyster festival and some of the steepest property prices in Northern Ireland. There's a little square next to the castle, which was built by the Hill family hundreds of years ago.

The race started from the square, hung a sharp left up the road towards Dromore and went straight into a massive hill climb. Just the sort of hill that would suit a certain young lightweight climber from Donegal. I'd travelled up from home that morning and signed on at the inevitable Orange hall on the Ballynahinch Road. I can't remember the exact distance, but it would have been around a hundred miles. The Tommy Givan was known to be an extremely tough race at the time and they don't run it over that course nowadays. All the top riders in Northern Ireland and beyond were there, some of them internationals.

Call it the arrogance of youth, but after two or three laps I thought to myself, 'I could do a job on these guys.' And I did. I just opened the taps and rode away from them. Halfway up that hill I was confronted by a guy called Jackie Corkan shouting from the roadside. Jackie was a respected figure on the local cycling scene and had parked himself in the hedge on a camping stool to watch the race. Not much of a day's entertainment when the bunch only flew past about once every half hour. 'Catch yourself on, young fella. You'll wear yourself out!' he yelled. Looking back on it, there was no sanity in the way I rode that day. Hitting the front near the start and going as hard as you can is not the way to win a pushbike race. It defies common sense. But at the finish I was six minutes in front of the second-placed rider.

What I hadn't realised was that the Tommy Givan was the final selection race for the 1982 Commonwealth Games in Brisbane. My rush of blood to the head caused quite a stir in the back pages of the *Telegraph*. Who was this kid who had blown away the entire Northern Ireland team? I'd won that qualification race by a country mile, or three. By rights a place on the team was mine, but the men in suits had made their decision months before. I have a heap of respect for the guys who went to Brisbane, but the selectors just ignored their own criteria and decided young Cinders would not be going to that ball. The whole episode left me with a bad taste in the mouth and the determination that when the next games came around, they wouldn't be able to ignore me so easily.

The day of the Tommy Givan holds another special memory for me. I remember sitting on the wall outside the Orange hall after the race with Debbie Kane, just talking nonsense and enjoying each other's company. It was around then that our relationship started in earnest. I'm pretty certain she'd won the women's race that day – she usually did. We were somehow travelling along this curve together. I found her incredibly attractive, just a lovely person to be with. We had this friendship based on riding bikes and racing bikes and winning races. Then I thought to myself, 'I've found my life here: this whole thing has become my life.' I was emerging as one of the top young riders in Ireland and I enjoyed Debbie's company immensely. It felt like it would go on for ever.

It's hard to explain quite how impressive Debbie was as a racing cyclist. She competed many times for Ireland and took part in the world championships in Italy. One year, it would have been '83 or '84, the two of us made a trip to the Harrogate Show in Yorkshire. The county is the heartland of English bike racing with some infamous climbs through the dales. It even hosted the opening stages of the Tour de France in 2014. The Harrogate event was a big trade show for the entire UK cycling industry, with exhibitions during the day and racing every evening. Dave had opened a shop specialising in top-class cycling clothing just a few doors down from his bike shop in Belfast, and Debbie was scouting for clothing for the shop during the day, and after hours we'd go racing.

On Tuesday evening of that week, I had a chance to ride Britain's most iconic time trial course, Boroughbridge. They called it 'the Borough' and it ran along the A1 dual carriageway in and out of the cars and heavy lorries bound for Scotland. The Borough was renowned as the fastest place to ride a time trial in Britain and records were regularly broken there. That evening I rode a 25-mile time trial and to this day it's the fastest 25 I've ever ridden. I was on a standard road bike with standard wheels and my time just blew everybody away, including a guy called Ian Cammish, who was the UK's top time triallist for the whole of the 1980s. Cammish set off one minute behind me and he never caught me.

On the Thursday night, Debbie and I headed down to the Borough together. We parked up in a grassy field, she got changed and we rocked up to the start line. That night Debbie became the first Irish woman to ride a 25-mile TT (time trial) in under an hour. We were ecstatic. She was already on the upward plane that would lead her to the international stage. Later in the week, I was invited to take part in a two-up TT and took Debbie's young brother Mark along as my partner. He must have been all of 13 years old but we still finished third or fourth. If someone asked me, 'What's your greatest memory of the Kane family?', that week in Harrogate was certainly one of them. When I think back on it, I would call it a golden era. Debbie and I were in a great place. Our relationship was blossoming and one racing success followed another. It felt like everything was on the up. It was a great period in my life.

In many ways my life can be measured in more than the results of my sports career. I look back and see the families I have passed through and how each of those families has moulded me and made me what I am. People have been very generous to me down the years, inviting me into their family circle and pointing me on to the next destination on my journey.

I'd reached a point where I'd had enough of sleeping in the car. I decided to ditch the long drives to Donegal and move to Belfast. I'd met two cycling brothers from west Belfast at the races, Brendan and Mark Graham. Mark offered to let me stay at his place and I jumped at the offer. He was a great guy but was sadly killed in a head-on collision with a British Army armoured car on the way to a cyclo-cross race at Kilbroney Park in Rostrevor, near Newry. Debbie and I were also going to the race, but we were ahead on the road. It was a shocking experience, not just for Debbie and me but for the entire Northern Ireland cycling community.

Moving to Belfast meant I'd be giving up my long-held allegiance to the City of Derry Wheelers. It meant I'd have to choose a club where I could develop my skills and I took the decision very seriously. Brendan and Mark belonged to a west Belfast club called VC Glendale. It's still a flourishing community club with a great reputation for bringing on young riders. People on the racing scene knew I was from Donegal and because I was a close friend of the Grahams there was a general consensus that I'd go to an NCA club. But I had my eyes set somewhere else entirely.

The Cyprus club was based in Glengormley, a largely Protestant area on the edge of north Belfast. Unlike most clubs it was essentially a team of high-performing competitive riders. There were no social cyclists at Cyprus. The club was firmly based in the NICF camp and its members regularly competed for Northern Ireland.

I wasn't out to make any political point when I chose to join Cyprus, although others may have read it as some kind of big statement. There was no intention to nail my colours to anyone's mast. I went to Cyprus because it was a high-performance environment where I could advance my cycling career. The top man at the club was Morris Foster. Morris was a big man who ran a tight ship. The ideal commander-in-chief. If you were one of Morris's boys you were pretty darn tough, and you were pretty darn good. Morris was also the coach of the Northern Ireland cycling squad. I'd heard of him when I was still riding with the juniors at City of Derry and I made sure I was on his radar. I always knew the way forward in Northern Ireland was with the people who made the decisions. For me it was the Morris Fosters who made the decisions, influenced by the Dave Kanes and the Commonwealth Games Council.

What I wasn't counting on was that there would be some resistance to me being in the club. Was it to do with who I was and where I was from? I've no proof of that, but given that this was Belfast during the Troubles you'd be naive to think those types of conversation didn't happen. I was certainly a bit wet behind the ears. I was still a hundred per cent convinced that the sport was entirely based on your capability – if you win, you get. Experience was to teach me a different story. I was a young kid full of enthusiasm, but I was trying to make my way in a sport that was utterly ruthless.

I have no complaints about my experiences with Cyprus. Morris was very good to me, and his wife, Maureen, was very supportive of Debbie and me as a couple. On the other hand,

Morris pulled no punches with any of his riders. He set the bar high and you either reached it or you didn't. Did I ever turn out to be Morris's favourite? Absolutely not – he preferred the big, muscular guys who could shine through his punishing training schedule. But I do think I earned his respect. I broke his 100-mile time trial record and his Ireland end-to-end record. He was proud of those achievements and I think he had some regard for me for matching and beating them.

Even a rolling stone like me eventually gets fed up with crashing on other people's sofas – not to mention my generous hosts getting sick of me hogging the bathroom in the morning. In truth, a big part of the motivation for the Belfast move was also to spend more time with Debbie. I started looking for a place for myself and hunted down a little bachelor pad on the Upper Newtownards Road, just a few hundred yards from Kanes' shop. The flat was on the top floor of a little red-brick terraced house, a typically east Belfast place. You couldn't have swung a cat in it but there was room enough for me, a few clothes and a pile of bike gear.

Parking a Donegal-registered car outside the house in that part of town probably wasn't the cleverest thing to do, and it didn't go unnoticed in those strange days. More than a few times I had unusual people ask me questions about who I was and what I was doing in deepest east Belfast. Once they'd heard about my association with Dave Kane and realised my sole interest in life was riding my bike as fast as possible, I was left in peace. That little suburb of Ballyhackamore used to be a village in its own right before it was swallowed up by the big city and it still had some of that friendly village feel to it. People may have been curious but they never said anything nasty to my face. I enjoyed my time in in the 'hack and made a lot of friends there.

The one disadvantage of my devil-may-care lifestyle was that I had no regular income. The amount of training I did and the racing all weekend just didn't fit with the discipline of a regular job. You couldn't be a plasterer or an electrician and dedicate your life to sport the way I was. There was no lavish National Lottery funding or big commercial sponsorship in those days. The result was that for years I was scrabbling for a few quid from wherever I could get it. I'd go back to Donegal for the odd bit of casual labouring or agricultural work; on afternoons when I wasn't training I'd sometimes help out Dave or Maggie in one of the shops. I'm not ashamed to say that my own family was also helping out; my mum was slipping me some money when she could afford it. It was a rough time financially but it was a self-inflicted rough time. And it got to the point where I'd be sitting on the bike at the start line thinking, 'I better get an envelope today with some ready cash or I won't be racing tomorrow.' Funnily enough, this feeling of quiet desperation could actually give you the hunger to perform better. I saw this later in my career when I raced against teams from behind the Iron Curtain: the Poles, the Czechs and the Russians. Those guys had no money either and they were hard as nails. The French say that cycling is the sport of the working man and the peasant and I saw that for myself when I lived and raced in Brittany. I look back on my early days and wonder how the hell I managed to achieve what I did when I was running on empty.

I could have got a job like everyone else but right from the start I only had one ambition – to be a pro rider. That was all I wanted. Everything else could wait. My attitude to life in those days was pretty cavalier. Throw caution to the wind, go for the adventure, forget about security. All that stuff. I'm not a silly twenty-something kid any more but I'm still able to tap into some of that.

In 2020, before I started my record-breaking time trial the length of Ireland and back, my partner, Jill, and I sat quietly for a few moments in the team vehicle. High winds buffeted the car and rain lashed on the windscreen. Jill looked me in the eye and said: 'Are we okay with this, Joe?'

'I have no fears,' I said. That inbuilt self-belief has always been with me.

CHAPTER 3

Meanwhile, in the Back Seat of a Peugeot

A sk anyone where the home of cycling is, and they'll likely tell you it's France. I'd been dreaming of the place since I was a kid colouring in those Tour de France cereal packets at my grandma's house in Newtowncunningham. That curiosity was stirred to fever pitch by the fan magazines with their talk of magical mountains like Alpe d'Huez, Mont Ventoux, the Tourmalet and the Galibier. The heroic breakaways and dizzying descents were things of legend. To be in France in the July heat watching the multicoloured peloton streaming down a switchback road from a mountain pass was as far from Donegal as you could imagine. The Tour, they say, binds the French nation together by taking the sport to people's front doors or under their balconies. Strangely enough, there hasn't been a French winner of the Tour for the guts of forty years, not since the legendary Bernard Hinault raced to victory in 1985. Hinault was a small, aggressive rider with a permanent scowl who dominated his fellow riders like an angry sergeant major. He was a farm boy from Brittany, and they called him the Badger. And Bernard has a walk-on part in my story.

If the thought of one day being able to ride in France had

been a recurring fantasy for me since I was nine or ten years old, the possibility of actually getting there seemed hopelessly remote. But shortly after I joined Morris Foster's Cyprus club it was suddenly revealed to me that getting to compete in France was not only possible but stupidly easy. If you've ever been stuck behind a group of cyclists out training, riding two abreast, you've probably noticed that they never seem to stop talking. It's part of the sport, riding along talking shite, about races, other riders, maybe even the football results if you're that way inclined. This is how I learned from two of the Cyprus guys that they had been racing in Europe. I was startled. There was, it seemed, no great secret to this. You didn't need to get picked by anyone, fill out a ton of forms, join a club or have your application approved by a man in a suit. You pretty much bought a ticket and went. I noted down the names of the races, and chased the organiser's contact details.

The only difficulty would be finding the money. On my next trip home to Donegal I approached a potential sponsor. As usual my mum was only too happy to indulge my teenage whims. It was about two hundred quid, money she couldn't really afford. I bought a plane ticket from Belfast to Paris and then a connecting flight from Paris to somewhere in Brittany. I'm not exactly sure where, but since I didn't make it that far it hardly matters. I grabbed my bike and stuffed a few clothes in a bag and went for it.

However, my meticulous planning hadn't stretched to checking if Paris had more than one airport. I arrived at Orly (or was it Charles de Gaulle?) only to discover that the flight to Brittany was from the other airport and I had no hope of making it to the plane in time. I can't help rolling my eyes when I compare my youthful efforts with the months of careful planning we spend before each of my endurance records attempts.

Having missed the connection, I opted for Plan B, a lengthy train journey to the west coast. I tried to take my bike into the carriage with me, but the guard was having none of it, so I had to get off the train and stow it in the baggage car. Unbeknownst to me, when it reached Le Mans the train split in two. I went in one direction and the baggage car with my bike in it went another. I felt such a mug when I got off the train to discover the bike had gone AWOL. The railway people traced it to a town called Quimper, the last station on the line. Plan C it was, then, and I set off to retrieve my bike and bag.

I had trouble sleeping and woke up on the morning of the race utterly knackered. After facing the horror of the continental-style toilet fixtures in my crappy B&B I stumbled into a nearby patisserie to load up on pastries for breakfast. Then it was off to the sign-on and my first experience of pushbike racing Breton-style. It was in truth a pretty low-level affair – what we back home would have classed as an open local race rather than a national race. It was no great shakes to the French guys massing by the start, but to me just to get to the starting line was a major triumph. I stood in the midst of this pack of big, self-assured Breton bikers and fretted about whether I'd be able to get past the race officials at the registration. Once you'd signed in, they gave you your race number, called a 'dossier'. There was a fair amount of confusion until they worked out that I was the 'Irlandais' on the list. I thought I detected a few sidelong glances along the lines of 'What the hell's he doing here?' and even a patronising wink from one character. Never mind that. I stood over the bike, leaning on the bars and drinking in the atmosphere. Over by the town hall that unmistakable red, white and blue tricolour turned in a warm summer breeze. I'd finally made it.

Then the starter's flag dropped and the race set off at a hell of a lick, faster than any start back home. Like Jackie Corkan in his

Hillsborough hedge, I thought these guys would burn all their matches and the race would slow to a sensible pace. But they didn't and it didn't. I'd travelled 700 miles to get the kicking of my life. It was instant death. They have a term for it in France – the 'lanterne rouge', the red lamp at the end of the race. I trailed home dead last.

To tell the truth I'd come to France with not a clue what to expect. I thought I'd be riding what we at home call a criterium, a short-circuit race around a town centre. They used to be a common sight in small Irish towns. In France they call them a kermesse and they're a different thing entirely. Where the criterium runs on a circuit of maybe 1.5 km, on a kermesse the circuit is maybe six or eight kilometres and the race runs for three-and-a-half hours. That would have been a full-blown road race for me. And the number of riders was astonishing, even though this was only a small local race. There were team cars with spare bikes on the roof and whole families of supporters. Back home cyclists were seen as oddballs, like pigeon racers or members of the local male voice choir. Over here it was the national sport and in Brittany it was taken very seriously indeed. It was an exhilarating experience for me, but it was a harsh one.

I suppose I learned a lot, but the trip left me feeling thoroughly disheartened and a little inadequate. Having set off full of a sense of adventure and ready to tell tales of my exploits in the home of cycling, when I got home I didn't really talk about it. I was kind of embarrassed because it had been a total crash and burn and it impacted me quite badly. In later years when I travelled to Europe to compete as part of an international team it was a very different experience. Someone else would have booked the accommodation and arranged the travel and you were in a protective bubble. Yes, we invariably got our butts kicked but it didn't seem so bad when you were sharing the kicking with a bunch of other guys. Travelling to France that first time when I was 19 was like being dropped into the ocean from a great height and being left to sink or swim.

My next experience of the tough world of Breton racing came a few years down the road in my cycling career. A potential deal to join a pro team in the UK had fallen through and I was nursing my wounds from the disappointment. As luck would have it, an invitation dropped onto the desk of the federation in Dublin looking for an Irish rider to join one of the top amateur teams in France. The invite was forwarded to me via Dave Kane. It wasn't the pro contract I'd been chasing, but VCP Lorient was a first-category, full-tilt French amateur team. It wasn't unusual to see young foreign riders taking their chances with the big amateur teams on the Continent. Most of the time they went home with their tails between their legs, but some struck it lucky and made it to the big leagues. Ireland's two most successful racing cyclists both started their European careers with French teams. Sean Kelly, one of the finest riders of the one-day classics of all time, started out at VC Metz, while Tour de France winner Stephen Roche raced as an amateur with the prestigious ACBB club in Paris.

Compared to my Irish experiences, the Lorient club was incredibly well organised and resourced. It was part-owned by the local council and sponsored by the big hospitality firm Eurest. There was no checking into a shabby B&B this time. The team had a block of apartments in the city centre where all the riders from other parts of France lived and I was instructed to check in there. I'd learnt my lesson since my first chaotic trip to Brittany and was first to show up. After a certain amount of linguistic confusion, the penny dropped that the apartments were not ready. I sat on the steps wondering what sort of situation I'd got myself into when a car pulled up and two men got out. They introduced themselves as Guy Trehin and his son, Roger. Luckily Roger spoke pretty good English and he explained that they were members of the club and I'd be staying with them for a couple of nights until the apartments were ready. I never went back to the apartments. In fact, I stayed with the Trehins for three remarkable years.

Lorient still has a special place in my heart. It's a seaside town with a population about the same size as Derry and strong connections to the glamorous sport of ocean racing. The Nazis built a massive concrete submarine base to house U-boats during the war with the result that the town was bombed flat by the Allies and most of it had to be rebuilt. The Trehins lived on the edge of town but they owned a little bistro/crêperie place in the centre. Jacqueline, Guy's wife, ran the family restaurant business. There were two daughters, Nathalie and Christine. Christine worked in the bistro with her mum, and Nathalie worked as a ski instructor in the Pyrenees through the winter. Nathalie and I became firm friends. We'd watch TV together in the afternoons when I came home from training. That's how I learned to speak French. Nathalie would pick out words from the telly or the newspaper and I would learn them. Sometimes it took me days to get the pronunciation right.

When I first arrived at the club I was pitched into a tough all-French sporting environment with little or no knowledge of the language. Once the team had assembled, we headed way down the coast to Biarritz in the Basque Country for a training camp. There were 17 French guys on the team, including an ex-professional called Hubert Graignic. He seemed to regard himself as the top dog and always sat up front next to the driver in the team car. We travelled the length and breadth of France in these big Peugeot estates with three rows of seats. I invariably ended up in the back row, often on my own. For about three months no one apart from Roger spoke to me on those long cross-country trips. We became close friends and it was through him that I was introduced to the cut-throat world of Breton cycling. The whole scene was run by what I can only describe as a mafia. A close circle of riders from all the teams would meet secretly to decide the outcome of the races. Roger had an inside line on the whole thing, and he was able to tell me 'so and so's going to win today.' Deals between riders are common at all levels in cycling but they're mostly hatched up between individuals out on the road. This was on an entirely different scale and if you messed with the mafia there were consequences.

Once the training stopped and the racing started in earnest, I found myself in a familiar place, kicked in the teeth and booted out the back door. Every time I started a race, I ended up second last, or last man over the finish line. My confidence was shot to shit and it was clear the team was getting frustrated by my pitiful performance. I'd come to France with a strong reputation. They'd been told I'd won a lot of big races back home and yet here I was riding like a kid in need of stabilisers. Then one day I finally came good. Roger and I were in a breakaway with two of the strongest riders in Brittany. It was my opportunity to pay back the Trehin family for everything they'd done for me. I managed to shake off the other two well before Roger and I approached the finish line. I've still got a big picture of us crossing the line one after the other.

I was feeling knackered but happy as we piled into the Peugeot at the end of the day for the long trek back to Lorient. Roger got in beside me and we shared a few jokes about a good day in the saddle. Just then the looming figure of Hubert swivelled in his throne up front and looked me in in the eye. 'Well done, Joe. That was a great shift you put in today,' he said, in perfect English. It seemed unlikely, but in chats with other riders I'd been told that one of the issues Graignic had with me was that I was Irish. He had been part of the Sem-France Loire team under the legendary directeur-sportif, or head coach, Jean de Gribaldy. This was the team in which Sean Kelly first sprang to fame, and Hubert had helped Kelly win the points classification at the 1982 Tour de France. Rumour had it that the two had not been best pals, but that may have just been team talk between the Lorient guys. In any case, after proving my willingness to put in a shift for the team the air of gloomy silence lifted, and I gradually became accepted by the other riders.

Meanwhile my immersive introduction to French life and culture continued at the Trehins' place. As a respected member of the local cycling community Guy took a personal interest in my development. He used to take me on training rides up the coast behind a derny, one of those funny little motorbikes they use in track cycling. He'd take me out for an hour or two, then come back and take Roger out for a spin. One of the funnier aspects of learning French in a family setting rather than from a schoolbook was the little idiosyncrasies that I picked up. After a while I was able to join in the craic sitting at the breakfast or dinner table. In the afternoons Roger and I would go to a café to meet some of his cycling mates. I thought I was holding my own, pitching in a few funny comments, but I could see some quizzical looks in Roger's direction as if to say, 'What's he talking about?' Then Roger explained that I was mixing up my French with words from the Celtic Breton language and the guys hadn't a clue what I was saying. It turned out that Guy, being the old-fashioned Breton that he was, freely mixed the two languages when he was with the family. I muddled my way through with French until I was able to go to the shops by myself. Eventually, I was helping in the café on Fridays when the queue for Jacqueline's delicious crêpes stretched out of the door and down the street.

Culture aside, France presented a massive education to me in how to race bikes. Back home you knew all the riders and you knew there were maybe ten guys in the race who had any chance of winning. In France there were as many as fifty riders capable of winning. It was like trying to read a constantly moving chessboard. You had to work out all the possible combinations and ride accordingly. You'd see a guy helping out another and start thinking, 'When's the payback coming for that?' Two days later it would help you to know whether to chase when someone broke away from the pack. It was Dave Kane's race brain again, but on a whole other level.

I also learned specific skills that you just didn't learn back home because the terrain or the weather was different. In Brittany you'd often be faced with fierce sidewinds. The first thing that happens if the wind starts blowing in from the right is that the riders all head for the gutter on the left. You're battering along at 50 miles per hour in single file and the wind's trying to put you in the ditch. And that's when the echelon starts to form. The riders fan out into a diagonal line abreast across the road. You move slightly to the side of the rider in front and just behind. It takes up the whole width of the road and there's always a big fight to get in the front echelon. I'd be desperately trying to keep control of the bike and maintain my speed, then suddenly there would be this massive six-foot Dutchman breathing down my neck and trying to push his way in. Echelons can look spectacular when you see them viewed from a helicopter on TV but for me riding in them was a terrifying experience.

I loved the whole French experience, but money was a problem and in the days before mobile phones and the internet it was hard to keep a lifeline with home. I didn't have any work, and I wasn't winning much at the races, so I was really struggling to support myself. I had to go to the public telephone at the end of the street with a fistful of old French francs and I'd be shoving them into the slot at a ridiculous pace. I'd get maybe three minutes on the line before the money ran out.

It put a great strain on my relationship with Debbie. We wrote a lot of letters. Looking back, the 1980s were probably the last great era of the love letter. We had some fleeting hours together at a big race meeting in Tipperary. I'd come over from France for a couple of days and Debbie came down from Belfast. We kissed goodbye and I caught the ferry back to France while she endured the long drive north in those pre-motorway days. My aim was to get a contract with a professional team in France and then Debbie could come over to live with me. Maybe I was being naive. Another year with me in Lorient and her in Belfast might have been too much. In the end, fate intervened and it never happened.

It was the same with my mum; a big chunk of my weekly spending money went on phone calls back to Donegal. My mum understood what I was trying to do but she struggled hugely with the financial stress of it, and she knew I wasn't telling her the half of it. There were times when she sent me money and it took two weeks to get there, and then I'd have had to find somewhere to change it. The Trehin family were so good to me. They pretty much looked after me like one of their own. I couldn't have stayed in Lorient without their help and I'll always be grateful for that.

I was able to make some money from racing but there was a bureaucratic catch-22 that meant you couldn't get your hands on your winnings. Prize money won by international riders had to be paid by the race organisers directly to the FFC, the French Cycling Federation. It would then be paid out to you at the end of the season. This defied all logic as far as I was concerned. In fact, the only reason I could see for it was that the money sat in the FFC's bank account for a few months earning interest.

There was another way of earning a few francs. Most races, especially kermesses, offered small cash prizes called 'primes' for intermediate sprints during the race; or there might be a prize for King of the Mountains or whatever in some of the bigger races. The great thing about primes was that they were paid in cash at the end of the race. I would have ridden two or three kermesses a week in the hope of bagging a prime. In effect I was riding purely for the brown envelope. My job for the entire day's racing was to win one sprint. You could have been winning 100 or 150 francs, just about enough to live on for a week. Everybody was in the same boat and that's what made it so damn hard to win those sprints. If you couldn't sprint you were in trouble. There was the odd day when I won a prime, but not many. I was a better cyclist than back in the day when I first won the Tour of Ards but I was still a crap sprinter.

Money was a problem for most of the young amateurs in Brittany, but poverty wasn't the motivation that led us to put up with the deprivations, the mental kickings and the humiliation that went with the sport at that level. I think everyone was on the same pathway with a desperate desire to make it onto a pro team. That's where the ruthlessness came in. You had to win consistently in order to get noticed, but getting noticed wasn't enough in itself. If you wanted a slot on a pro team you needed to have people with influence working for you. They could make phone calls for you, lobby for you, try to open doors. It was such a steep curve that to make it on riding alone was almost impossible. Looking at it this way you can understand why so many successful pro cyclists seem to have had fathers and grandfathers who were in the pro ranks before them. Contacts count.

One of the ways the Breton cycling fraternity used to network was by going on hunting expeditions. 'La chasse' is a big deal in France. If you're ever in Decathlon, the French-owned sports superstores, you'll notice the massive section devoted to camouflage waders, duck decoys, that kind of thing. It seemed a bit strange at first, but I came to recognise that they were just like businessmen doing deals on a golf course. Hunting may have been a great way to make contacts, but I only went once, and for two reasons. First, because it absolutely wiped me out. Stick me on a bike and set me off to climb to some crazy mountain pass in the Pyrenees and I'd be fine, but 12 hours up to my arse in marshland carrying a shotgun absolutely totalled me. The second thing was that I just didn't get off on killing animals and birds. Maybe it was because I grew up next to a nature reserve with all those harmless birdwatchers pottering up and down our road, but shooting small creatures just seemed cruel and unnecessary. The hunters sometimes met up in the Trehins' house before heading out with their guns.

One morning I was just arriving back at the house from my early morning run and stepped in through the back door into the kitchen. There was a guy sitting at the table who seemed strangely familiar. I did a double take. Surely not? It was the Badger himself. The legendary Bernard Hinault was taking some time out in the off-season to do a spot of bird shooting. I exchanged a few friendly words with one of history's finest cyclists before heading off to the shower.

Some of the clubs would have shown you the door after a single season if you weren't cutting the mustard. A quick word from the directeur sportif and that was it. 'Pack your bag, sonny, and don't come back.' They were much more forgiving at Lorient and riders were given a fair chance to prove themselves. I think one of the things that helped me was that I'd started to make a lot of friends in the club and around the town. Cycling in Brittany had a reputation for being tough, but they were prepared to cut me a fair bit of slack.

Guy Trehin had been around cycling in Brittany for a long time. He knew everybody who was worth knowing. They were all old mates and sometimes they'd come around to the Trehins' house for dinner. One of Guy's pals was this guy Ange Roussel. I'd been riding for Ireland during the latter part of my stay in France and it must have seemed a novelty having an international riding for a Breton club. One night, Roussel arrived over for a chat. I wasn't exactly sure of his importance, but I'd heard the name and it was obvious he was giving me the once over. In fact, he turned out to be one of the top officials in Breton cycling. During his long career he coached the French national team and worked with Tour de France winners Bernard Hinault and Laurent Fignon and world champion Luc Leblanc. He started talking about his son, Bruno, who was doing great things with a club in Paris.

Roussel introduced me briefly to Bruno, and I tried to figure out a way in which these two could give me a leg up to the big leagues. I'd been there long enough to know young Breton riders who'd joined big pro teams, even some who'd ridden in Le Tour. Surely there must be a chink I could squeeze through. In the end, the Ange Roussel thing came to nothing. It was probably just as well. Bruno went on to be a high-profile directeur sportif. Rather too high profile, as it turned out. In 1998 he was manager of the Festina team when a shedload of doping materials was discovered in the boot of a team car on the eve of the Tour de France. Festina was booted off the Tour and Bruno was given a 12-month suspended prison sentence.

Doping has dogged the sport of cycling since its very beginning. You hear stories about riders in the early years of the sport raiding bars along the side of the road and necking bottles of brandy – anything to keep the pain at bay. The list of substances those guys were pouring into themselves is shocking. Strychnine, nitro-glycerine, cocaine, ether – the entire contents of the devil's medicine cabinet. I never saw any overt signs of doping in Ireland. You were riding against the same relatively small group of riders every weekend, which meant you had an intimate knowledge of what they were capable of and what conditions they were suited to. Every so often a rider would pull off a result that was absolutely off the Richter scale, but it was only after I went to France that I started to realise what I might have been looking at. I'd always believed that the highest sporting performance was built on proper nutrition, training and recovery. This was an eye-opener that began to change my view of the sport.

The first time it became blatantly obvious was after the initial training camp in Biarritz when I'd first joined the Lorient club. I'd had a great winter's preparation back home and was in peak physical condition. I reckoned I was riding as well as, if not better than, the 17 other guys on the team. Even the coaches were commenting on how well I was doing. Days later, at the first race in Brittany, the guys I'd been dropping at the training camp were blasting off up the road leaving me behind. At first, I thought I was getting sick, that there was something wrong with me. I couldn't understand how the hell I'd gone from blowing everyone away to struggling just to make it to the finish. Then it dawned on me. There were probably a range of factors, but guys using dodgy substances had to be one of them.

In terms of doping eras, if you want to look at it historically, the time when I was racing was just at the end of the end of the

Tommy Simpson or Eddy Merckx era, when riders were mostly accused of using amphetamines and, later, steroids, and the punishment for being caught amounted to little more than a slap on the wrist. It would probably be regarded as Mickey Mouse stuff nowadays, but it was highly effective. Use of the infamous blood-doping drug EPO (erythropoietin) didn't begin in earnest until the 1990s. Doping was a regular subject of discussion in the cycling world, but people didn't go into specifics. Most of amounted to little more than idle gossip – 'Oh, yes, of course!' They all said it was going on, but that's where it stopped. No one ever dished out the evidence.

I was never offered doping products the whole way through my career, possibly because I had a bit of a reputation as someone who had a particular interest in nutrition and healthy eating. It has always been a hobby horse of mine. Not so much a hobby horse, really, more an obsession. It's the key to all my ultra-cycling success, and it's hardly surprising that my partner, Jill, is also an experienced performance nutritionist. I struck it lucky when I was billeted with the Trehins. They were basically a family of chefs. They weren't into the rich sauces people associate with French cuisine; they went in for peas and beans, fish, tons of salad and soups. Jacqueline would come home each evening from the bistro and immediately set about cooking for the family. Those meals became the focal point of the day and they sometimes went on for three hours. The food just clicked with me. Alcohol was a different matter. I was a complete non-drinker – I didn't have my first glass of wine until 2009 and now I'm very careful with it. I didn't even drink coffee before I went to France, but that didn't last long once I'd got there. Coffee oils the wheels of the average cyclist. They drink it until it's coming out of their ears.

There was a forest out the back of the house and each morning I'd be up at seven and off on a run. When I got back, I'd do an upper body session. I was fit as the proverbial butcher's dog. People knew the effort I was putting in and that was another reason for my frustration. The Roussel thing was just one of several occasions when I really got my hopes up that I was on the verge of a breakthrough but, as time passed, I began to think, well, maybe I'm just not that special as a rider. I started to realise that there was another level of riders above me, possibly two, and I felt I was approaching the absolute limit of what I could achieve in racing. These were dangerous thoughts. They came to me in the night and I pushed them away, hoping they would disappear.

CHAPTER 4

Blacked Out under the Flyover

Riding in representative teams, whether for Ireland or Northern Ireland, was a big part of my years in mainstream racing. When I was living in France, I was a regular pick for the Ireland team's forays into Europe. It was quite comical, really. The guys would roll off the Cork to Roscoff ferry with all the gear in an old Toyota Hiace van. There would be a volunteer manager, a volunteer mechanic and a volunteer masseur. I was a cheap option because they didn't have to pay for the ferry ticket. I also had a lot of experience in French racing. For the guys who weren't used to it, riding in some of the toughest amateur races could be a brutal experience. To be competitive you needed to be racing regularly at that level but there just wasn't the money available to send teams away, so the Irish lads would set off a number of times each year and get their butts kicked.

I was lucky to be in a position to represent both countries. I may have grown up in Donegal, but I can honestly say that the first time I was selected for Northern Ireland I couldn't have been more proud. All the Northern Ireland guys were eligible to ride for Ireland but I was one of the few born in the Republic who represented the North. Morris Foster would have been the main

Northern Ireland selector. You didn't get a letter or even a phone call to say you'd been picked. Morris would drift over to you after a race and say, 'Hey, boy, get your bag packed; you're going to wherever next Friday.' He really was that laid back about it but in truth you might as well have got a letter from the Queen. There was the question of my citizenship, of course. I was actually born in Palmerston, County Dublin. My dad was working with his brother, who owned a hotel in Dublin at the time. I never knew much about that time – even my mum was vague – and I only lived in Dublin for six months before we moved back to Donegal. Ironically, all my siblings were born in a nursing home in Derry. A few weeks before I was selected for the team, Morris took me to one side to check if it was true that my Dad was from Northern Ireland. He was born in Derry, so that was me sorted. There was no official request from the board of selectors to see my passport or anything.

Once you'd been selected there was none of the hi-tech, science-based training you'd get in the twenty-first century. Morris would have got the team together in the car park of the Valley Leisure Centre in Glengormley at stupid o'clock in the morning. He would then proceed to get us hammering up and down the Glens of Antrim for hours on end. It was all about big hills and big mileage. Then you'd come back and do it all again the next day. Those were hard school days. Morris had been a big, physically robust cyclist himself and he tended to favour guys who could cope with that kind of battering. In hindsight, I can think of fifty better ways of preparing for a big race or a Commonwealth Games, but Morris only had his life experience to work from. Sadly, he's no longer with us but you have to give credit to the big man for the sheer level of raw passion he brought to the sport. He had enormous respect and you couldn't help but feel immensely proud to be one of the riders he'd chosen to take with him. Every time I pulled on a Northern Ireland jersey all I wanted to do was perform.

It was hard to attract international teams to the small number of stage races held in Northern Ireland. The Tour of Ulster and the Tour of the North would attract some riders from the home nations and if you were lucky there might have been a smattering of foreigners. Morris had a special relationship with the organisers of the Girvan Three Day Race in Ayrshire and that was a real step up. You would have been confronted by the full-blown GB squad and teams at that level, including guys from Belgium, Holland and the like. Another event Northern Ireland sent a team to was the Rás, Ireland's biggest stage race. It ran for nine days, attracted a big international field and had a tough reputation. The Rás was also a shop window for Olympics qualification.

When we went to these big events, I always made an effort to strike up friendships with members of the other teams. It's always useful to have contacts, and not just from a selfish point of view. I liked to be able to walk over to another team car and have a yarn. It got to the point where the entire GB national squad once spent the afternoon in Newtowncunningham with my mum serving them tea and buns. They were on the way back to England in a Ford Cortina via the Larne–Stranraer ferry. There was no flying around in those days. That was the year I got thrown off the Rás, the only time I've ever been disqualified from a race.

That day's stage ran through the Glengesh Pass, a high, winding climb through bleak Donegal hillsides. I had punctured and was chasing back to the front group after changing the wheel when a police motorbike came by. I couldn't resist the opportunity to get in his slipstream and hitch a free ride. I flew around a blind bend to be greeted by a dozen guys on bikes stopped in the road. The race had been halted, possibly because of an accident, but from the looks on people's faces it was clear I'd been rumbled. I couldn't possibly have caught up so quickly without help. I was hauled in front of a Dutch race commissaire who asked me if I'd breached rule number whatever it was. I just held my hand up. It was all rather embarrassing.

One of the visitors my mum plied with her finest scones that day was Gary Fryett, a GB mechanic from Essex. In later years I stayed at his place when I was on the professional circuit in England and he was my mechanic when I competed in cyclo-cross for Ireland. Gary's a big guy with a loud laugh and a broad Cockney accent. He's a joy to be around. He also had a proper job working as a stockbroker in the City of London and ultimately it was some of his clients who helped bankroll my doomed 2012 RAAM – Race Across America – attempt.

The Northern Ireland team didn't take part in the Olympics or the world championships, of course, so the Commonwealth Games was the big stage. I'd missed the 1982 games despite winning the Tommy Givan that time so the 1986 games in Edinburgh were on my radar from a couple of years ahead. I had a great season in 1985, so that just left Morris Foster's rigorous selection process to deal with. He'd taken a team of big hitters in '82 and they had been expected to come back with a medal in the team time trial (TTT). When they returned from Brisbane with a fourth place there was great disappointment. At that point there should have been a complete rethink, but Morris's mindset was that he wanted big, strong guys who could knock down a brick wall and keep riding. Morris already had the bedrock of his team in place in the form of Alastair Irvine and Martin Quinn. There were two places up for grabs.

It was going to take some work to change Morris's thinking, but we'd just reached a watershed in cycling where the scientific understanding of training was emerging. This was when the first pulse meters (which enable the rider to measure their high-level intensity training) appeared and when coaches began to take a serious look at how physiology functions and where it fits into training. Getting to understand how the physiology of the human body works is one of the key processes for any rider to improve their performance. Nowadays you could be swamped by the sheer amount of data that's available. Back in the eighties it was more about piecing together what little information you had. To this day the heart rate is the basis of all training.

Among the select group invited to audition for Morris's latest blockbuster production was a Belfast lad called Cormac McCann. Cormac was obviously following the developments in scientific training. To the best of my knowledge he was the first cyclist in Northern Ireland to possess a pulse monitor. I was intrigued by this electronic device strapped to his handlebars. It was big – half the size of a mobile phone. This technology wasn't exactly witchcraft, but it was certainly the first sign of a new era in bike racing. With the help of the monitor, Cormac was able to sustain a level of speed that meant other racers had to adjust their riding style to keep up. And there were points in the race where he had so much speed that you couldn't do anything to keep up. You can imagine the challenge this posed to Morris's coaching style. He would have dismissed it as a load of trendy bollocks and said you needed to go out and get 200 miles in your legs.

The scientific approach was the sort of thing that has always appealed to me, nutrition being another example. To me it was blindingly obvious that if Cormac was able to achieve those speeds out on the road I needed to investigate his technique. I wasn't as academically savvy as him but I kept asking questions until I had a decent grasp of the principles. I made it a priority to track down and get hold of a pulse meter as soon as I could.

Cormac was working all this out off his own bat, but the official line was still that we pounded up and down the roads of

County Antrim until we were worn out. I remember one winter's day when the four of us, Martin, Alastair, Cormac and myself, sat on the kerb by the side of the road in Cushendun, up in the Glens. It was snowing heavily and so bitingly cold that Alastair was literally weeping into his hands because he couldn't feel them. Morris disappeared off to some local shop and returned with four pairs of cheap woollen gloves. We were ordered back on the bikes and told to get moving. It was what we'd all signed up for and the impression we were given was that if we dropped the ball once there was no going back.

The Commonwealth Games selection process consisted of a series of time trials, or TTs, on a circuit from the outskirts of Belfast out to Larne and back. Each run consisted of Martin and Alastair accompanied by a couple of riders challenging to be on the team with them. The Commonwealth Games event is run over 100km with a team of four riders each setting off at one-minute intervals. As the name suggests, it's a straight race against the clock. You'll see time trials if you watch the Tour de France on TV, but there are lots of variations; you can have individual TTs or races with eight riders. The skills required for a TT are very specific. You can't get out of the saddle, for instance, because it pushes the bike backwards into the guy behind you and the next thing you know there's a high-speed crash. Teams ride in single file to make the most of the slipstreaming effect known as drafting. You could only spend 22 seconds on the front before making way for the next guy. You're belting along at 30–35mph and there's no room for error. Then your heart rate is banging it out at 185 or 186 beats per minute. There's a slight recovery window when it gets down to maybe 178 and then you're accelerating again. Try keeping that up for two hours. It's brutal.

The trial runs out the Larne road were gruelling, with contenders dropping like flies. They just couldn't keep up with the speed and were spat out the back. Alastair and Martin would do a debrief with Morris after the run and it would be, 'Okay then, he's no good. Who's next?' I was one of the riders who took part in all but two of the test runs, and there must have been 16 or 20 of them. It got to the point where I was getting pissed off because I wasn't getting dropped off the back and yet there seemed to be this reluctance to move me from the possibles to the probables. I sort of knew what the problem was. In Morris's book I was just too small, no shelter for the guy behind, all that nonsense. There was only one way I could be sure to get that ride and that was to drop the whole team – fire the whole lot of them out the back.

So I came up with a plan. That night I played along with the game until five miles to the finish. It was just at the crest of a hill next to a place called the Airport Inn that I opened up the taps. Alastair, Martin and Cormac were left for dead. Bang. End of discussion. Martin's dad was in the team car that night. He wound down the window and said, 'That's been a bit of a conversation stopper.' 'No, it hasn't,' I said. 'Just put my name on the page and build the rest around me.' Even Alastair and Cormac were saying to me afterwards, 'Bloody hell, where did that come from?' As the little climber, I'd always been in their shadow, but I had decided to take control of the situation and it worked.

Dave Kane's influence with the Commonwealth Games Council and contacts with Raleigh also played a role in my getting to the games. The wrong size frame was ordered from the bike makers and Dave was able to intervene to get the order changed. There was no real question of me not going after that.

If the eighties was when cyclists started to learn about how to use fairly basic electronics like pulse meters, it was also the era when aerodynamics first came to the fore, especially in time trialling. Some of the bikes they were coming up with were fairly outlandish. I had a sponsorship deal with Raleigh at the time and I politely asked if we could have some of their bikes for the Games team. The company had a Specialist Bicycle Development Unit based at Ilkestone in Derbyshire that made bikes for the Panasonic racing team. Their latest Wacky Races invention was a time trial bike that had a 27-inch rear wheel and a 24-inch on the front. You leaned forward at a terrifying angle with your bum in the air. I'd been doing some R&D work with the Ilkestone people and that helped when I asked for the bikes. They were identical to the ones that Panasonic had for the Tour de France, except theirs were white with blue front forks and stem and ours were white with emerald green at the front. When the frames arrived, it was given to me to assemble all the Northern Ireland bikes in Morris's garage in Glengormley. To this day I do all the work on my own bikes – going right back to the time when I used to take the Chopper apart in the kitchen.

My last hurrah before the team was announced was the Northern Ireland road race championship. I won the race in a solo effort near Lurgan, partly, it must be said, because Martin and Alastair sat back and didn't chase me.

I punched the air when the letter came from the Commonwealth Games Council to say I was on the team. 'Yes!' It felt like another big step up towards the big leagues. As we set off for Edinburgh my objectives were to deliver what the Northern Ireland guys in 1982 hadn't been able to do, and to prove that it's not the biggest and strongest who win – it's the smartest. It's a pity the Games venue wasn't a bit more exotic, but holding it in Edinburgh saved a few quid for the home nations, I suppose. Morris was an old hand at this sort of thing. He'd competed for Ireland at the Mexico Olympics in 1968 and even carried the flag for Northern Ireland at one Commonwealth Games. He encouraged us all to go to the opening ceremony. You could be cynical about it, but he was right when he said it could be the only chance we'd get to take part in something like that. I felt really proud to walk out in front of that massive crowd at Meadowbank Stadium. It's not as though bike racing is a big spectator sport in Ireland. I still have my fancy team blazer.

We stayed in university halls of residence during the Games but all the cycling preparations took place in a different part of the city. Each team was allocated a big shipping container to act as a base for the bikes and all the equipment. On the morning of the race we set off to ride across Edinburgh to the start. We were on public roads and it was a normal Edinburgh rush hour. The great fear was that one of us would damage one of those little 24-inch front wheels because only four had been made and we had no spares.

I hadn't got a hundred yards down the road when I suddenly felt something was wrong with my bike. 'What the fuck? Today of all days!' I pulled over and set the bike against a wall to take a look. No puncture, but my mechanic's eye soon noticed that the chainset had been swapped: 170mm cranks were pretty much the limit for me but the bike had been refitted with 180mm. The guys rode on while I hightailed it back to the big container. Sure enough, the original chainset was lying in the corner. I worked flat out and fixed it in ten minutes flat. I should never have let anyone else touch my bike. When I do all the work myself there's no room for silly mistakes. That left me to pretty much sprint to the starting point, and my pristine white handlebar tape was slathered in black oil. I arrived there ten or twenty minutes after my teammates, who were wondering where the hell I was. It actually worked out pretty well because I was nicely warmed up while they'd been left standing by the side of the road for an age.

The general consensus in the cycling community back home was that we hadn't a hope in hell of getting a medal. We were up against three of the best TTT teams in the world: Australia, Canada and England. If someone had said we'd get a place on the podium they'd have been laughed out of the room.

The race was run over a closed section of motorway and we knew as soon as we recced the course that it was going to be fast. There was one section where you hit a roundabout after a long downhill section. By the time we reached the roundabout we were going so fast that the four of us were swinging like a snake's tail. It must have been all of 40 or 50mph from kerb to kerb and you could barely keep the bike upright. There was no GPS tracking back then to tell you exactly where you stood compared to the other teams. As you passed through the start and finish area you could see the timings and how you were positioned compared to the others. Going into the last lap there was something like 35 seconds between us and the third-placed team and less than a minute and half from the second place. England were well in the lead, three minutes ahead of us.

What transpired was a crazy last lap race for the bronze medal. We'd lost Cormac by that point. It's not unusual to drop one of your team during a TTT and Cormac had blown up with two laps to go. We were going so fast that if you slightly mistimed coming down the line or were hanging on at the back you were gone. It didn't reflect badly on him, but it meant the remaining three of us hit a vicious pain barrier, our lungs searing. Martin Quinn looked across at me as I was coming down the line and shouted: 'Whatever you do don't let go!' Then Alastair started screaming, 'I can't come through!' I had to shut the gap in the middle to make sure he stayed in the line. Then I was coming off the front and plugging the gap to give him a rest. He would then come around me and shut the door again and we'd be back in formation. All sorts of crazy shit went on in the last five miles.

I remember crossing the line, but total exhaustion hit me as I climbed off the bike and I passed out in the middle of the motorway under a flyover. When I came to I was looking up at a concrete sky. A team doctor who'd been in the car with Morris was shouting, 'You did it! You're on the podium! You've got a medal!' In that batshit crazy last lap we'd managed to overhaul the Australians and undo the failure of 1982. I looked over to the rest of the team and there was Morris Foster, the original tough guy, wiping the tears from his face. I still have a massive sense of pride when I look back on that time trial. I may not have been the greatest rider in the world, but moments like this gave me a sense of possibility. I could look back at my dad and those schoolteachers and anyone else who told me I would come to nothing and laugh in their faces. If I kept on striving I could overcome and triumph.

When I'd been riding regularly for Northern Ireland for a while it became obvious that riding for Ireland would be the next big step up. The thing about the Northern Ireland set-up was that, okay, you're an international rider on one level, but on another you're not. Getting on the Irish squad would be a pathway to possible selection for the world championships and the Olympics. I also had this perpetual issue of being seen as a Donegal man when I was racing in Northern Ireland but a northerner when I was racing in the Republic. As far as a lot of people were concerned, I was neither fish nor fowl. Getting on Irish teams was all about how well you were performing and getting noticed by the international selectors. I'd always gone to a lot of races down south, but now there was more of an edge to them. And the sport was changing. The governing bodies of the various sports were signing up to government grants that were dependent on success measured by podiums, medals and international championships.

The first time I got picked for Ireland was in 1985. It would have been hard for the selectors to overlook me; I'd had a fantastic season, culminating in winning a thing called the Classic League. It included all the top races on the country, maybe ten of them. Once I'd been selected for the international squad I was on a whole new learning curve. The guy who ran the Ireland team at the time was Pat McQuaid. He went on to have a major career in cycling administration, including what you could probably describe as a turbulent period as the president of the sport's world governing body, the UCI. I only know him through my experience as a cyclist on his teams decades before all of that. Coming from the Northern Ireland experience under Morris's wing, the Ireland set-up immediately alerted me to the fact that this was on a different level entirely. We were treated like professionals and made to take responsibility for our own behaviour. Pat had no time for shirkers. He would have reprimanded you for not sitting up straight to eat your food at the table.

I was selected to ride for the Irish team in the Tour of Britain, known in those days as the Milk Race. The experience was pretty spectacular, but not in a good way. It was a 14-day stage race that was widely regarded as one of the hardest amateur races in the world. Talk about a baptism of fire. The first stage started in Bournemouth and ran for 113 miles. It wasn't overly long but the problem was the weather. It was lashing down with rain, an absolute biblical storm. Then I punctured forty miles out the road and was faced with trying to chase back onto a group that was headed up the road at 35mph. It just wasn't going to happen. I rode on feeling like shit and thinking how it would look if I failed to make the cut-off time and got bucked off the race on the first day. The road ran through a big cornfield somewhere near Cheddar Gorge and I came spinning around a bend to see three big Russian cyclists standing by the roadside. One of them had punctured and the other two had waited for him. They rolled off just as I came around the corner and I sat on the back getting drafted along. It was like sitting on a freight train and they towed me right back to the main group of riders. I wasn't in the bunch three miles before I punctured again and was dropped off the back. Just my bloody luck. There were no big Russians lurking by the side of the road this time. It pissed with rain all day and as I rolled across the finish line, I can remember seeing litter blowing around like tumbleweed. The crowd had all disappeared. I was nearly an hour down on the stage winner but I'd somehow managed to remain within the time limit. Just like during that first kermess in Brittany, I'd finished up holding the lanterne rouge.

You can imagine what the atmosphere was like at the Ireland team dinner table that night. I couldn't justify what had happened, but equally there was no attempt by the team to put the matter to rest. In hindsight, I would have expected the directeur sportif to take me to one side and say, 'Look, we understand what happened here and it's not your fault. We're going to regroup tomorrow. We'll get you to work for the team and you'll get to the finish.' But there was none of that. I felt completely isolated. I caught the odd disparaging glance, as if to say 'He's dead wood', but most of the time I felt ignored. You need mutual support to thrive in a team environment but there was none forthcoming and as a result I was getting more battered, mentally and physically, as the days passed. At times like this my head would drop and doubts would slip into my mind. If others thought I wasn't good enough maybe they were right. It takes a lot to pick yourself up and fight on. I have a tendency to turn in on myself at times but I also have the mental strength and resilience to fight my way back to the surface. It's a sense of defiance I can draw on when the going gets tough.

My troubles with the national squad came to a head when I wasn't selected for the Ireland team to go to the 1988 Olympics in Seoul. I came back from France in 1987 to show my face and prove that I could be one of the top five or six riders in the country who would make the trip to South Korea. I made a great showing in the Rás, where I finished third overall and was in the winning team. I was also in the top ten in the national road race championship. To get on the team you had to achieve a certain level of results within a defined set of races. I believe I fulfilled all the criteria and yet I wasn't selected.

That year I came as close as I ever would to winning the Rás. I was second in the overall race for six days in a row, about four seconds down from the leader, Paul McCormack, but for the life of me I couldn't make up those four seconds. My last chance to catch him was a time trial at the Devil's Glen in County Wicklow. I've always been a climber and I knew I could make it faster up the hills. The riders set off in reverse order according to their position in the race, so there was a lot of waiting around before I set off second to last. There were time checks all the way up the hill and I knew I was ahead on time. Halfway up the hill there was a narrow stone bridge, so narrow you could barely get a car through without scratching the wing mirrors. As I approached the bridge a race marshal on the far side let a car drive on to it. It was sheer incompetence. I threw my hands in the air. 'For fuck's sake!' In the end I actually had to get off the bike, lift it in the air and slide along the wall to get past the car. That's how I lost the 1987 Rás. At the end of the race I found myself in third place. It was a punch in the gut alright.

Even with losing the Rás in that way I was still easily within the top five or six who were a shoo-in for the Olympics. I'll never know why I wasn't selected. Call it a chip on my shoulder if you like, but it still hurts. Ask a competitor in any sport and they'll tell you the Olympics is the pinnacle of their ambition. This was the year after I'd won the medal at the Commonwealth Games up against the best time triallists in the world. My thinking was that if the team got a good result in Seoul there would be a queue of professional teams waiting to sign me up. I'd discussed it with Debbie and Dave and with Martin Quinn and it seemed to be a goer.

The result of my profound disappointment was that I decided I was done with amateur racing. I would have to take my career by the scruff of the neck and find my own route into the professional ranks.

CHAPTER 5

Never the Same Again

One afternoon in the spring of 1988 I was getting my stuff together prior to heading back to France for the new racing season. The phone rang. It was Dave Kane. There had been an accident, he said, a terrible accident. Debbie was hurt. Things were never the same after that.

Debbie and I had started dating in 1982 and we'd been an item ever since. It started with us being out on the bikes training together or working in the shop and just snowballed. In the evenings we might have gone to the cinema but more likely we'd have gone back to my little flat and chilled in front of the telly. We didn't really have a social life outside racing, but there was such a rich sense of fellowship in the cycling community that there was no need for drinking and dancing. Debbie used to come with me to Donegal and had a great relationship with my mum.

Things weren't always so easy. Keeping in contact when I went away to France was a nightmare. Racing can put a lot of strain on a relationship because you're away so often. After Boroughbridge, when she rode the 25-mile TT in under an hour, her racing career really took off. She won numerous national titles and rode for Ireland at the world championships in 1986, the year I was in Edinburgh at the Commonwealth Games. I have a copy of the *Sunday Life*, the Belfast newspaper, from around that time that has a double-page spread on the two of us. It was a kind of 'cycling's golden couple' thing.

That was the point we'd reached when Debbie had her accident. She'd been competing for Ireland in an international race in Essex and had run into a truck. Dave and Maggie were heading for the airport when Dave called to tell me. I couldn't get a flight right away but flew to Stansted the next morning. The race organisers sent someone to pick me up from the airport and take me to the hospital. It was Gary Fryett, who, as I've already mentioned, went on to become one of my great friends. In the car that day was the first time I met him. He'd been one of the first to reach Debbie on the road and had cleared her blocked airway, probably saving her life.

It was only when I reached the hospital that I learned the whole story. The race had been held on a public road with a rolling road closure. The police were stopping traffic and pulling vehicles that were coming towards the cyclists over to the side. In the middle of all this Debbie had a puncture so she'd stopped to change her wheel. Once that was sorted, she needed to get back to the front of the race. I think one of her teammates may have been helping her to get back up there. In any case, she was on the outside of a bunch of riders as they came into a corner. There was no way she could have known there was a 45-foot articulated truck on the far side of the bend. It was parked up but it hadn't been taken off the road. As the cyclists swept downhill around the bend, they must have been doing thirty-plus miles an hour and Debbie ran straight into the front of the truck. The impact was colossal. She hit the front of it full tilt and didn't even have time to hit the brakes. Debbie had a litany of fractures, and her back was broken.

When I arrived at the hospital she'd been given a heavy dose of painkillers. She was badly burned by water from the truck's radiator and had cuts everywhere. I couldn't believe that anyone could be so badly injured coming off a bike. I'd seen many crashes, but nothing like this. Then the doctors were checking her over and discovered Debbie couldn't move her lower limbs. The thought that she might be paralysed came as a horrendous shock. When something like that strikes a person you love, everything else in life becomes insignificant in a split second. I instantly knew that cycling was over for me. France was over. My place was at Debbie's bedside.

The cycling community rallied round, raising money to get her flown home. I think it may have been a military aircraft that brought her back to Belfast. Debbie was admitted to Musgrave Park Hospital in Belfast, which specialised in orthopaedics. I went to the hospital every day. It became a routine. I went in the morning and covered the day shift while Dave and Maggie were running the shop. I fed her and gave her drinks and was there for her as best I could. At 6.30 in the evening her parents came and took over. I sat by her bedside for months and months. It developed into a routine. The ward sister was a bit of a Morris Foster type. She kept her nurses on a tight rein, but her plain speaking meant she was good at explaining medical matters in layman's terms. She laid out for me what the future held for someone in Debbie's position. The sister wasn't particularly well liked by her staff but she was good to me in her fashion. One day she marched into the room and said, 'If you're going to be moping around the place here you night as well make an effort to help out.' She gave me a white coat that was about four sizes too big and set me about fetching food and drinks, running errands and generally helping out with the four patients on the ward. They were a varied bunch from all walks of life. One had fallen off a horse and another had fallen off the balcony of a block of flats – that kind of thing.

Then something really bad happened. It's a difficult part of my story, one of the most difficult. One evening, Dave and Maggie had already gone in to see Debbie and I was coming out of the front door of the hospital. Two men approached me. One looked me straight in the eye and told me never to return to the hospital. He said I was to leave Northern Ireland and not come back. It was an order. He made it clear what would happen to me if I disobeyed. The other had his hand in his coat pocket and was pointing it at me. He was clearly holding something. Either it was a real gun or he wanted me to believe it was one. He scared the life out of me. You could get shot in Belfast for walking down the wrong side of the road in those days.

It just so happened that a cyclist I knew well, he'd been one of Morris's Cyprus lads, was going in to see Debbie and saw what had happened from across the street. It must have looked very strange because he came up to me and asked if I was okay and who those guys were. God knows what had registered on my face, but I just felt stunned. 'No, it's okay, mate. I'm fine. Hundred per cent,' I said. I usually walked home from the hospital to my flat. It was quite a hike but it was the only exercise I was getting. That night I took a taxi. I threw all my stuff into my car and drove to Donegal. I arrived home to my mum's house and I didn't leave Donegal for six months. It was an impossible situation, the worst. All through my life I would have told my mum anything but I was reluctant to talk to her about this. When I did, she was terrified for me. Sometimes I look back and feel that I didn't act with enough courage. Maybe Debbie and I would have stayed together, but I will never know. I was just plain afraid to go back to Northern Ireland because I didn't know who would be watching me.

Debbie and I arranged to meet up again a few years ago to discuss those times. Her husband, Stephen, dropped her off at a hotel in Templepatrick, near Belfast. I had always wanted to set things straight with her about our past. It was awkward at first. Debbie seemed to be angry with me. She'd come to the meeting thinking I wanted something from her – forgiveness for what had happened. All I wanted to do was to explain to her very clearly what had occurred. As I explained those events of from thirty years previously, I could see it was beginning to make sense for her. I described the incident with the two guys at the hospital and she said she understood. I think it was a relief for us both and we went on to reminisce about happier times. In the end, Stephen phoned Debbie to say we'd been talking for a couple of hours and maybe it was time to head home.

From that meeting onwards there was a kind of reconciliation with Debbie. On another occasion, she came to my house and we spent hours talking about the old days. Debbie even made the trip to Donegal to spend the afternoon with my mum. It was like she had never been away. Those two always got on well. Life dealt Debbie a terrible blow on the bike race that day. She remained paralysed for the rest of her life. Her husband, Stephen Barclay, is a great guy and was so very good for her. Debbie sadly passed away from cancer in 2020. I told her about this book shortly before she died to ask if she would like to add her thoughts, but it was not to be. Debbie was a well-loved member of the cycling community in Northern Ireland and there was a great outpouring of sympathy for her family when she died.

I was like a hermit when I got back to Newtowncunningham. I didn't even walk about the house, just sat in the living room staring blankly at the crap on the TV. It was like I'd had a mental breakdown. There were people with guns who were prepared to kill me. What the fuck was I supposed to do with that? For a long time, it just repeated in my head. I don't know to this day what their motive was.

After several months sprawled on the sofa I decided to get back on the bike. It was either that or become some sort of basket case. I had no other skills; racing pushbikes had been my life. I persuaded myself that a gunman wouldn't come looking for me at a crowded bike race. When I did go back, I took a tremendous amount of flak from the cycling world that I had been part of. It was understandable from their point of view, I suppose. Some ganged up on me in races. Others told me to my face what they thought of me. This went on for three or four years. The consensus was that I'd walked away from Debbie when she needed me most. I couldn't help feeling angry about the treatment I was getting considering that there was only one person who had actually seen me being approached by those men outside the hospital.

If I was going to go back to racing then I had to have a plan. I couldn't just let things drift. It was moving into 1989 and I'd be hitting my thirtieth birthday soon. I'd realised some time before that my career seemed to advance at half the speed of other riders. That's okay when you're 21 or 22 but I was already beginning to sense the closing of my window of opportunity. Kind of ironic when you consider I'm more than twice that age now and going stronger than ever, but that's how it seemed at the time. I was still angry about not being selected for the Olympics and France was no longer an option. The Commonwealth Games was coming up in New Zealand. I had stopped riding for months. Could I get my shit together and make it onto the team?

I started riding again seriously at the start of the 1989 season. I was rusty as hell, but it didn't take me long to hit my stride. New Zealand was just the motivator I needed. I was selected for the Northern Ireland team again and was back with Alistair and

Cormac in the TT chain gang. Morris was still at the helm and he'd made one significant change. He'd dropped Martin Quinn, the man I still think was the best time triallist Northern Ireland ever had, and replaced him with Davy McCall. I knew Davy really well and we were friends. Sadly, he was killed when his bike was hit by a car during a race in County Antrim in 2008. Davy wasn't really a TT specialist. Being more of a sprinter he had a tendency to move from side to side in the line and even to get up out of his seat. Given the speed that we were moving at it was quite unnerving for the rest of us. 'This isn't working very well,' Cormac said to me, trying to be diplomatic. 'It isn't working at all,' I replied.

Despite the gloomy portents, the Auckland games was a remarkable experience. There were new faces on the rest of the cycling team. Dave Kane's son, Mark, was there and Northern Ireland had its first woman cyclist competing. I couldn't help thinking that if Debbie hadn't had the accident she would probably have been there. The team's training camp was in a remote little resort town near Rotorua on North Island. The four of us TT lads shared a cabin with its own swimming pool. The training rides were strange. This was in the days before GPS, of course. We discovered that if you set off on a road that went up into the hills it could abruptly turn into a dead end. It just ran out of tarmac. One day a 'short' training ride took us about 160 miles around the back of a mountain.

As race day approached, we rode our bikes the hundred or so miles up to Auckland and checked into the athletes' village. I remember watching the boxer Wayne McCullough finishing his early-morning training session just as we were getting up. The 'Pocket Rocket' won a gold medal at the games and later held the WBC world bantamweight title. It was the height of the New Zealand summer and as the days passed it got hotter and hotter.

This was bad news for Davy as the heat just wiped him out. He had that typical Irish complexion, pale skin and freckles.

The race was held on a big motorway sector near the city and by the time we got started it was 12.30. The sun was fierce and it was a case of mad dogs and Irishmen go out in the midday sun. From the get-go it felt wrong. We just couldn't get into a proper rhythm and then Davy dropped out. He couldn't hold the speed. It was about ten miles into the 62-mile race and it left the three of us to wrestle with this monster. Then one of the guys got some crap caught in the front wheel; I think it was a wire coat hanger. Once we'd untangled that we were dead in the water and trailed home in sixth place. All that way and months of training for zip. Fair play to Alistair, he made the most of a bad job. They put his name down for the track racing. I must admit I laughed at him and the crappy track bike they knocked up for him. Then to everyone's surprise he won a bronze in the points race. Cormac and I didn't even go along to the velodrome. We watched it on TV and both regretted not being there to congratulate our teammate. I was really chuffed for him.

Auckland was a setback for my hopes to get a place on a professional team. It didn't matter where. I'd met some guys who were racing in America and by this stage I'd have been prepared to go to the ends of the earth to get signed by a professional outfit. I knew from the range of opportunities that had opened up after Edinburgh that a half decent result could pay dividends. No team was going to prick up its ears when I boasted I'd finished sixth, but my persistence is legendary.

Just before setting off for the Games I'd met two brothers, Brendan and Michael Clarke, who ran a big plastering and flooring business. Not very glamorous, you might think, but some of the biggest teams in world cycling have been sponsored by companies making glue, concrete, sausages, lemonade ...

The Clarkes had just got into cycling. They saw Greg LeMond winning the Tour de France on a very special, very expensive TVT bike, went down to Dave Kane's shop and said, 'We'll have two of those Greg LeMond bikes, please!' And Dave, with his mysterious contacts, was able to source them.

The guys set up a club called Bann Valley at Portglenone in County Antrim and started a series of club races on Tuesday and Thursday nights. Brendan invited me over to have a crack at it. 'If you survive one of these you'll be doing well,' he warned me. I was taken aback by the number of riders; the place was hiving with them and they weren't exactly skilled in bike handling. There was a good bit of banter and I ended up going a couple of weeks in a row. Over time, I became good friends with Brendan and his wife, Maria. One evening over dinner Brendan leaned over towards me: 'Joe, I could listen to you tell your cycling stories till the cows come home, but I know there's one thing missing. If you really want to turn pro I can sort it for you. Clarkes will sponsor you. It would be my pleasure.' I smiled to myself as a door opened on a whole new set of challenges. And that was how it happened that I turned pro in England and Clarke Brothers sponsored me.

Criteriums were a big thing in the UK at the time. Channel 4 ran a series called *Kellogg's City Centre Cycling*. It was very popular and if you take a look on YouTube you'll see there were thousands of people out on the streets in London, Manchester, Cardiff, Birmingham. I rode in all those places and in the big national league races as well. There were maybe ten full-blown professional teams operating in England at that time. Then there were guys like me, individual professionals who had private sponsorship. It was a very fluid environment in the teams, with riders coming and going all the time, so there was always the possibility of picking up a team contract. Clarkes' sponsorship got me into the pro ranks and I went to England because I knew some of the big teams were also racing in Europe. It was still my ambition to be racing on the professional stage in Europe. The conventional door that had been taken by the likes of Kelly and Roche had long since closed to me. I knew the only way to get what I wanted was to go out and grab it for myself.

I spent a lot of time camped out at Gary Fryett's place in Essex, using it as a base to travel around the country for races, but when I was back home I was usually to be found up in Portglenone with Brendan. He and Maria had a massive house that always seemed to be full of dogs and cyclists. Some of the club members used to drift in and out of the kitchen there as if it was a clubhouse. I was training with Brendan most days and I ended up moving into the house. I still have a lot of friends in the area. The Clarkes were my kind of people. They were from the country, relaxed and easygoing. After all the disappointments, the stress and failures of recent years, I finally felt at peace. It was one of the best times I had in mainstream cycling.

It was during the time that I was riding as a professional in England but living in Northern Ireland that a very special person came into my life. Anyone who knows me or my wonderful partner, Jill Mooney, knows we are joined at the hip in every part of our lives. If you watch the videos of me knocking my pan in on my crazy ultra-cycling challenges it's Jill's soft, Canadian-tinted voice you'll hear gently urging me on. I met her in 1993. It's a rather convoluted story.

My physio, Micky Kerr, had been doing some work with City of Derry Rugby Club. Micky is a very gifted osteopath. He's worked with all sorts of sportspeople, from Cuban boxers to badly injured motorcyclists. Jill's dad was a coach at the rugby club and when she hurt herself while out running, she came to Micky for treatment. The pair of them got talking about sports nutrition, which is Jill's speciality, and Micky was very impressed. The next time I saw him, Micky said, 'Seriously, Joe, you should go and see this girl. I reckon she could sort out some of the nutritional stuff you're concerned about.'

I picked up the phone and booked myself in for a session at her consulting room. She'd just come back from university in Seattle at this point. She held her clinics in a little room in the flat where she was living above her father's optician's shop on Queen Street in Derry city. When I saw her I kind of went 'Wow!' She was an absolutely stunning-looking young woman with beautiful eyes and brown hair. It was like having a consultation with Miss World.

I've always had an interest in nutrition and I knew a fair bit about how food and the actual nutritional content of it works. I'd also done a fair bit of work with Micky on supplementation with vitamins – vitamin C, vitamin E and all that stuff. And I had a fair idea of how the body functions; but chatting to Jill that day made it clear that she was working on a whole new level. As I remember it, by the time the consultation had finished I had Jill's phone number in my pocket and our first date in my diary.

Jill would tell you a different story, mind. 'You waltzing out of the consulting room with my telephone number and a first date pencilled in your diary? That didn't happen,' she said, flat out, when I brought it up. 'Maybe in your head it did. But it was a couple of months down the line that you phoned and said you were going to a mountain bike race down south and did I want to come. So we drove down, and I watched you race – and that became our thing.' That's the bit we're in total agreement on. 'Right from the start, I was handing you bottles and doing your food.'

Soon we were spending a lot of time together and Jill started coming racing with me up and down Ireland. She was with me the day I lost the national cyclo-cross championship. At the same time, Jill was building her business and had her own life. We weren't living together and I wasn't in her pocket every day. Gradually my feelings for Jill started to get more serious. At least I felt it was getting serious for me and I thought it was for her, too. But we never got to the point where we had the big conversation about commitment. Looking back, I can see it was a huge mistake. When I've told Jill since how I felt about her back then, she says it makes her realise just how good I was at pushing my feelings down in favour of the one thing that always won out – the bike.

The other mistake I made was signing up to ride with a team in Belgium. At first sight this was what I'd been dreaming about for years, an opportunity to ride as a professional in Europe. Maybe it wasn't quite the golden ticket, but it was halfway there. The opportunity came through connections in England – a former GB pro road race champion, Tim Harris, was putting together a team in Belgium as a rider-manager. He was signing a lot of UK-based riders for this new Maestro team. I approached Tim and we hatched up a scenario where I would race under the Maestro banner while the Clarkes continued to sponsor me on a personal basis.

Maestro were based in Mechelen, midway between Brussels and Antwerp. It has a beautiful medieval town centre surrounded by a lot of industrial sprawl, and it has a famous football team. The Maestro team rented a lot of big open-plan apartments, above a furniture factory, where the riders lived. We had Belgian coaches and managers who were wired into the local race scene. That's how the team managed to get invitations to most of the big Belgian races. But I hated Belgium. There's a photo of me with the Maestro team lined out in our fancy new purple-and-blue kit, and if you look carefully, you'll notice that I'm freezing cold and it's pishing with rain. That pretty much says it all about Belgium as far as I'm concerned. There's nothing about the entire experience that I'd want to repeat. It was a pity because the guys on the team were a great bunch from all parts of the world. The country is crazy for cycling and has produced some of the world's best cyclists, including the greatest ever, the Cannibal, Eddy Merckx.

The thing about Belgian cycling is that it's all about hardmen and big, gnarly one-day races like the Tour of Flanders and Liège–Bastogne–Liège. The Flemish races in particular are infamous for their brutal cobblestone climbs and filthy weather. It was just the wrong place for a lightweight climber like me. I even got frustrated by the training. By law you had to ride almost everywhere on cycle paths. The only place I could ride on tarmac was on the canal towpaths. I'd ride out of Mechelen for fifty miles past the windmills, sluice gates and piles of rotten turnips, buffeted by the wind blowing off the muddy fields that stretched to the horizon. Then I'd turn around and ride the same tedious fifty miles back.

I rode a lot of the top Belgian races. One in particular I remember was E3 Harelbeke. It's one of the big spring races, what they call the cobbled classics. The granite cobblestones were brutal and as usual I was bouncing all over the road. It was, of course, pissing down and blowing a gale, pretty much par for the Belgian course. E3 is about 200km long and there was no way I was going to make it to the finish. My head went down and I stopped the bike. It's just something that happens in racing. It happens to everyone but you can't help but feel that black cloak of failure on your shoulders. I took the numbers off my jersey and waited by the side of the road for the broom wagon, the bus at the back of the race that 'sweeps up' riders who have dropped out. As I got on board I glanced around the group of hunched, freezing riders, peering out of the window. Every time something like that happens you sense that heavy ball of inadequacy. Every time I picked myself up. Like every dad says to his kid, 'Get back up on the horsey.' But you can only do that so many times before it starts to mess with your head. I wasn't right for Flanders. I was a lightweight climber, perfect for those high, sunny mountain passes in France or Spain.

Belgium had been a great opportunity for me, there's no doubting that. It was top-class racing against the best in the sport. After all those years of trying I'd earned my ticket to the big leagues, but when I got there it just wasn't right. I stuck it for a year but every time I had the chance I came back to Ireland. That's not the way it should be if you're living away from home and you're enjoying it. When you're in it you must stick with it and even when it gets tough you fight it out. Somehow Belgium drained the fight out of me and left me in a dark, bad place. As I looked at the way forward there seemed to be precious little there.

Worst of all, I'd fucked up my chances with Jill. She was young, she had great prospects and enthusiasm for life, and just around the time I went to Belgium she decided she was going to go to Canada. Her mum was Canadian and she had a sister there. Neither of us has ever been scared to take a big risk, and within three weeks of making the decision, she was gone. By the time Belgium was finished for me I'd realised that I should have gone to Canada with Jill. It was another twenty years before we got back together. They weren't bad years by any means but I often think about those lost decades when we should have been together, what turnings we would have taken on life's journey.

So that was it. I'd raced in England and lived the pro cycling nightmare in Belgium and I'd lost Jill, for ever it seemed. Inside my head I was spiralling downwards. I had no plan of escape. Things were headed for a crash.

Brendan Clarke asked me to come and ride with a Clarkes team in the Rás. Four or five of the Maestro team came over from Belgium and rode for Clarkes in that race. I think I rode the Rás 16 times in my career so forgive me if that particular one doesn't stick out in my memory. I drifted home on the Sunday after the race to see my mum and spend some time chilling in Donegal. Deciding to set off to get a few miles on the bike and turn my legs over, I followed a circuit I'd followed many times in the old days and, funnily enough, it ran by the end of the road where Jill's mum and dad lived. As I was heading back home through Derry over the Craigavon Bridge across the River Foyle, I was looking forward to a smooth run home, some home-cooked food and an evening with my feet up in front of the TV. The bridge is a pretty odd construction: a big blue, double-deck job with the bottom deck originally used for hauling railway wagons. I came to a set of traffic lights with a yellow box junction painted on the road. I was headed left, down to the lower deck. It was a junction I'd been through a million times in perfect safety.

Then a car, a Peugeot I think, swung across the road and crossed the box junction right into my path. The driver didn't see me at all and I smacked straight into the side of the car. I flew clear over the top and my bike's front wheel went into the passenger door like a knife. There was a baby in a child seat on the side where the bike hit. It was one of those old-style chairs where the baby sits in the front seat facing backwards and restrained by the seatbelt. As the bike bent the door in, the car seat was pushed over towards the driver's side. It happened so fast that I didn't even get to hit my brakes. I turned my head to the side, my helmet stuck the edge of the roof with an almighty smack and the sunroof sprang open, spraying the baby with shattered glass. I slid across the junction, my skin cut to ribbons through the Lycra kit. My mind's a blank after that. The helmet saved my life, but even with that protection the massive impact fractured my skull. A doctor later told me that the only reason I didn't break my neck was because the sunroof popped open, allowing the roof to buckle.

I remember waking up in Altnagelvin Hospital doped to the eyeballs. Apart from the fractured skull, I had smashed a cheekbone in the impact and you can still see that one cheekbone is higher than the other. Then there was a long tear in the flesh down the side of my face where they had to fold the skin over, leaving another big scar. That was just the visible stuff. I also had a broken arm, a broken collarbone and a broken leg, all down the left side where I hit the car. I had big patches of skin missing from my back, my hips and my legs, and my knees were skinned to the bone. Most painful of all, my fingernails had been torn off when I slid along the road.

Once they'd patched me up, I returned to my mum's to recuperate. A couple of weeks later she had a phone call from a lady who'd seen the accident. 'I've got your son's bike,' she said. She had picked it up from the side of the road and wanted to hand it back. More important, she was able to tell me that the baby had slept through it all. The emergency services had cleared away all the glass and the child was completely unhurt.

CHAPTER 6

A Bright Red Ducati 916

I t may seem ridiculous, but while I was lying in bits in the house in Newtowncunningham I became obsessed with replacing my bike. That was my best race bike and it had been trashed. I needed to be on the road. There was an element of desperation about this, I admit. The old mindset that only a bike could make things right rose to the surface again.

Rehabilitation was painfully slow. The internal injuries on my left side were much more difficult to heal than the broken bones. I was working with Micky Kerr on my rehab, and the first day I started with him, I shuffled hand over hand along the wall to get to his table where the work could begin. I went back to Micky week after week, and slowly we were able to regain movement and flexibility. At last, I made my way back to the bike, even though I carried weakness on the left side for years. I got out on the roads again in the winter and was racing again in the new year. And in spite of all the crap that had been thrown at me, I decided to give it one last throw of the dice.

The Commonwealth Games was coming up again in 1998 in Kuala Lumpur. I was almost 40 by then, but I somehow convinced myself that if I could get picked for the Games then things would be all right. Life would have a meaning again. Cycling was all I knew and I wasn't about to give it up without a fight. I was back into competition and winning races. There were seven places up for grabs on the Northern Ireland team. When the time came to announce the riders, I should have been fifth on the list. The criteria were clearly laid out and I fitted all of them. Then came the day and I got a phone call: 'Sorry, Joe, you're too old.' As blunt as that. I qualified under every single one of those criteria but they just swept them clean away and said they wanted to give some younger guys a chance.

I put the phone down and walked into the hall, looked at my face in the mirror and said, 'That's it. I'm finished. I'm not doing this any more.'

I felt utterly crushed. Like a pile of bricks had fallen on top of me. I'd thrown so much of my life into cycling, heart and soul. You could call it a dream, but that wouldn't be right – a dream by definition isn't real. I'd sweated blood over this for 25 years. The most frustrating part was the role played by the unaccountable amateurs who ran cycling in Ireland. The volunteers who acted on a whim and messed about with people's lives. It seemed like a cruel joke. I look at some of the stories coming out of sport now about how young people are treated by coaches and federations and it makes my stomach turn.

For me, trying to put up a fight had become a fruitless task. The experiences of the previous couple of years, the Belgian fiasco, losing Jill, the crash and now this rejection, put me into a tailspin. I withdrew into a very dark place. Racing bikes had given my life meaning. Lost and without any sense of how to put my life back together, I would sit for hours staring out of the window in Newtowncunningham. At times I jolted awake in the night, the sense of failure tensing my body.

In the half-light of an early Donegal morning I took my bike out of the garage and set off along the road towards the village and up into the hills. It was the first time since I was a kid that I recovered the sheer joy of being on a bike. That's how I learned that cycling wasn't the issue. When I was living with the Kanes in Belfast all those years ago, they would go out on a big club run every weekend, just a bunch of guys having a laugh, talking crap and riding their bikes through the countryside for the sheer fun of it. Debbie used to go with them, but it just seemed so alien to me. Dave could read me like a book and he saw my problem. 'You know, Joe, you need to learn how to enjoy riding your bike. It's not about going balls-out all the time.'

Now, at what seemed like the end of a failed career, I felt the wind in my face and my body moving in harmony with the machine. I had time to glance over the hedge to see the cattle waiting to be milked or a heron rising from a river. So that's what I did for many years, just rode my bike with my head full of thoughts until I reached that point where it was just me and the long view over the fields.

I could spend only so much time licking my wounds after the decision to quit racing. I'd always lived hand to mouth through the racing years, whether it was digging spuds, helping out in Kane's shop, scrapping for primes in France or waiting for a sub from my mum. Now, here I was, almost 40 years old, a man who had never had what you'd call a proper job. My life hadn't had space for a Plan B. The shocking thing about being an athlete, and you never realise this until it hits you, is that when you retire the sport walks away from you and keeps walking. The circus leaves town and you're standing there with a worthless ticket. I didn't have a home, I didn't have a job, I didn't have a pot to piss in.

At first, I couldn't even sign on the dole. I'd been moving around so much I was struggling to find a country to call my own. You walk into the dole office to try to sign on and they ask you for paperwork to prove you are who you say you are. It's like in the movies when the Gestapo ask you for your papers. I had nothing, not even a National Insurance card, never mind six months of electricity bills or whatever. To get into the system you had to prove you were part of the normal world, and travelling from country to country, sleeping in other people's houses, didn't count as normal. It was a bewildering experience and seemed to take months to sort out. And then when I'd finally proved my existence and started getting my few quid of dole money everything ground to a halt. Derry and its hinterland, Donegal and Strabane are usually to be found near the bottom of the employment statistics. At a pinch I could probably have made a badly paid living as a bike mechanic if the opportunity arose but I was forced to busk it and discover skills I didn't know I had.

I have to thank my brother Mark for giving me a bit of a leg-up. He was a logistics and procurement manager for Seagate, a big US company that makes computer hard drives and that has a factory in Derry. Mark had an event coming up that involved getting together all the big logistics suppliers, their CEOs or whatever, for a slap-up dinner at the Guildhall in Derry. He asked me if I'd like to come along to help fill a table. It wasn't what you'd call my natural environment but since the alternative was another night slumped on the sofa watching *A Question of Sport* I decided to tag along.

The Guildhall's a very impressive venue; big stained-glass windows, a high-beamed ceiling and wood-panelled walls. And there I was in my rented tux chatting away to these businessmen while they tore into the brandy and cigars. I didn't know any of them from Adam but I got talking to a guy called Graeme Hanna from Belfast. He was interested in my cycling stories and I was only too happy to oblige. I explained to him I was living in limbo since I'd finished racing. Graeme was the managing director of a pretty big global logistics firm, IFS, and at the end of the evening he passed me his card. 'If anything comes up, I'll give you a shout,' he said. I thought no more of it but a few weeks later I got a message through Mark to go and see Graeme at his offices near Antrim. I was headed up to Belfast anyway so I thought I might as well drop in, nothing to lose. I took a seat in a waiting room for a few minutes flicking through magazines with words like Warehouse, Supply Chain and Haulage in the titles. Graeme called me in and over a cup of coffee he explained that the company was hoping to expand into the northwest. They needed someone to test the water, to draw up a report on the financial prospects for the expansion. I'd never done anything like that before. I'd pretty much lived my entire life on a cash-in-hand basis. But I walked out of Graeme's office with a contract to carry out a six-month feasibility project, gathering information and preparing a presentation.

I suppose you could say it was barefaced cheek on my part but I got the feeling Graeme had a fair idea from talking to me what I might be capable of. Plus, I knew every hole in the hedge from Muff to Magherafelt. As I drove home over the Glenshane Pass I figured that if I found myself struggling, I could always ask Mark to give me a few pointers. My main problem at the start was my total lack of contacts in the business world, and my brother was of enormous help to me with that. I spent most of my days driving around the countryside chatting to people over a cup of tea and trying to gauge whether Graeme could squeeze a few quid out of the market.

At the end of the six months, Mark gave me some advice on how to do the presentation. As it turned out, there was a significant opportunity for Graeme in the northwest and my presentation went down pretty well. I'm not saying it was a spellbinding performance but they could see the numbers and that's what mattered. Then it was handshakes all round and I was left with a 'We'll be in touch'.

And then nothing happened. There was radio silence for several months. I moped around the house and went out and rode my bike. Finally, my determination never to race again went out the window and I signed up to ride the Tour of the North. It was 1999, and I was 40 years old. Let's face it, I'm an addict. The race start was in Dundonald, my old stomping ground in the Dave Kane days. A reporter from BBC Radio Ulster approached me and we were in mid-interview when a black Porsche 911 pulled up across the street. It was Graeme. He nipped over and we had a word before the race started, and then I went to see him a couple of weeks later. 'There's a job here if you want it,' he said. 'If it doesn't work out, we'll let you go, but it's up to you if you fancy it.'

And that's how, in November 1999, I hung up the multicoloured Lycra and swapped it for an M&S pinstripe. There was nothing fancy about the job, no company car or lavish expense account. I sat down on the first day and drew up a list of potential clients. Then it was a case of cold calling and trying to get past the company reception desk to get to speak to the manager. It was a complete blank sheet to me. My patch was Derry, Coleraine, Ballymena, maybe over as far as Magherafelt and down by Dungiven. Really, it was an open book, anywhere that there was global freight that needed moving. Then I'd be out on the road meeting people and trying to develop relationships, so I wasn't just a desk jockey, which suited me. There was a lot of stale coffee drunk in ring-road industrial estates.

I made loads of mistakes but it turned out I was pretty good at the job, which was just as well because it was boring as hell and it never really challenged me. When you're racing, the ask is so great, physically and mentally, and you've got to step up to it every day. I persevered with the new job only because I convinced myself that I had to make myself fit into that world. At the time, I didn't realise how detrimental it would be to my mental health. After a few years of it I felt my life had shrunk. The work was easy and I wasn't delivering a quarter of what I felt able to deliver. I looked around and said to myself: 'Is this all there is to it?' I was hammering square pegs into round holes all day, every day. I didn't fit into that world. I kept telling myself that I had no choice but to knuckle down and comply. There were days when I seriously thought of running away, to just go and live in a caravan and do nothing. But most of the time it seemed that logistics could be a relatively lucrative way to an easy lifestyle. I bought a BMW, but it was just a way of driving between appointments. When I was a rider, my greatest ambition was to become a professional cyclist, but that was never to do with the money that sporting success could bring. Now that racing was finished, I told myself I had no right to have ambitions any more. In trying to fit in I managed to nail myself into a tiny box.

My life changed again in 2002. Seagate always had a lot of small last-minute deliveries and quite often they were out of hours. One evening I found myself driving down to the big warehouse at the back of the factory with a small package to hand over. There was a woman there who signed for it. Her name was Sinead Lynch, petite and pretty. We had a chat and a bit of a flirt and I asked her out. I enjoyed being with Sinead. She was great company and she came from the real world. Up until then I had lived in a kind of cycling bubble. We started seeing each other on a regular basis but we had to keep it under the radar because my brother was her line manager.

Our relationship became more serious and we bought a new house in Eglinton, just outside Derry. I was beginning to live a normal life. I'd done a lot of travelling when I was cycling but

I'd never really been on holiday. Sinead and I went on many trips to all the usual Mediterranean holiday spots – Spain and Turkey are two I remember. On one unforgettable trip we got stuck in a snowdrift on the M6 in England driving home from Euro Disney. Things that other people might have found utterly normal were somehow a bit exotic to me. We had been living together for a number of years when I asked Sinead to marry me. We had a big party with friends and family at the Everglades Hotel in Derry on our wedding day and everything seemed set fair for the future.

Through all this time I'd kept up my friendship with my old mate Gary Fryett in Essex. We were talking on the phone one night when he suggested we travel to France to watch the Tour de France. The idea was that we'd do the trip on motorcycles. I was a bit out of practice with motorbikes but I jumped at the chance. I mentioned it to Graeme Hanna and he said he had a bike I could borrow, which seemed very decent of him. It turned out that Graeme had a taste for exotic Italian superbikes. I followed the Tour that summer in the saddle of a bright red Ducati 916, often described as the most beautiful motorcycle in the world.

On the way home I stayed overnight at Gary's place and set off for the long motorway run up to Scotland and the midnight ferry from Cairnryan. The heavens opened somewhere between Carlisle and Gretna Green and by the time I checked in for the boat I was sopping wet. A man in a hi-vis directed me to the front of the line and I pulled up next to another guy on a motorbike who was equally soaked to the skin. I got talking to him and we laughed at the absurdity of the situation. He'd just ridden down from Fort William in the Highlands. We met up in the lounge on board, drank coffee and had a really good conversation. As we chatted on the boat he said he lived near Dungiven, which is on the road to Derry, so we shared the ride part of the way home and said we'd keep in touch.

That's how I met my best friend Alan. He's been through thick and thin with me over the years and been my wing man on many ultra-racing exploits. As with so many of my friends, he's the complete opposite of me. He's a big fella – six feet tall – with a fondness for fried breakfasts or a sausage bap. Alan comes from a staunch Protestant family, but that has never meant anything between us. For me people are people. He's a witty guy with a dry sense of humour and he has a great integrity. Alan was by my side through some of the most difficult times of my life and he's also top of the pile when it comes to driving a crew car.

That was really the start of my getting involved in motorcycling. A lot of people who know me from cycling are surprised to learn that I was so deeply involved with the other sort of bike racing. I had a motorcycle, a Honda CBR 600, that lay in the garage at my mum's house for the best part of a decade. To be honest, I wasn't a very good rider and I was always scared of falling off. I picked up a motorcycle magazine one day that had an advert for a guy in Ardglass in County Down who repaired bikes. If I'd thought it through, I could probably have found someone round the corner in Eglinton to give the Honda the kiss of life, but I ended up doing a four-hour return trip to a fishing village at the back end of County Down. The mechanic's name was John Donnan and at the time I had no idea that he was one of Northern Ireland's best-known road racers.

John said it was okay to come after work, so it was already getting fairly late when I drove into his farmyard. He worked part-time on the farm but he had a big workshop in one of the outbuildings with a load of racing bikes parked up. After John had cast an eye over the Honda, he invited me in for a cup of tea.

We really hit it off and sat talking until one in the morning. We were both racing guys at heart and he took a genuine interest in my cycling. John had a really open way about him. He was what I'd call a people magnet. There's a strong bond of friendship in the motorbike racing community and people naturally seemed to gravitate to John. At the end of the evening, as we shook hands, he said to me: 'If you're interested, why don't you come racing with me? We'll be in Cookstown at the weekend and you'd be more than welcome.'

I found his Ford Transit in the paddock area at Cookstown. The racket from the race bikes was deafening. John had a business supplying tyres, and other riders were constantly up and down to the van. What with the business and actually competing himself, John was a busy man on race days. After I'd watched the race at Cookstown I started going regularly. The next step was to help out with the team. I was a pretty good mechanic when it came to pushbikes but I wouldn't have known where to start with a motorcycle, so I was really just a gofer, carrying wheels or getting stuff from the van. And the thing was, I really loved it. I was racing again and that was exciting. I went to the North West 200 with John, and to the Isle of Man TT. Bike racing has a huge following in Northern Ireland, and many people look forward to the North West all year. It's not just bikers that follow the sport. Whole families will spend the day lying below a hedge or perched on a wall watching their heroes burning past at speeds of over 200mph.

Motorcycle racing on public roads is also, of course, one of the most dangerous sports in the world. These are not purpose-built race tracks with perfect surfaces and wide run-off areas. They are often narrow roads with all kinds of street furniture, trees, fences and walls, concrete kerbs and cut-up tarmac. If you come off you will in all probability hit something very hard. In the end, I got fed up with road racing because some great guys I knew started to get killed; young guys, guys withs kids and lives ahead of them. The sport went through a dark period when there was a spate of deaths. I knew all the riders. Eddie Sinton died in the 600cc race at the Carrowdore 100. It's a course that runs over little country roads around a village in the Ards Peninsula. I'll never forget that day. Eddie came over to John's van to get a tyre fitted. I stood chatting with him while the wheel was sorted. Minutes later he hit a grass bank on the second lap of the race and was killed. He was 35. That sort of thing just didn't happen in cycling.

So many riders were getting killed that it felt there was almost an inevitability to it. The law of averages says that if you keep on doing this long enough, eventually it's going to get you. John never took stupid risks, but the nature of the sport meant the threat of a catastrophic error was always there. In 2001, he had a big crash at the Tandragee 100. John had always raced Yamaha R1s and the new fuel-injected R1 had just been launched. He told me he just couldn't get a handle on it. For whatever reason it just didn't have the power of the previous model. At Tandragee we were experimenting by swapping between the two bikes, trying to judge the difference and come up with a solution.

In the middle of one of the races John came off the bike in a spectacular fashion. He was lucky to escape with a broken leg. I drove him to the hospital and on the way home I levelled with him. I told him he had to stop racing because he was going to get killed. John was too good a friend to lose. He had a young son and a successful business. I told him he'd done enough in the sport to retire a success. The problem with motorcycle racers is that they become addicted to the speed. Try as hard as you like to persuade them, they will never give up. Looking back, I can see that asking John to give up was as pointless as asking me to give up cycling. It's an obsession and without it your life becomes colourless. I told John I wouldn't be coming racing any more. I told him, quite plainly, that I didn't want to be bringing him home in a box. He wouldn't take my advice and said he'd really miss my company.

John was killed in an accident at the Tandragee 100 in 2008. He hit a safety bale that had been dislodged by another rider. John was catapulted to the side of the road and died at the scene. A journalist rang me at my home in Eglinton to tell me the news. John's passing was a sore loss to me. I thought back to the times he brought me for a walk across the fields the family farmed at Coney Island, a place made famous by a Van Morrison song. There was a big picture of him in his leathers smiling out of the front page of the *Sunday Life* with the headline 'Race Ace Tragedy'. John was my friend. He was 42.

While I was going racing with John, I became friendly with Philip Neill, who ran a team called TAS. The team later became one of the big names in the British Superbike Championship. Philip and I got talking about things like training and nutrition. Those were new ideas in the motorbike world, where nutrition probably meant a pizza and a bottle of Bud. Philip was open to new ideas and he asked me if I was interested in coming to work with his young riders. I called up my old physio, Micky Kerr, and we started work on a fitness programme with the guys embracing the physiology knowledge we had gained from cycling. One of them was Tom Sykes, who later became World Superbike champion.

I was still working full-time in the logistics job while the bike thing was developing and I suppose it was a helpful distraction from the mundanity of the nine to five. The job was all wrong for me and it was driving me to distraction. Sinead had never had an interest in cycling but she came to the motorcycling with me and we were making friends in the bike racing scene. As time passed, I was spending a lot of time away from Eglinton because I started travelling to races in the British 600 Championship to work with Tom. This was the right place for me if I wanted to continue my involvement with motorcycle racing. It was all on race tracks; there were no lamp posts to hit or manhole covers in the road. What was the likelihood of anyone getting killed? A lot less, almost nil.

I was back to regular travel to England at the weekends, just like my pro cycling days. I handled all the riders' nutrition, hydration, stuff like that. We were one of the first teams in the British Championship to work with the riders in those areas, to try to prevent them getting fatigued towards the end of the day. If you feel drained, you're more likely to make mistakes, which obviously isn't a good thing when you're constantly making split-second decisions on the track. I worked with Tom for a couple of years. We kind of bonded because his grandfather, who had brought him up, had been a competitive cyclist as a young man.

My time in motorbike racing came to an end after I became involved with a team called Vitrans. The owner, a Scottish businessman called Robbie Burns, believe it or not, asked me to help run his superbike team. It was very intensive work. I was travelling up and down the country and constantly flying back and forth. It took up more time than my day job. I did it for a year, burning the candle at both ends. In the end it was just too much. I was exhausted. I threw the head up and walked away from motorcycling.

There's no question that it was exciting. Having that escape was enough to convince me in my head that I was okay. The reality was that I was a pushbike rider to the core and nothing else could fulfil my needs. The nature of motorbike racing just didn't lend itself to real physical performance and good health, and those were things that I needed for myself. I have this intense mental drive to compete that requires me to reach the peak of physical conditioning. All that travelling and sitting around and stress went against the grain for me. I still keep in contact with guys from the motorbike world, but I needed to find something else.

It would have been 2003 or 2004 when I discovered sportives. I'd been riding the pushbike for fun and to try to build up my fitness when someone suggested that I have a crack at the Inishowen 100. 'It's like a race but it's not a race,' was how it was explained to me. My ears pricked up like a retired greyhound when it spots a squirrel in the park. 'No, no. If it's a race, it's a race. You can't go halfway with a race,' I said. I'd never heard of a sportive but I knew what a gran fondo was from my days in Europe. Gran fondos are like the London Marathon. There's a proper professional race at the front and then there are 20,000 participants at the back. This sportive thing was a gran fondo with no race at the front, just a rag-bag of cyclists of every different size and capability. You paid your entry fee, anything from a tenner to thirty or forty quid. Then you went for a ride with all these other folk. On the fancier ones you got a medal or a T-shirt, sometimes a freebie set of tyre levers. For most of those taking part it was the closest they'd ever come to a real race.

I struggled with the concept. Did you just ride around a course, or what? Why would I pay good money to go out and ride 100 miles? I could do that any day of the week by myself. So I decided I was going to make it count. The sportive set off from Templemore Sports Complex in Derry, across the border at Bridgend, through Buncrana and right around the Inishowen Peninsula. There were some serious climbs on the way, including

Mamore Gap, that would test the strongest pair of legs. I later learned that the Inishowen has the reputation of being one of the hardest sportives in Ireland. The thing that cracked me up was that there was a coffee stop half way around. You don't stop for lunch when you're on a 100-mile ride.

It felt strange to be at the start of what appeared to be a bike race without any of the familiar faces on show. There were the usual racing rituals of unloading the bike from the car, signing on at registration, sorting out bottles and pumping up the tyres. Everyone enjoys a bit of craic with old colleagues but I kind of liked the fact that there were no expectations of me in this car park full of strangers. No one knew my backstory, all those years of busting a gut to make it as a pro. Sportive was a new thing and the people in it were new. They were ordinary guys who'd come to cycling later in life through watching the Tour de France or whatever. There were the weekend warriors, who were properly fit, took the sport pretty seriously and rode some seriously expensive bikes, and there were the Mamils, the middle-aged men in Lycra whose dad bellies strained their tight cycling kit.

They didn't know me but they knew pretty soon that I was a rider who could handle himself. What happened, of course, was that the old instincts took over and I was soon racing myself, pitting myself against the course. We set off and after ten miles or so there was a core group of ten or a dozen half-decent riders at the front. I just held the pace I was riding at and then suddenly everyone else had disappeared. And that pretty much became the pattern with all the sportives I did. My attitude was, 'Right, as soon as this thing gets out of the car park I'm going to ride as fast as I can to the finish and the hell with everything else.' It was straight back to the mentality I'd had when I was a 16-year-old racing for the first time. That wasn't entirely the philosophy encouraged by the people who organised and took part in sportives – for them it was more of a fun run. I just wasn't capable of anything else.

Once I got a taste for the sportives I started travelling all over the island to take part. There was one in the Sperrin Mountains that was infamously tough, there was Kells in County Meath, a big one in Sligo, Dungarvan, Galway. An Post, the Irish postal service, sponsored a whole series of them and I went to all of those. As usual, there was no such thing as half measures when I developed a new obsession, particularly when it involved cycling. I roped Alan into the enterprise. He was a motorbike man really, but when I decided to chuck in the motorcycling he said he'd help me out at the sportives. It meant I was able to take the 'racing' to a whole new level. Alan was effectively driving a service car out on the course with spare wheels, food, drinks, whatever. I'll admit it must have seemed absurd to the average hobby cyclist that here I was essentially riding a professional race in the middle of a sportive. Alan and I always referred to them as races. I taught him all about how I prepared food, how I dealt with bottles and the whole tactical side of racing. He became a skilled service car driver. If it was far enough away, we'd stop over in a B&B, or we'd just have our dinner on the way home. It was all good craic and didn't feel like it would develop into anything more than that.

Then my sense of restlessness took over, as it always does, and I began to get a bit bored with the Irish sportives. I'd done them all. In fact, some of them I'd done twice or three times. One night over dinner after one of our races I said to Alan, 'What would you think of trying out a proper gran fondo in Italy?' His eyes lit up. 'Let's do it,' he said.

The Gran Fondo Nove Colli is known as the Queen of the Gran Fondos. It's the original and, the organisers would no doubt say, the best. Unfortunately, it's also insanely popular. Nove Colli, meaning 'nine hills', is based in a little port town called Cesenatico on the Adriatic. It's a beautiful little place arranged around a port canal designed by Leonardo Da Vinci. It was also the home of Marco Pantani, 'Il Pirata', the tragic hero of Italian cycling. With his headscarf, earrings, goatee beard and shaved head, Pantani looked every inch the pirate. His death in 2004 from a cocaine overdose was emblematic of a turbulent era in cycling.

The tickets for Nove Colli go on sale in November for the event held the following May. Entries open at midnight and they're sold out in ten minutes. Sold out means 13,000 riders. The town can hardly hold 13,000 cyclists. Each rider is assigned a colour at sign-on and each colour lines up in a particular street. So there could be 2,000 oranges in one street and 2,000 reds in the next. The idea is to start the colours one after the other to avoid congestion. As soon as one street empties it's time to open the next.

The first time I rode the Nove Colli I got my entry through Jamie Burrow, a friend who'd ridden on the US Postal team with Lance Armstrong. He was riding for a top gran fondo team in the Italian championship, the races that were held ahead of the mass-participation event. That first gran fondo was a shock to the system. Despite the best efforts of the organisers and their colour co-ordinated start system, the tsunami of cyclists spilling onto the streets led to an instant gridlock. You literally couldn't move and the heat was intense. When I did manage to get the bike rolling I had to stop because I was running into the back of another rider. Someone was evidently making a packet of money out of this. I kept thinking the crowd would clear and we'd be away, but it took an age. Once we were out on the road there were two or three water stations along the way with boxes and boxes of bananas. The place was a death trap, carpeted in slippery banana skins and dumped water bottles.

Alan and I went to quite a number of those gran fondos. There was the Gran Fondo Il Lombardia, held two days before the big UCI World Tour race that's known as the Race of the Falling Leaves. Il Lombardia is one of bike racing's five great 'Monuments'. It's held around the beautiful Lake Como in northern Italy in October. Then I went with Gary Fryett to the Tour of Flanders sportive, another of the Monuments. We needn't have bothered. It was another wet, bone-chilling day in Belgium. I really should have known better. I never went back to that one again.

The fondos were pure fun, really. It was an opportunity to spend time with good friends and it wasn't an expensive hobby. We'd fly over on Ryanair and stay in a cheap hotel. The entrance fee was peanuts. More important, they fulfilled a psychological need for me. As soon as I sat on my bike and put myself into that race environment, I could feel the stress of trying to be someone else, the man in the grey suit, just falling away. There was this sudden realisation, this clarity, that my life was about cycling, not about trying to impress anyone to get picked for a team. There was just me and the bike, and the race.

I enjoyed what I now think of as my sportive phase but I gradually came to realise that I was fooling myself on those gran fondos. I'm not one for hobbies. When I take something on it eventually becomes serious. I need a physical and mental challenge to overcome. This wasn't really racing; it was just me telling myself a good story, but it was a story I needed to hear. When I wasn't doing it, I felt like the life was being sucked out of me. There came a day when I looked in the mirror and said to myself: 'You never smile. You don't like life. There's just this deadpan face.' I had the house, the marriage, the BMW. I was able to go away and ride my bike in far-away places. I had it all, but it wasn't fixing the thing that was broken in me. It wasn't fair on me and it wasn't fair on the people around me.

I was living in a world that wasn't real, and I was slowly drowning.

CHAPTER 7

The Tap of Metal Shoe Tips

I was a late joiner on the conveyor belt of proper job, marriage and kids. Before I moved into the house with Sinead I'd been on the road for my entire adult life, whether it was on the bike, travelling the length and breadth of several countries to race, living on other people's sofas or in their spare rooms; even my job involved driving around the country setting up contracts. My mum always said I was a loner and would always live out of a bag. And here I was, well into my forties, moving into a brand spanking new bungalow on an estate of brand spanking new bungalows on the edge of a small village.

If you've ever moved into a newly built house you will know the amount of work that needs to be done to get it up to scratch. I've yet to meet a man whose idea of a good time is to spend the afternoon shopping for curtain fabrics, but I couldn't work up any enthusiasm for even the most basic DIY. I didn't care about keeping the grass cut just to impress the neighbours, painting a fence or papering a wall. None of that registered with me. As I set off on a training ride, I'd see the house-proud guys in our street working in their gardens, polishing the cars on a Sunday or slumped on a sofa while Sky Sports blinked on a massive TV screen.

If living up to the responsibility of my first real home was a challenge, the level of commitment needed in my relationship with Sinead was something I never truly grasped. I'd experienced a very intense relationship with Debbie, but this was different. It was different because Debbie and I had had our own lives: we'd been footloose travellers to an extent, joined by our love of racing but separated by the need to be in different places in order to compete, driven by the need to win. There was a disconnection between Sinead and me that was partly to do with my desire to maintain a high level of fitness and performance. I couldn't see it from her perspective at the time, but I know now that from her point of view I was totally addicted to training and riding my bike. That was perhaps one of the core reasons why we never found a balance in our relationship. We looked at life from two completely different perspectives.

Sinead was also a very sociable person. She loved going out for the evening and spending time with groups of friends or family. I just didn't feel comfortable in those kinds of situations. I'd rather eat properly and get to bed early than go out and collapse into bed in the early hours. Being in a crowd of people set me on edge. I found it difficult to get into conversations because I felt I had so little in common with other people. Then, if we got into conversation about my cycling career, I would end up talking about myself endlessly. I had similar feelings about fitting in with Sinead's big family circle. Being part of that wider family unit was important to her and she was obviously disappointed by my failure to fit in.

Our first son, Reuben, was born in 2005. I was overjoyed when Sinead told me she was pregnant. It's that overwhelming feeling that a little someone is about to arrive in your life and change everything for the better. I went with her to all the scans and we made all the preparations for his arrival. I think I may have been rather naive about the responsibilities of family life, the amount of care and attention a baby needs and the shared role of the parents. I have enormous pride in my sons and I love them to bits, but I struggled to be a great parent for them, the parent they deserved. It seemed that I had absolutely no internal parenting sense in me. There's a picture of me taken the day Sinead and Reuben came home from hospital. I was sitting on the sofa in my training gear, about to go out on the bike, when someone handed me Reuben to hold for the photo. I look so awkward, as if I just didn't know what to do with him. When I hold the picture in my hand now, I can feel again that sense of shock that this fragile little thing needed to be looked after. From now on I was responsible for someone else in my life.

Sinead was very good with Reuben when he was a baby. She always has been a very good mum, an excellent parent. It didn't come naturally to me, but I did my best. I didn't dodge my duty when it came to nappy changing or any of the practical stuff that goes with caring for a baby. It took a long time to happen but eventually things started to fall into place. Reuben wasn't always an easy baby. He cried a lot and we struggled to get him to sleep. There's no rule book with babies but we got there, making it up as we went along like other mums and dads.

In October 2007, our second son, Ross, appeared in our lives. Reuben was still only two at the time so there was that air of controlled chaos about the house. Like any mum, Sinead was hyper-sensitive about her baby's health. When she sensed something was wrong with the shape of Ross's head she raised it with the health visitor. She was determined to have his head checked and was quite pushy with the nurse. It only took a moment to measure Ross's head and confirm Sinead's fear that it was a lot bigger than it should have been.

There was no panic at that stage; we could see Ross's head looked a bit odd but we thought he'd been born with a minor deformity. Sinead took him to his appointment at Altnagelvin

Hospital. We were not expecting anything dramatic, so I went to work as usual. It was about 11.30 in the morning when the phone rang. It was Sinead and she said, 'Joe, you've got to get over here. They've found something and they want to talk to us.' It took me all of 15 minutes to get to the hospital. My head was spinning.

It's a bit of a blur now. We sat in a featureless hospital office while three or four medics told us our baby son was dangerously ill. They told us they'd found a big dark spot on Ross's brain. The hospital in Derry couldn't deal with it; we would have to go to Belfast. I could sense they were trying to tell us how serious it was without actually destroying us in the process.

The meeting with the doctors in Derry was around midday, and by late afternoon we were checking Ross into the Paul Ward at the Royal Belfast Hospital for Sick Children. A few short hours ago we'd been sitting at the breakfast table chatting – a normal family on a normal February morning. Now we stood by as a nurse made Ross comfortable in the first of many identical hospital cots. The Paul Ward was a specialist unit for children with cancer. Across the room other children lay in little beds or cots. Some of them were clearly very ill, with feeding tubes in their nostrils and intravenous lines into their arms. IV pumps bleeped. Beside each bed a mum or dad sat anxiously looking over their little one. This was to become our world. Sinead was clearly shattered. I noticed her hands trembling. I felt sick to my stomach with shock. Was this really happening? To our little boy? I took a deep breath.

Then the practicalities kicked in. It soon became clear that someone would have to be with Ross 24/7. Reuben was only a toddler; he needed his mum with him back home in Eglinton. I was going to be spending most of my time in the ward with Ross. I asked a nurse where I would sleep. 'You sleep there,' she said, motioning to the floor beside the cot. There were four or five other children on the ward and each night I joined the other parents wrapped in duvets on the tiled floor desperately trying to get a few hours' respite. The nights were broken by children crying, parents quietly hushing them back to sleep. Occasionally, there would be a flutter of activity and raised voices as the night nurses responded to a call for help. As I lay in the dark on that first night my mind raced and the truth of the situation sank in. This wasn't a nightmare I would wake from in the morning. It was real and it couldn't be wished away. All Sinead and I could do was to listen to the experts and follow their instructions to the letter. We eventually settled into a routine where I did three or four nights with Ross while Sinead mostly looked after Reuben and spent one or two nights at the hospital.

Things moved quickly in the hospital. Ross was allocated a neurosurgeon, Mr McAuley. From what I'd heard it was a bit of a lottery when it came to allocating surgeons but the nurses on the ward seemed to rate him very highly. 'You've got the right man for the job,' one of them assured us in a quiet moment.

Sinead and I were ushered into the surgeon's office. He showed us an X-ray and explained that there was a large tumour attached to Ross's brain stalk. I took a deep intake of breath and put my head in my hands.

'That bulge in his forehead is there because the bones in your son's skull haven't fused and the tumour is pushing his brain forward,' Mr McAuley said. 'It's what we call a stage four neuroblastoma and it'll have to be removed.'

My mind was racing. 'How can you do that? Surely he's far too small?'

Mr McAuley explained that he would have to cut the tumour out – but that if he so much as touched the stalk it could leave Ross with serious brain damage.

'I'll be straight with you. The chances of such a small baby surviving the operation are fifty-fifty. The only guarantee I can give is that I'll do my best.'

I felt offended at the way he had spoken to us. We were already beaten up and here was this brusque doctor beating us up some more with his blunt assessment of our child's prospects. It was all new to me and I later reflected that he was just being honest with us. He laid the cards on the table and let us see clearly how he would set about trying to save Ross's life. The date for his surgery was set and we were given a pile of waiver forms to fill in. I started to read them before signing but soon gave up. If any of the scenarios they referred to actually happened, Ross wouldn't have survived in any case. There's a saying about surgeons that you put your life in their hands. We were putting our son's little life in their hands and it was a massive responsibility.

We had a final briefing with Mr McAuley the day before Ross's surgery. 'I'll be in at seven in the morning,' he said. 'This is going to take as long as it takes and I'm not going to be in any hurry. I won't be contacting you until I've finished and, whatever the result, if he's alive or not, you won't hear from me until I'm done.' Did we have any questions?

'What do you need from us tomorrow?' I asked. Surely there had to be some role for the parents?

'Take yourselves into town and do some shopping,' he suggested.

I was taken aback. Did people really do that? Pick out a jumper in Debenhams? Try on some shoes while their child's life hung in the balance? I left the room feeling numb. There wasn't much sleep that night.

At seven the next day, Sinead and I accompanied a nurse as she wheeled Ross down a long grey corridor to the preparation area. I heard the tap, tap of metal shoe tips behind me. It was Mr

McAuley, smartly dressed and carrying a briefcase. He smiled. 'We'll do all we can to save your son.' We kissed Ross goodbye and as we walked out the door the thought ran through my mind that we may have seen him for the last time. Needless to say, there was no shopping trip. We spent the day wandering the corridors, slumped in a café downing endless cups of instant coffee, surfacing now and then for a breath of air outside the building.

The hours crept past, through lunchtime and into the afternoon and still there was no word. Darkness fell and finally a nurse appeared. 'I can't give you any details. Mr McAuley says you've to go to the ICU.' We followed the signs to the intensive care unit and were directed into a small office. The surgeon was sitting there, still in his scrubs. 'Ross is alive,' he said. 'It's gone very well and I'm very happy with how everything's worked out. You can go and see him now.'

We were ushered into a large white room. In the middle was a little cot on a pedestal. And there was Ross, this tiny, red-faced baby of five months, his head wrapped in a big white bandage. He was hooked up to all kinds of wires and drip lines into his arm and nose. My first thought was how could he, so small and vulnerable, have survived such massive surgery on his brain. And the second was, 'Now we're in the fight, we're in with a chance here.' That was the day of Ross's surgery, the day they removed a tumour the size of a golf ball from his brain stalk.

The next stage of his treatment was a very aggressive protocol of chemotherapy. I was told that children can withstand a very high level of chemo. It's hard to fathom but I saw it in action. The amount they were giving Ross would have floored an adult.

It seemed to me that they were just pouring it into him like Coke. The big problem with chemo, for patients of any age, is that it destroys the body's natural immune system, and patients become very prone to infections. Sometimes the treatment designed to save a life can prove fatal. When Ross developed a chesty cough, Sinead insisted that he should have an X-ray. She wouldn't give up on this and I have to admire her for sticking to her guns. When the doctors finally agreed to the X-ray it revealed something entirely unexpected. The bones in Ross's ribcage were split toward the end that joins the breastbone like a wishbone. They're known as bifid ribs and are one of the signs of a condition called Gorlin syndrome. They checked Ross for other symptoms and confirmed the diagnosis.

Gorlins is incredibly rare. When Ross was diagnosed, I think there were something like a half dozen kids like him with Gorlins in the entire UK. It meant he became a bit of a curiosity in the hospital for the medical staff. We felt we had to protect him from the unwanted attention. Gorlins can affect many parts of the body, including the skin, nervous system, eyes and bones. It can also cause a non-life-threatening type of skin cancer. To this day, Ross has to cover up and wear a hat at all times. The one stroke of luck we had, if you could call any of this lucky, was that Ross never received radiotherapy for his brain tumour. Radiotherapy can cause big problems for people with Gorlins as it encourages the spread of numerous small cancers.

When Mr McAuley had completed his work with Ross he was placed in the care of a treatment consultant, Dr McCarthy. He took us to one side and explained the way forward. Many of the children on the ward were so weakened by the chemotherapy that they were being fed through a tube inserted in their nostril. This was where the infection could start, he said. 'It won't be easy because he will be in such a state that he won't want to eat, but

I'd advise you to do whatever you possibly can to keep your son feeding from a spoon,' Dr McCarthy said.

This rapidly became our sole purpose in life. I sat by Ross's bed with a table spread with little bowls trying to find a food he was prepared to swallow. Every tiny mouthful from the plastic teaspoon became a major victory. At one point we nearly lost him. He became so weak they had to put a feeding tube into him. Thankfully, it was only there for a day. It annoyed him and he rooted it out of his nose. I remember thinking: 'That's a message. We need to keep spooning the stuff into him.' We struggled along, day after day, and the feeding tube never went back into him.

Some of the other children were not so lucky. There were five children in the Paul Ward on the day we arrived and two of them are no longer alive. You get very close to the other parents when you're in the hospital day and night. I remember we went to the funeral of one little girl who didn't make it. Sinead and I both took it very badly. You couldn't help but be shaken by it. Everyone talks about the cancer journey, and the thought that this could be where we were heading with Ross was too much for me. I started lying awake through the long nights thinking about how I would have to carry him into the church if the time ever came. It was getting out of control and I knew I had to stop these dark thoughts or they would drive me insane. My solution was to block them out. But that was only storing up trouble for the future.

The hospital ward became my life. It was a strange kind of bubble. The Royal Victoria Hospital site is in the heart of west Belfast and it's hemmed in by some of the busiest roads in the city. Life was going on out there, but when I entered inside the bubble, I was rarely more a few yards from Ross's bed. Day and night kind of melted into one. At two in the morning, the kids might settle down for a bit and someone would volunteer to make tea in the tiny kitchenette along the corridor. Sometimes I think the NHS runs on tea and toast. I had some real heart-to-heart conversations with the nurses and the other mums and dads, people I would never have met in other circumstances. The subject of conversation rarely strayed beyond cancer. 'How was your day?', 'How many spoons did you get in?', 'Did he sleep?'

The time of day was marked by the comings and goings of the staff. The doctors and the day shift nurses would slip away to their homes and families, and the late shift drifted in with their midnight snacks of sandwiches and Cup a Soup. The cleaners arrived at the crack of dawn with a 'How is the wee pet?' I got to know them all and the realisation came to me that, from the lady cleaning the floor to the likes of Mr McAuley performing miracles in the operating theatre, they were all members of the same team and striving for the same goal. They wanted you to be a step further forward than you were the day before. When I started my ultra-riding adventures I didn't set off on my own. It's vital to have a cohesive group of people with the right skillsets to back you up. I had to think carefully about putting together the support team and how their specialist skills would fit together. The last thing you'd want is a shouting match between a mechanic and the social media guy in the middle of the Arizona desert.

The other thing I learned in the hospital was how to cope with the endless nights that run into day and back into night. It's not a skill you set out to learn; you do it because you have to. You look out the window for a moment and realise you've been awake since the day before yesterday. It was only when I signed up for my first ultra, the Race Around Ireland, and saw that I'd have to stay awake on the bike around the clock, that I knew I had a hidden advantage. Keeping going is what the sport is all about. Most first-timers would have looked at the schedule and gasped at the thought of it. I just thought, 'I've been doing that for months.'

As Ross began to improve a little, I would occasionally nip out of the hospital for an hour at lunchtime to fill my lungs with fresh air. I'd become really unfit for the first time in my adult life and lost a huge amount of weight, which is quite something for a cyclist to say. I'd run down through the hospital site, past the big sculpture they call the Balls on the Falls and out along the Boucher Road. It's a part of Belfast that teems with traffic and shoppers. Sometimes I'd stop off in Marks and Spencer for a bowl of soup and a cup of proper coffee. I'd sit and people-watch for a few minutes. There's this invisible wall that comes down between you and the outside world when you're spending your life in a children's cancer ward. The couple at the table next to me eating carrot cake and drinking tea were living in that world I'd left the day we brought Ross to Belfast.

There's a huge amount of suffering going on in the world and it's not just in far-off countries. There are hundreds of families going through what we went through, and hundreds of professionals working to dig them out of that situation. There are about twenty kids a week going through that cancer ward. I didn't know that before Ross became ill. We're only interested in things when they affect us.

Dr McCarthy once said to me, 'By the time this journey is over you will know who your true friends are.' He said it very clearly and he'd obviously seen it happen many times before. I knew an awful lot of people, through cycling, motorbikes, work, whatever. But he was right: one by one they began to fall away. The phone calls and the texts stopped coming. Part of it was clearly embarrassment – they just didn't know what to say. They were scared to even ask about Ross. It didn't help that I started to get irritated by people who said, 'Oh, I know. I understand.'

Even I didn't understand what was happening and I was living in it. In hindsight, I know I was being unreasonable. People were just trying to bridge an impossible gap. When I meet someone who has cancer, or whose child has cancer, I say, 'I'm sure your world is difficult.' When the period of Ross's illness was over, I knew I had three good friends: Alan, Gary Fryett and my brother Mark.

Family was another matter. Sinead's family were very good; they were supportive in every way they could be. And I knew I could rely on my family, but they were so far away up in Donegal, far from the coalface. There were times when I didn't bring the whole story home because it would have been too painful for my mum.

Almost imperceptibly I started slipping into a kind of downward spiral. I remember sitting with Ross on one of those days spent leaning over the bed with the little bowls of food and holding the spoon to his lips. I was fully concentrated on getting him to eat when my phone rang. I lifted it, switched it to silent and threw it on the bed. It angered me that the world should burst in when I was concentrating on trying to keep my little boy alive. That was me finished with ringing phones. To this day my phone has never been off silent. I hadn't realised it but I was shutting down on the world again. It was a process that continued for years, probably dating back to when my dad taunted me as a boy. To be honest, I've really only recovered from it in the past couple of years, with the help of my present partner, Jill. That's the only reason I can write about it now. Jill has helped me see that, beneath everything, I'm resilient. 'You use all that darkness to add grit to your performance,' she said to me once. 'Many extraordinary people have had trauma in their early lives. It's what they do with it that counts.'

As Ross began to get a little better, he would come home to Eglinton for short periods, returning to the Royal for more treatment or for check-ups. Sometimes he would develop an infection or he'd have to go to the haematology ward for an infusion of blood platelets. There were times when you could drive the two hours to Belfast and not be allowed in to see him because of the danger of infection. You just had to turn around and head home again. I'd say it was roughly fifteen months to two years from the time Ross was first admitted until I felt I could say, 'Okay, we're done with the hospital.'

Sinead and I were invited with the boys to stay at a respite care centre for families of children with cancer. It was in Newcastle, County Down, the little seaside resort where the Mountains of Mourne famously sweep down to the sea. Shimna Valley House was simply a detached house that had been bought by a charity, the Cancer Fund for Children. Three or four families could stay there at a time. Special activities were laid on and the idea was to let you decompress. I really didn't want to go. The idea of spending evenings in a TV lounge with other couples with only one shared experience did not appeal to me. There was a list of activities but most seemed to be aimed at the mums, whether it was Indian head massage or beauty treatments. I spent a lot of time lounging in the garden. And then there was the cancer talk, always the cancer talk. Shimna was a well-meaning place but it was still inside the bubble and inevitably there was a lot of talk about the children and what they'd been through.

By this stage I felt completely saturated in cancer talk. I felt trapped by it and it was sucking the life out of me. The things that I had done every day – the sport, the goal-setting, the planning, the looking forward, all the things that made me feel alive – were gone. All gone. I couldn't envisage anything good happening, ever. I sometimes talk about being trapped in a dark rabbit hole. Should I have seen a therapist? Probably, but in those days there wasn't the same emphasis on mental health that there is today. Because there was nothing wrong with me physically, I wouldn't even have thought of going to see a doctor who could have referred me to a therapist. My response to these feelings of stress or depression has always been to blank them out and forge ahead, seeking out new goals for myself. I have to admit that other people have sometimes suffered as a result of this driven side of my nature.

While I was undergoing these personal difficulties, there were aspects of Shimna that were doing the family a lot of good. It was serving an important need for families in crisis. The charity was also very ambitious. They had a vision to expand their services and, above all, to transform the small-scale operation at Shimna Valley House into a full-blown therapeutic centre, known today as Daisy Lodge. At the time we first visited Shimna, the plans for Daisy Lodge were ready, but it seemed that time was running out with the official planning process and the Cancer Fund still needed to raise a heap of money.

I'd been away from the bike for a couple of years, but I needed a project to straighten my head, and Daisy Lodge needed a fundraiser. If I was going to be able to raise a good chunk of cash for them it was a bike race or nothing. That was the only skill I had. Prior to Ross's illness, my brother Mark and I had run a big sportive called the Tour of Ireland. It was the first multi-stage sportive ever held in Ireland or the UK. The idea was that cyclists would get a taste of what it's like for professionals to ride in a big tour, like the Tour de France or the Giro d'Italia. The riders stayed in hotels, and they were taken by coach to the start and on to the next hotel from the finish. There were professional mechanics, that sort of thing. If I could find the right sort of cycling project, I was pretty sure we could raise plenty of sponsorship and get a lot of free PR for Daisy Lodge.

Then I struck lucky. One day when it was my turn to take a break from hospital duties, Alan took me to a sportive and I got into conversation with a guy who asked me if I'd heard about this big new Race Around Ireland thing. I knew nothing about ultra-racing. If someone had asked me if I knew anything about driving a Formula One car the answer would have been the same. Anyway, I kicked it around and decided to call Alan. 'Do you fancy doing this thing?' I asked him. 'Well,' he said, 'the worst thing that could happen is that you win and we would have to keep doing them.'

This, it seemed, was the project I had been looking for. It involved riding 2,500km around the whole island of Ireland without stopping. To the sane observer this immediately screams pain and exhaustion; to me it said five days of unbeatable fundraising exposure.

CHAPTER 8

Nailed to a Fence in Navan

The Market Square in Navan isn't the sort of place from where you would expect to set off on a journey to change your life. The occasional passer-by turned and glanced across at the flurry of activity by the start line before heading to the local shop, the bookies or the pub. I leapt out of the rented motorhome, suitably suited and booted in my bright-yellow Lycra, and waited for my turn to roll out on the biggest cycling challenge I'd ever faced. Apart from my own crew, I didn't recognise a single face in the square, which would have been unimaginable during my years in Irish road racing. This was a different sporting world.

In their wisdom, the organisers had decided that I should be the final starter. Ultra-cycling world champion Fabio Biasiolo was in front of me on the start line, which hardly seemed fair. As I circled the warm-up area I listened with interest to the PA as the Italian was interviewed. He was a big unit, tall and long-haired with a pony tail and a cocky air to him. Some of the stuff he was coming out with scared the life out of me. 'I'm not getting off the bike for fifty hours,' he said. That's when I hit the panic button. 'Fucking hell, I'm not doing that,' I thought. We had been so caught up in organising this escapade that I hadn't thought too deeply about whether or not I was actually capable of finishing it. I'd be pretty much flat out for 120 hours and if I didn't make it the whole way around, I'd end up with a lot of egg on my face. Flying under the radar wasn't an option because we'd stoked up so much media attention. No pressure, Joe.

The longest mainstream race I had been in before was probably around 550km. Race Around Ireland was 2,500km. I had attempted a number of long-distance records organised by the UCI, the mainstream world cycling body, earlier in my career. It must have taken me ten years to break the Irish national 100 miles record, previously held by Billy Kerr, one of the most respected figures in Irish cycling. I didn't break it by much, about 40 seconds. There were only two opportunities a year to try for the record, one in the North and one in the South. They were always at the end of the season and it was typically blowing a gale. I then started thinking about the end-to-end record. In those days it ran from Fair Head in County Antrim to Mizen Head in County Cork. The record was held by my old mentor, Morris Foster. I had already done the 100 miles faster than Billy or Morris, so this seemed the obvious next step. My first attempt at the end-to-end finished in failure. I blew up in the final quarter, completely busted flat. Determined to have another crack at it, I went again and triumphed in a time of 19 hours and four minutes. I had knocked an hour off the record and I believe it stood for a good 15 years before it was broken.

There was an adventurous aspect to these long-distance record attempts that appealed to me. The sheer distance meant it was more than just a bike race. You were setting off into the unknown, and digging deep to master the challenges along the way gave me huge personal satisfaction. Men like Morris and Billy were a kind of yardstick for me. Breaking their records was bittersweet, but I was proud to see myself on their level. Ultra-cycling wasn't on my radar in the eighties and nineties, so once I held the end-to-end there was nowhere to go with the long-distance stuff.

I didn't go into Race Around Ireland thinking it was something that would change my life. It was purely about fundraising and publicity for Daisy Lodge. I had ridden in charity events before but they were organised by other people so it was just a matter of showing up and riding your bike without really thinking about the cause. The journey we had been through with Ross meant that this was a different beast entirely. I had seen things on that cancer ward that will stay with me for ever and this was an opportunity to do something, anything, to ease the pain of those kids and their families.

The race also gave me a feeling of self-worth, a feeling that I was overcoming the sense of inadequacy that has dogged me all my life. My dad always told me I was no good and I would never be any good. I've found that I can turn these feelings around and put them to my own use. If someone doubts my ability to compete well in a race, my attitude is always: 'You think so? Just watch me!'

When Alan and I started looking into the technical aspects of the race it became clear that we wouldn't be doing this on a one-man-and-a-car basis. I had somehow got the idea into my head that it would take about seven days, so when I read that the winner was expected to be home and hosed in around 120 hours, I took a sharp intake of breath. I also knew we needed the maximum possible media coverage. Sport sells newspapers and generates TV viewers, so it's a great way to get publicity. We hooked up with a freelance TV producer called Molly Stack who agreed to collect the footage to make a documentary. Alan's friend Mickey Price and some of his biker mates agreed to handle the cameras. If it sounds like I knew what I was doing, let me assure you I did not.

I had kind of panicked and made a list with two of everything I thought we needed, with the result that we finished up with a crew of 18 people and three or four vehicles plus two motorbikes. All we needed was a couple of helicopters and we could have rivalled ITV's Tour de France coverage. The crew met up before the race and we had some publicity photos taken at Lord Henry Mountcharles' gaff, Slane Castle. To be fair to them, the crew all worked their asses off during the race and the skillsets I needed just fell into place. I wouldn't be where I am today without them.

Race Around Ireland is a firm fixture on the ultra-cycling calendar nowadays, but the 2009 edition was the first time it was run. The organiser, Alan Heary, had been involved in an Irish team that went to the epic Race Across America, or RAAM, and he saw the potential for a similar race back home. Importantly, Alan got the support from the World Ultracycling Association (WUCA) for inclusion in the sport's World Cup and negotiated for it to become a RAAM qualifier. In 2012, Alan was on the team that supported me on my first, doomed RAAM attempt. As far as the route of Race Around Ireland was concerned, the clue was in the title. We started in Navan and rode anti-clockwise around the edge of the island, through Newry and Belfast, up to the Giant's Causeway, round to Malin Head, down through County Donegal and on down the west coast through Sligo to Mizen Head. Then there was the long loop along the south coast via Waterford and up through the Wicklow Mountains to finish just along the road from where we'd started.

I set off about three minutes after Biasiolo. It was a September afternoon so there wasn't a lot of time before it would start to get dark. As the time ticked down, I clung on to the thought that I had put in long riding shifts through the night during those end-to-end attempts, and I'd stayed awake for days on end holding

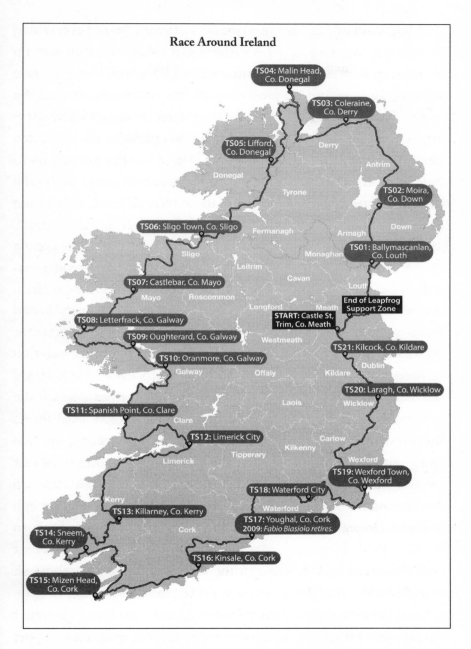

Race Around Ireland

TS04: Malin Head, Co. Donegal
TS03: Coleraine, Co. Derry
TS05: Lifford, Co. Donegal
TS02: Moira, Co. Down
TS06: Sligo Town, Co. Sligo
TS01: Ballymascanlan, Co. Louth
TS07: Castlebar, Co. Mayo
End of Leapfrog Support Zone
TS08: Letterfrack, Co. Galway
START: Castle St, Trim, Co. Meath
TS09: Oughterard, Co. Galway
TS21: Kilcock, Co. Kildare
TS10: Oranmore, Co. Galway
TS20: Laragh, Co. Wicklow
TS11: Spanish Point, Co. Clare
TS12: Limerick City
TS19: Wexford Town, Co. Wexford
TS18: Waterford City
TS13: Killarney, Co. Kerry
TS17: Youghal, Co. Cork
2009: *Fabio Biasiolo retires.*
TS14: Sneem, Co. Kerry
TS16: Kinsale, Co. Cork
TS15: Mizen Head, Co. Cork

Ross's little hand. If needs be, I could bully myself through the first day at least.

Riding through the countryside of County Meath takes you through a vast sweep of Irish history and the first few miles of the race spun along past the incredible prehistoric monument of Newgrange before dipping through the site of the Battle of Boyne. The battlefield sign with its crossed swords caught my eye for two seconds as I refocused my attention on chasing after the big Italian lad. I caught up with him along a narrow country road between Dunleer and Castlebellingham. We had only gone about twenty miles from the start and it was my usual road-racing pace that did the job. I heard him before I saw him. There was a young woman leaning out the window of his crew vehicle, a Volkswagen Transporter, screaming at him through a loudhailer. I later discovered that all the Italian ultra-crew cars do this, bellowing instructions and playing loud music to keep them awake at night. It would be enough to drive me up the wall.

I was clearly outpacing Biasiolo but I needed to hang on until the road widened a bit in order to pass the van safely with my crew car. When we reached a suitable stretch, I pulled out, but the van swung in front of me, blocking my way. 'Holy shit! Will you let me out!' I shouted. The driver pulled back over but when I made another attempt to pass, the van swung out again. Alan was driving my crew car, a BMW Tourer, with Alastair Irvine, my old teammate from the Commonwealth Games, navigating in the passenger seat. I shouted out over to them: 'What the fuck's he at?'

In the meantime, I was getting an earful from the woman with the bullhorn. They seemed to think that I was trying to get an advantage by drafting on the back of the van. I noticed that Biasiolo was riding up the inside of the vehicle, so I decided to chance my arm and dive in there – they were hardly going to pull in and risk knocking him off. I nipped into the gap and got up beside him. But if I thought his crew hadn't been happy with my attempt to overtake – well, let's just say that Biasiolo also showed his displeasure very openly. It wasn't pretty ... but I was past. I caught Alastair's eye as we pulled away up the road and he shook his head in disbelief.

I only saw Biasiolo three more times during the race. By the time we hit Sligo I was 45 minutes ahead of the Italian on the road but I was feeling wrecked. I was dehydrated and my nutrition was all wrong. All through my cycling career I've had this problem of not drinking enough. It's not the sort of race where you can get by on a diet of brown bread sandwiches and whatever the lads could pick up from some petrol station shop. We were 24 hours into the race and I had no choice but to stop and grab some sleep in one of our two motorhomes. I was awoken by the blaring racket of disco music and Italians shouting. It could only mean one thing. By the time I got up and on the road again he was maybe 10km ahead of me.

As we rolled down along the beautiful west coast, through Castlebar, Clifden, Oughterard and Galway, I was gradually gaining on Mr 50 Hours. I now had the advantage of a sleep in my legs. In fact, I was always going to be one sleep in front of him. He knew how close I was and it spooked him. I just kept going, and going, and going. Half of the race is in your head, and I thought of the kids on the Paul Ward, of their daily struggle to make it through to the next day. They were my example. As we approached Mizen Head I had shut the gap right down on him. He was only about three or four kilometres in front of me. We passed each other on the road as he was coming out of Mizen and I was turning in. It was a vital psychological moment; he now knew he really had to put the hammer down. But did he have it in him? I felt I had him on the ropes and I was pouring on the hurt.

Just as it seemed I had the beating of this guy, fate threw a massive spanner in the works. After meeting Biasiolo on the road, we looped down to Mizen Head and headed back up and out towards Kinsale. To this day I still don't really know what happened. We were on a narrow little road; Alan was driving but by this stage Damien Keys, a top-class mechanic who had worked with me in my mainstream racing days, was in the navigator's seat. We reached a hidden dip and a big truck appeared heading towards us. Suddenly there was a bang as the service car struck my back wheel. I felt that split-second stab of panic you get when you know you're going to come off the bike. I went straight down on the asphalt and a horrendous pain stabbed up my left leg. The bike was sucked under the car and spat out the back. The guys couldn't see me. They just heard a massive rattle under the car and presumed I'd gone under with the bike. They leapt out of the car but still couldn't find me as I'd been thrown into a hedge. Alan was convinced he had killed me and was physically sick by the side of the road. We've rarely spoken about it since then. It's just something that happens in racing. Put it down there and move on.

The car's front passenger wheel had gone over my foot and done some serious damage. I'd always worn these white Sidi cycling shoes with really strong carbon soles. They protected my foot to a certain extent as it was dragged on its edge, but they had a ratchet strap with a metal buckle. The weight of the car bore down on the buckle and broke a little bone on the top of my foot. The plate was completely torn off the sole of the shoe. Damien leapt into action. He grabbed a new pair of shoes, cut away part of one shoe and reached for the gaffer tape. The bike was completely trashed, along with the fancy Zipp wheels I was rather proud of. The shattered frame is still hanging on the wall of my garage as a kind of grisly souvenir. When Damien had taped up the shoe he took my E1 Colnago bike down off the roof rack. 'Get on the bike and keep riding. When your foot swells up, we'll stop and retape it,' he said. The next ten miles were some of the most painful I have ever experienced on a bike, and we still had hundreds of miles to go.

The incident was traumatic but the two lads handled it well and the panic slowly settled. Above all, we didn't let the race HQ know what had happened. They could have pulled us out of the race or let our rivals know we were flying on one engine. So I rode on in excruciating pain that didn't seem to be easing off. I couldn't even get off the bike without help because my foot wouldn't come out of the pedal. If I wanted to stop, I had to put one foot on the ground and Damien would cut the tape to free my shoe

Cork is the biggest Irish county and it's a hell of a long drag along the southern coastline until you reach the little town of Youghal before slipping into Waterford. Sir Walter Raleigh had some sort of holiday mansion in Youghal and rumour has it he imported the first spuds to Ireland there. You can bet that wasn't on the mind of Fabio Biasiolo as he approached the outskirts of the town. I don't know how long he'd been there before I eased around a bend and caught sight of him stretched out on an airbed by the side of the road. He didn't look great, to be honest. The VW was parked up alongside and the loudhailer woman was on her mobile looking distressed. Shortly afterwards, Alan got the message from race HQ. The big Italian lad was retiring from the race due to exhaustion. My relentless progress had pushed him into a corner and he had snapped. You don't like to see anyone in pain but there was a profound satisfaction in knowing I had outfoxed the world champion.

With 300 miles to go and riding with a broken foot the race was mine to throw away. Biasiolo was lying in the road and my nearest rival, Mark Pattinson, was 14 hours behind me. This was quite an achievement in itself as Mark has finished second in RAAM five times. He was born in the UK but has lived in Connecticut for much of his life. I didn't know him from Adam back then but in later years he gave me a lot of help with techniques for dealing with night riding and racing in the desert. I kept tapping out the miles and the guys in the car calculated that even if I took a few rest stops Mark was never going to catch me. The fight between me and the Italian guy had been so ferocious that we had wiped out the rest of the race.

Looking back, it was probably the way he reacted when I first overtook him that did it. From that moment on I was running on fury. I became massively angry and all the pent-up frustration of recent years became focused on beating this guy. I was up against someone who knew what they were doing so I needed to channel a huge amount of self-belief into my riding abilities.

The nights were the worst for me. The sleep deprivation was building day by day and I started to fear the arrival of nightfall. Then the anger would swell up and I'd think: 'No, you're not. You're not going to beat me here. You're not going to beat me in Ireland.' The strange thing was that I never for a moment doubted that I could do it. I didn't have the training or the experience but somehow I managed to make it up as I went along.

As I ploughed along the south coast and into Wexford there were moments when I could easily have crashed and burned. I got into trouble at the Quay in New Ross. Sometimes your body can just pull up like a horse before a high fence and refuse to go on. I don't know how I got going again, but I did. Then came the Sally Gap, high in the Wicklow Mountains, and the wheels almost came off the wagon. I was cold and utterly bone tired. Knowing that I was so far ahead of Pattinson, I gave in to my body's demand for some respite. I stopped at the side of the road and they cut me out of the shoe before I fell into bed in the motorhome. Once the pain in my foot subsided, I slept for the best part of four hours. The relief lasted for as long as it took me to blink my eyes open and realise I had to get back on the bike. As they gaffer-taped me into my shoe once again my eyes roamed over the bleak moorland landscape. It took an age to get down off the mountains. If you watch bike racing on the TV you'll see the riders struggling to get their warm jackets on before the descent. As I came down from the Sally Gap my whole body was shaking with cold and my fists held the bars with an iron grip. At the bottom, near the chocolate box village of Enniskerry, the crew wrapped me in a foil sheet, like a disaster victim, and fed me hot coffee. My body had taken such a beating that it was nearly in bits. I had no power in my legs and my brain was befuddled. It was going to take the best part of a year to recover from this.

I rolled into the finish at a not-so-glamorous industrial estate in Navan 112 hours after I had set off, the winner of the inaugural Race Around Ireland. You don't get huge crowds at the finish of ultra-races. There are no bunch sprints or fans banging the barriers at the finish line. After all, the guy in second place was still hours away down the road. But all the people who mattered were there. Reuben and Ross were there with their mum. Our wee man wasn't out of the woods yet but he was able to take a day away from the treatment to see his dad win this crazy race. My crew were all there, the TV people and the bikers and even a smattering of local people from Navan who had heard through the grapevine what was going on. Alan Heary could see the state I was in. 'Are you sure you're okay, Joe?' he asked. And I said, 'Well, it depends what you call alright. I've busted my foot but I think I got away with it.' We unbound the gaffer tape, pulled away the shoe and rolled down the sock. My foot was black and blue, a real mess. Alan couldn't believe I'd ridden all the way from west Cork in that state. Our decision to keep the accident hidden from race HQ staff had paid off.

I've never experienced anything like it. In my head I was on an absolute high, immensely proud of what I had achieved. There was never any intention to win the damn race; I was only there to finish it and do the fundraising I had set out to do. My body was beaten to a pulp and I had dragged my ass to the end of that finishing straight. For the final 300 miles it had felt like I was being nailed to a fence. I had no feeling in my hands or my feet and could barely change gear. My groin was so badly battered that I couldn't go to the toilet and when I did manage it the pain was horrendous. The dehydration gave me the worst headaches I have ever experienced. The very bones in my body were aching from the ceaseless vibration. I think it's fair to say I got a good kicking over those four-and-a-half days. It was much, much harder than I thought it would be.

The physical intensity of the experience had left me stunned, but while I was out on the road the thrill of the race had been instantly familiar. I felt completely at home, particularly on that stretch down the west coast where I was going flat out to catch Biasiolo. It wasn't pure physical effort. All the while I was working on my strategy and trying to mess with the Italian's head. After all those years away from it, all my racing instincts came back.

It took a while to sink in but my life was never to be the same again after winning Race Around Ireland. If it hadn't been for an innocuous conversation at that sportive, I wouldn't be sitting here spilling my life out into a book. I didn't get off the bike that day with a burst of exhilaration thinking I wanted to do it again next year. In a way I felt glad that I didn't have to do it any more. But I suddenly had something in my life that was positive. I wasn't just talking about cancer all the time.

I don't think the Cancer Fund people entirely grasped what I was up to. Their response was 'Okay, that's great. Thanks very much.' To them I was probably just another dad who had come through the painful cancer ward experience and wanted to give something back. In some senses that's just what I was, but I was prepared to put myself through hell for this and there were great opportunities for publicity. I've got enormous respect for the young people working in the fundraising office but I got the feeling that they were more used to people running coffee mornings. The money we raised from the race went into what is now a fantastic facility and a very special place. I still think of what we achieved as a team back then with a sense of pride.

The publicity side of things went through the roof when BBC Northern Ireland got involved. They could see the potential in my story, and the fact that we had already collected the bulk of the footage made it a lot easier for them to commission a documentary. We spent a day up at the Silent Valley in the Mourne Mountains recording interviews and bike footage. It was great fun putting it together, and seeing the finished product was a real pleasure. The documentary, No Ordinary Joe, was only supposed to be screened on BBC Two, but there was such a positive audience response that they found it a prime-time BBC One slot and in the end it was shown a number of times.

The big difference for me came after the TV documentary was aired. It was almost embarrassing how some people reacted to me. Strangers would come up to me in the street, start a conversation and shake my hand. One man even ran across a supermarket car park towards me. I thought he was going to hit me or something but he just wanted a handshake. There was no expectation of me doing another ultra-race and it was just viewed as a one-off fundraiser. I went back to riding the occasional sportive where I didn't have to put on a performance.

People in the cycling community were always keen to have a chat about my experience.

What I think of as the post-Race Around Ireland phase went on for a good ten months. It dug me out of the black hole I'd been in for the previous two years. The sense of release was almost physical, like a valve allowing the pent-up anxiety to release. I also got a lot of satisfaction from the feeling that I was helping people. I didn't really get my head around this until I had a conversation with my American friend Len Forkas. Len was in the same boat as me – a dad with a young son who had cancer. I met him at RAAM in 2012, where he was also raising funds for charity. 'Joe,' he said, 'you've got to understand that what you're doing is a whole lot more than just racing bikes. You become an ambassador for what you do and you have to take ownership of that.' Once people started looking up to me, I knew I had to measure up to their expectations. Len gave me a whole new perspective on that.

I kept in touch with Mark Pattinson after the race. He's a lovely guy and a veteran of the ultra game. He's a big lad, looks more like a construction worker than a cyclist, and he clearly hadn't been expecting what he got from this little Irish guy. I think Mark saw a lot of potential in me and he said I should really consider looking at the sport more seriously. When you lack confidence, hearing one of the top guys praising your abilities is a real boost. It was nice of him, I thought, but I had the real world to deal with. We still had to spend a lot of time at the children's hospital with Ross.

A number of years passed before I came across Fabio Biasiolo again. That was in 2017, at the start of the Race Across Italy in Nettuno. I went down to the start area before the race to sign in and bumped into Angela Perini, an Italian ultra-cyclist. We always have a chat when we meet so I gave her a wave and strode across. Just then I noticed the pony-tailed figure standing beside her. Our eyes met briefly and there was a flare of mutual recognition. 'This isn't going to end well,' I thought, but it would have looked ridiculous to turn on my heel and walk the other way. Angela greeted me in her usual effusive way and she never clocked the frosty atmosphere. But Fabio said nothing and I had nothing to say to him. I suppose we let sleeping dogs lie.

CHAPTER 9

Interlude – Downing a Mud Milkshake

'Fancy going to the cross this afternoon?' said Debbie.

'The what?'

'The cyclo-cross at Belvoir Forest Park,' she explained.

It was a dull Saturday afternoon in November. We'd been working in the shop until late the night before and were at a bit of a loose end. Nowadays, cyclists can stick their bike on a turbo trainer in the garage in mid-November, hook up to a computer and be racing up a sunny Alp with riders from all over the world. Back then, the off-season was pretty dull. Long, solitary miles on filthy country roads was the norm. Of course I was aware of cyclo-cross but I'd never actually been to see a race. What I saw intrigued me. For the uninitiated, cyclo-cross is a mixture of cycling and cross-country running. It's the dirtiest, filthiest thing you can do with your clothes on and I love it.

The set-up at Belvoir in Belfast was a tight, twisting course running through the trees. It was one or two kilometres long and marked out with tape. There were steep, short climbs where riders had to dismount and run, carrying their bike on their shoulders. The knobbly tyres tore up the grass and in no time the riders were slipping and sliding. I couldn't resist it. I had to have a go. There were lots of meetings locally in town parks and forests across Northern Ireland, in Bangor, Carrickfergus, Cookstown and Ballymoney. I got an old road bike, adjusted the brakes and put on some knobbly tyres. I was crap at the start but soon got the hang of it. The great thing about cyclo-cross is the bike-handling skills it teaches you. I also found it a great way of bridging the fitness gap between one season and the next. You're belting around this course at a speed that puts your heart rate off the scale. It's a great cardio workout.

Within about three years I was getting properly good at cross. Bloody good, in fact. In 1985, I won the national championship at Phoenix Park in Dublin. Frankly, I surprised myself; I really didn't think I was that good. From then until the early nineties I was the top rider on the Irish cross scene. I was national champion four times and represented Ireland in Europe many times, including at world championships.

If cycling is a minor sport in Ireland, cyclo-cross is a niche within it. In Europe it's a different matter. It's surprisingly popular in countries like the Czech Republic, Italy and Switzerland. It's big in the Netherlands and massive in Belgium. Go to a big cross race in Flanders and the crowds will be in their thousands. They're lining the side of the track, full to the gunwales with strong Belgian beer and chips with mayonnaise. The atmosphere is outrageous. Unlike a road race where you might get to see the peloton zip past in thirty seconds, when you go to a cross race you get to see the riders numerous times and they're really close up. I once took part in a race where the course ran through a massive beer tent full of roaring punters.

The 1986 cyclo-cross world championships were held at Lembeek in Belgium. The Irish federation had arranged for me to stay with Herman and Elise Nys before the race. The Nys family home was a kind of shrine to Irish cycling, and to Sean Kelly in particular. Herman and Elise took many young Irish riders under their wing during the early years of their cycling careers. Kelly actually lived at their home near Brussels for six years. The pavement around their corner house was painted with tricolours and Kelly's name. In the conservatory the walls were lined with jerseys from his greatest triumphs. There were so many trophies in there you could have spent half a lifetime polishing them. On a shelf by the window I noticed the most famous trophy in cycling, the granite cobblestone awarded to the winner of Paris-Roubaix, the Hell of the North. Kelly had won it twice. I was about to discover my own particular hell in the mudbath that awaited me at Lembeek.

The cross courses on the Continent were in a different league from what we had in Ireland. Where we had grassy banks they had man-made obstacles that were like a muddy pit with a climbing wall to get over. The start of a world championship cross race is not for the faint of heart. You set off along a strip of tarmac about 500m long, before swinging 90 degrees to the left or right on to the mud. Everyone wants to get to the turn first so they don't get caught up in the carnage at the back. They're literally belting into the corner at 40mph. The whole bunch slides to the side and you've got to be able to go with it or you're toast. It had been pissing with rain for most of the week before the big race at Lembeek and the course was knee-deep in mud that was somewhere between the consistency of cake mixture and chocolate milkshake. It didn't taste like it, I can tell you. Apparently, the farmer who owned the land had broken an agreement not to plough the land prior to the race. There were vociferous complaints after the race that a UCI rule that two-thirds of the course should be accessible by bike was ignored. It went down in cyclo-cross history as the world championships of disgrace. I spent my first worlds running around in the clabber for an hour with my bike over my shoulder and finished 47th. The only way was up.

With the help of my friend Gary Fryett I became a one-man Ireland team at the big continental races. The federation was only too happy to have the country represented, but there was little or no money to get me there. Gary would organise a whip round of his well-heeled colleagues in the City of London and we soon had a thousand quid for another adventure into deepest Europe. It was all done on the flimsiest shoestring you can imagine. Gary was my mechanic. We'd throw everything into the back of a big Volvo V70 estate and set off from his home in Essex headed for the ferry. Those road trips with Gary were unforgettable. He loved cross as much as I did and the craic in the Volvo was mighty. We went to a worlds at Pordenone in Italy back in the days when there were no satnavs. Maybe someone was holding the map the wrong way up, but we ended up on top of a mountain somewhere in Germany completely snowed in. Stale bread and pickled onion crisps that you've found in the back of the car is hardly the breakfast of champions. The race was only a day and a half away but we got there in time and I proudly flew the flag for Ireland.

The starting grid in the world championships is like Formula One. All the best guys are lined up at the front, which pretty much meant a crowd of Belgians in their sky-blue jerseys sprinkled with Dutch riders in orange. I started off right at the back at Lembeek but over the years I gradually improved until I was halfway up the grid. I always said that if I climbed one line in the grid each year I'd be happy.

The cross community at the top level is really close-knit and friendly. The big teams have a truckload of bikes – we only had two or three. The idea is that there are pits around the course where you can swap your mud-clogged bike for a clean one.

Gary was good mates with some of the GB team and they used to take one of my bikes into their pit and powerhose it for me. Cyclo-cross is about as far as you can get from the ultra that I do now and still be racing a bike. There aren't exactly a heap of transferable skills, but what I learned in cross has probably saved me from some nasty crashes where I've momentarily lost control of the bike. Mostly, though, thinking of my days as a cross champion just brings a big smile to my face. Cross was special and really, really awesome.

CHAPTER 10

Half Dead on Wolf Creek Pass

In all my years as a bike racer I'd never seen anything quite like this. A beautiful southern Californian morning on the seafront at Oceanside, San Diego. From the start line I cast my eye along a wooden pier stretching way out over the Pacific surf for a quarter of a mile. Big pelicans perched on the railings, sunbathers lounging on the beach, palm trees along the boardwalk, you name it – it was pure Americana. It was a beautiful sight and the kick-off point for a massive challenge – the Race Across America 2012.

After that year of basking in the glory of Race Around Ireland I suppose I started to feel a bit antsy. What was coming next? I needed something to take me out of the ordinary. When you sign up for these races, they always make a big thing of being Race Across America qualifiers. It was obviously a way of enticing people to sign up and since I was just doing the race for charity, I didn't pay too much attention to it. It was only after I won the whole shebang that I went back and checked the small print. I was intrigued. The RAAM qualification lasted three years. If I was going to do it then the last possible year was 2012. I mentally folded up the paper and put it away. If someone had said to me in 2010 that I was going to do Race Across America in 2012 I would have laughed out loud. The costs would have been astronomical.

And that's how I found myself gazing up at the star-spangled banner while rock music banged out over the PA and a commentator announced the riders to the people crowding the roadside. I'd had a lot on my mind, not least the seventy grand I'd had to scrape together to fund this escapade, and thoughts of Ross, whose illness had brought me into the crazy world of ultra-cycling. For the moment, though, as I leaned on the bars of the bike and waited my turn to start, the only thought in my head was 'Holy shit, I'm not getting off this thing for twelve days. This is three thousand miles long and the razzmatazz is over.'

Race Across America is a unique long-distance sporting event. To put it simply, you get on your bike and ride as fast as you can across the USA from the Pacific to the Atlantic without stopping. It is about a third longer than the Tour de France and the riders complete the distance in about half the time. Unlike the Tour, there are no rest days. This is ultra-cycling at its hardest. It's as much to do with the rider's strength of character as their ability to deal with the massive physical demands.

It was surprisingly chilly on the seafront and I thought about slipping on a jacket – quite ironic considering the catastrophe that was to unfold over the next few days. It started to warm up as soon as I reached the end of the opening straight and hung a left through what I can only describe as a hole in the hedge. It swiftly became a superfast bike path with lots of local cyclists wondering what the heck all these people on racers were doing there. After a few miles, race marshals directed me off the bike path and onto the public road. The race timer started, and I was on my way into the Californian orange and lemon groves. That fresh citrus smell hung in the air as I pushed over the sharp inclines. For the next 25 miles I would be on my own, hoping I had no mechanical problems until I was reconnected with the team vehicle.

The first hint I had of how tough this race was going to be was the ferocity of the heat out in those orange groves. It was over 40°C and we were still only in California, nowhere near reaching Arizona, where I'd been warned to expect the worst. Fifty miles on and into the Mojave Desert. The heat was just incredible. It's so hot out there the sweat doesn't even drip off you, it just evaporates off your skin. I was forced to stop and put on zinc sunblock when I felt my skin sizzling. As for the heat coming up off the road – you know when you're cooking your Sunday dinner and you open the oven to lift out your roast? You know that surge of hot air? It was like some sort of blast furnace.

And it was so dry I was struggling to breathe. The guys in the crew car were constantly handing me bottles to keep me hydrated, but the drinks were warm. It was the first example of the unknown. Not having chilled drinks was one of the many rookie mistakes that blighted my first attempt at RAAM. At best you could say I was naive, at worst stupid.

The heat was killing but the roads themselves fairly rolled along until we hit the famous descent of the Glass Elevator. The Grand Canyon State, as they call it, isn't level with California. The Glass Elevator is where you literally drop down into the base of Arizona. Standing at the top it feels like you're in a plane looking down on the tiny houses far below in the desert town of Borrego Springs. We're talking almost four thousand feet down through ten miles of fast hairpin bends where riders can hit 60–70mph. The problem is there's this tremendous updraught that can catch the racing bike's deep-section wheels and flip it over like a Frisbee. When you set the bike into the corner you have to be totally in control. You've no idea which way the wind is going to lift the bike and if you hit the Armco barrier it'll cut you like a cheese grater. There have been a lot of scary crashes with guys getting badly hurt there. I've seen a rider lifted clean into the air and dumped on the road. He looked seriously injured, and his bike was literally smashed in two. It happened in a split second and I just closed my eyes and rode through the wreckage. The first time I went down the Elevator it scared the life out of me. I couldn't get a grip on the ferocity of it and it almost blew me over. I thought, 'This thing's going to kill me,' and I shut the gas right off.

My back of a cigarette packet calculation told me RAAM was roughly twice the length of Race Around Ireland. It couldn't be that hard, surely? Wrong. Race Across America is on a level of its own. We're talking 3,000 miles, 12 states, endless deserts, the Rocky Mountains and 170,000 vertical feet of climbing. I had all these simplistic ideas in my head that I had no real evidence to back up.

I was 53 years old when I set off from Oceanside that day. No spring chicken. Self-discipline and training have never been a problem for me but I'd never embarked on a challenge quite like this before. To be honest, I was just making a lot of it up as I went along. Do I have a talent for riding pushbikes? Obviously – I won a lot of top races in mainstream racing. But I worked incredibly hard with the level of talent I had. It's not the sort of talent that's instant and comes ready-made out of a box. When you look through my career, you'll see I was there or thereabouts

The one smiling childhood
picture that I have.

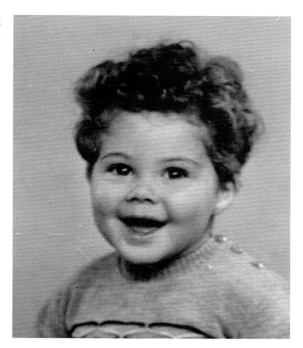

My beloved Bimbo bike in my granny's hen coop – two things that saved me from
my childhood.

Relaxing with
Debbie in Donegal.

With Tommy
Pyper, my mentor
and the person
who mapped out
every page of this
book, even though
he may not have
known it.

In the Vendée area of France in 1995, with Gary Fryett, my manager and great friend, who deserves a whole book to himself.

With Guy Tréhin during my early days in Brittany. Being taught by someone of this magnitude was an unforgettable experience and changed the way I understood bike racing.

At the Cyclo-cross World Championships – another day in the mud proudly wearing the green of Ireland.

KELLY'S FAREWELL RACE

WORLD'S BEST

■ **WINNER'S PODIUM:** Laurent Fignon, Bernard Hinault, new Irish cycling professional Joe Barr, Stephen Roche and Sean Kelly enjoy some champagne spraying

I took fourth place that day but still found my way onto the podium, and I pinch myself every time I see this.

Team time trials at the 1986 Commonwealth Games. I was so proud to win a bronze medal alongside Alistair Irvine, Cormac McCann and the great Martin Quinn.

The race that started my love affair with endurance: the 2009 Race Around Ireland.

Winner of the 2009 Race Around Ireland. A podium I will never forget.

The first time I held my son Reuben, and my first understanding of unconditional love.

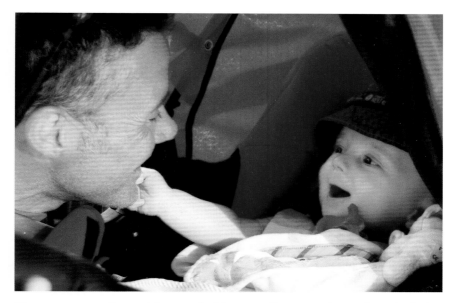

My younger son, Ross, giving me the biggest smile on a welcome day trip during his chemo treatment.

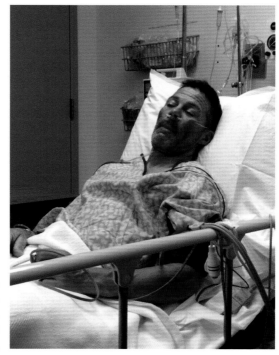

A humbled cyclist in South Fork hospital in 2012, when my first Race Across America attempt ended in disaster. But I would be back.

My mum, Elizabeth, who taught me kindness. I think I made her proud.

The 2015 No Country for Old Men dream team: Alan Hamilton, Ian Struthers and Jill.

Taking a well-earned break alongside my three amigos – Alan, Ian and Jill – after a training day in Donegal. (*Courtesy of William Kelly*)

Making it onto the top spot of the 2017 Race Across Italy podium – always the smallest one!

A big hug before the 2018 Race Around Ireland. The last time I was on this start line, Ross was tiny and still in cancer treatment, so having him there in 2018 meant more than I can say. (*Courtesy of Gavin Connolly*)

My beloved Donegal. I've always said that if you can race the roads in Ireland, you can race anywhere in the world. (*Courtesy of William Kelly*)

My team for the 2018 Race Around Ireland, when we managed to get it so right. One of the most enjoyable races of my career.

This is what endurance looks like: the day after winning the 2018 Race Around Ireland. *(Courtesy of team member Andrew McMullan)*

With my inspirational and supportive friend Len Forkas, who walks the same road I do.

The biggest show in ultra-cycling: the Race Across America. There's no start-line experience like it. (*Courtesy of RAAM media*)

Heading up, up, up towards Wolf Creek Pass during the Race Across America in 2019.

Battling the US heat in 2019. There's hot, and then there's Race Across America hot! (*Courtesy of RAAM Media*)

Safety first: snatching a 10-minute nap with my helmet on during the 2019 Race Across America.

With my handsome son Reuben at the 2020 Belfast Telegraph Sports Awards.

Smashing the 2020 Irish End-to-End & Back Again World Record, when my world put their arms around me. Home. (*Courtesy of Gavin Connolly*)

My compass – Jill. (*Courtesy of William Kelly*)

No matter what, there's always another horizon – just keep the bike moving forward. (*Courtesy of William Kelly*)

in all the big races, especially the world races. I always performed better at the higher end than at domestic level, but I never made it to the very top of the sport. There was always that level of disappointment that fuelled my sense of inadequacy, but this late in the game I'd found an outlet that might just allow me to prove myself to the world.

Training for RAAM was only half the battle. The money side and the logistics of the event are huge. You need the right people on your side. Alan Heary, the organiser of Race Around Ireland, agreed to come on board my team, along with a number of guys with the knowledge and experience to ensure my RAAM attempt didn't crash and burn before I'd even got the money together, among them Emmet Roche, PJ Nolan, Simon O'Dea and Killian Galligan.

The heart of the team, though, was my old pal Alan Hamilton, who knows me better than anyone and probably saved my life on the Colorado mountainside. The joker in the pack was our young cameraman, Ian Struthers, who dealt with all the media side of things. Damien Keys, who had been Alan's right-hand man since Race Around Ireland, recruited Ian. I only met him the night before we set off for the States. He was straight out of college with training in filmmaking; more important, he kept the crew car in stitches. My long-time kit sponsor, Garth Young from Powerhouse clothing, and Mark Taylor, a family friend, made up the rest of the crew.

It was just a loose collection of people who wanted to help me, with not a lot of the required structure. The guys from down south had been there before, and they knew the RAAM organisers, so I was reliant on their knowledge. They were across the whole procedure from start to finish. I'd never even been to California. Ask me to point at Oceanside on a map and I'd have been scratching my head.

Somehow we scraped the money together. PJ brought in a couple of quality backers from the States. He really helped a hell of a lot with the financing. It's not just a question of jumping on the bike at the start and away you go. There were two cars to be paid for: a direct service car that follows immediately behind the rider the whole way across; and a gofer car that chases off to the nearest Walmart or garage or whatever when you need stuff. In 2012 we also had a big whale of a motorhome that we discovered was a complete waste of money because no one ever got any sleep in it. It cost $10,000 to hire one way, not forgetting the five grand we paid for fuel.

The service car idled down the Glass Elevator as I wobbled along through the switchbacks. When we finally arrived in Borrego Springs, a little desert town at the foot of the hills, the heat went through the roof. At 48 degrees it's hardly surprising that one of the local tourist attractions goes by the name of Hellhole Canyon. The landscape is straight out of the old cowboy movies: tumbleweeds, sand, more sand and those big old cactuses that look like they've been told to stick their hands in the air. And the roads are concrete. They can't use tarmac because the heat would melt it, so you're left with this completely dead road surface. It feels like you're riding through mud.

The heat now was beyond belief. Even the crew were suffering. Oddly enough, I started to get used to it, but the toll my body was paying was huge. There was the dehydration, certainly, but the big issue was that my core temperature was soaring, and I felt like I was going to faint. My body was being burned alive, but I was trying to push the bike along at as high a heart rate as possible to keep my speed up. Nowadays I know what I'm doing, and I've got ice vests that cool my core temperature down. It's another of those simple things that I should have known but didn't – another dumb rookie mistake.

As night approached, I had to keep stopping to take time off the bike, but it wasn't helping me. I still felt crap and I was losing time, sitting out in the middle of the desert achieving nothing. It got dark and I was back up and riding. But despite what you hear about it getting cold in the desert at night it didn't really cool down. It stayed about 28 degrees. I rode in the headlights of the crew car as trucks barrelled past in the dark. Hunched over the bars, I kept the cranks turning, but I was already panicking about the sun coming up in the morning.

When panic takes over the doubts come flooding in. Every rise in the road felt like someone had a rope pulling me back down the hill again. I just didn't have the strength to push the bike. It went on and on and on and I thought, 'Shit, I can't do this. What am I going to do? Three thousand miles? What the hell was I thinking of?'

So that was the heat. Next came the altitude. The route of RAAM takes you from sea level to 5,000 feet in a couple of days. The problems start to kick in as the atmosphere thins and you begin to lose oxygen. All the way across Arizona it was gradually ramping up. By the time we reached the town of Flagstaff we were at 7,000 feet and we still hadn't reached the Rockies. I'd been struggling with the heat, both physically and mentally. But suddenly it was like somebody gave me a slap on the head and said: 'By the way, sonny boy, we're about to switch the oxygen off!'

The team were doing all they could, to be fair, but they couldn't magic up an ice vest when we didn't have one. Instead, I was riding so slowly on the inclines they were able to run alongside with one of those big garden sprays and water me like a plant. Thirty seconds later I'd be boiling again. We now know that what I needed was slushie drinks like the ones kids have. They kill the dehydration and help chill your core. We never thought of it because we didn't know about it. Ignorance struck again.

Out of Flagstaff there's this swooping downhill that goes on for miles out into the desert. Head down, arse in the air, you can easily hit 60mph on a road like that. Then suddenly there's an abrupt 90-degree right turn in the middle of nowhere and next to it, on top of a sand dune, a dusty billboard the size of a house advertising a McDonald's in a place called Tuba City. It's one of those surreal sights RAAM throws at you when you're least expecting it. The little town belongs to the Navajo Nation; it's the biggest chunk of Native American territory in the USA. The few miles between that billboard and Tuba City was for me the hottest on the Race Across America. I had to stop and get off the bike. I could hardly stay on my feet. A scorching blast of air from the crew car's radiator had me reeling.

I lost a heap of time there by the side of the road, about five or six hours. I stood under a cold outdoor shower next to the motorhome, then got inside and we put the aircon on full blast. But I still couldn't get on the bike. The place was a roasting pot. If truth be told, there's not much to see in Tuba City. I rode on past the McDonald's – Trip Advisor gives it four out of five in case you're ever passing through.

Next up was Durango, home of the Durango Kid, the hero of dozens of old black-and-white cowboy movies. More important, it was also the town at the base of the Rocky Mountains. The road out of Durango heads towards Wolf Creek Pass, a name I can't hear now without a faint shiver down my spine. The country singer CW McCall wrote a song about it. He called the road '37 miles of hell', but the whole length of the uphill runs closer to 60 miles.

At the top of Wolf Creek, you're on the Continental Divide. There's a big 'Great Divide' sign there explaining it. On one side of the mountain all the rivers drain into the Pacific and on the other they drain into the Atlantic. The divide runs the length of the Americas, from the top of Alaska to the southern tip of South America, so it feels like a big deal when you reach it.

The endless drag out of Durango took me up to a little mountain resort called Pagosa Springs. The road up to it is hard going, relentless. I finally got to the stage where my body was just screaming, 'I can't do this!' It's hard to put into words how I felt. Mentally I was just falling apart. You get to a point where you're so overwhelmed by the physical punishment that your mind orders you to get off the bike and 'Ah, fuck this!' Somehow, I kept on. I'd have to get comfortable with intolerable levels of discomfort that go on for days.

I reckon my mind was already losing its connection with reality as we came through Pagosa Springs. We passed a pizza restaurant and I caught a gust of a delicious aroma. I had to have pizza. Immediately. I was completely dehydrated, I had heatstroke and here I was trying to push up the side of the Rocky Mountains with no air. I had only eaten a fraction of the calories that I should have eaten that day. The guys tried to humour me. They passed me a cardboard box and I tried to eat the pizza. It was a huge mistake – I'll spare you the details.

Other riders were passing me with a depressing regularity now – I did tell you this was a race, didn't I? I kept stopping, getting off and getting on again. A lot of the people doing RAAM, particularly the team riders, are fitness fanatics fairly new to cycling. The old bike racer in me was humiliated. I felt totally wasted and there was nothing I could do about it. It got to the stage where I couldn't eat; I was just so trashed I didn't have the energy to put my hand in my back pocket, take out some food and raise it to my mouth. So everything was going downhill apart from the gradient, and that was unmercifully upwards.

That's the thing about Wolf Creek: it's not the steepness itself – that's actually fairly gradual. The problem is that the climb never eases off. From Durango to the top of the pass is the best part of a day's ride. If you try to hammer it out on the pedals your heart rate goes up. The elevation also lowers the oxygen in your blood to dangerous levels. Nowadays we have an oxygen saturation meter that warns you if you're getting into dangerous territory. At that height your oxygen levels can drop to the low 70s, and when your oxygen's down at 70, 73, 74 it's not a nice place to be – you just cannot breathe.

The trick is to find the sweet spot that allows you to keep moving forward at a speed that's sustainable. If you have a meter you can see when your oxygen's getting low and ease back to get yourself over the mountain. If you don't have the equipment you're going to be in trouble, and that's where I was in 2012.

I cast my eyes up to the mountains from the bottom of the pass and watched the road zig-zagging way up through the trees. I knew just then how it was going to be. With the heart rate and the lack of oxygen I'd be sat there at six to eight mph for hours on end. All you can do is get the head down and flick it away yard by yard. I think the glance up the road momentarily cleared my muddled head because within a few minutes I kind of knew it was over. It was over but I kept going. From time to time, I'd get off and walk and then when I got too tired to walk, I'd get back on the bike for a bit.

All the while, the big lumber trucks were heading down the hill with the engine brakes on, restricted to 25mph. They even have these escape ramps in case they burn out the brakes and the truck runs away with itself. There are lots of cop cars on this part of US Route 160; they police the trucks and speeding motorists. Brakes were going to be the least of my problems on the climb, but my gear ratios were all wrong. They were set far too high and I was pulling a massive gear for the conditions. I hadn't considered it properly beforehand. Another rookie mistake – I didn't factor in the impact of terrain on physical capabilities and how to alter the bike to suit. In later attempts at RAAM I learned the set-up I needed but the gears I had in 2012 slowed me down and made pedalling more difficult.

I stopped at a parking place near the top of the pass and just hung over the bars. The guys gathered around me and their faces told a story. Alan had seen enough, and he knew me well enough to know I was in a really bad way. The fact was that I didn't have anyone with the correct level of medical training on the crew, no one who could actually call it and say: 'You've x, y and z. Get in the van. It's over.'

I wanted to keep going. The English bike racer Tom Simpson famously died of heart failure near the top of Mont Ventoux in the Tour de France back in the sixties. He's supposed to have said 'Put me back on the bike.' I can think of better ways of going down in history, but the top of the pass eventually emerged from around a long curve. There's a big sign up there: 'Wolf Creek Pass Summit Elev 10,856 ft'. It's the sort of place tourists pull over at for a flask of coffee and, even in June, there was still some snow on the ground. I was somewhere else, deep inside myself. My body and mind were fighting to keep life's show on the road.

I spoke to Alan again. He has years of experience of dealing with roadside emergencies. He's seen a lot of people in trouble and I'd trust him with my life. We finally agreed that our RAAM dream was over. I'd done a thousand miles and still had two thousand to go. I'd have needed a week of recovery before I could have continued. It had been over since Flagstaff, to be honest, unless we'd managed to come up with some drastic solution.

Here's the mad bit: I rode the bike to the hospital. I didn't say 'Put me back on the bike' exactly, but it was all downhill and sure I thought maybe I'd come around a bit before we reached the bottom. I was doing everything possible to delay that inevitable and overwhelming feeling of failure. The road swooped down nearly twenty miles to a town called South Fork and by the time I got near it I could hardly keep the bike in a straight line. I rode into the car park and we then had the usual tussle every foreigner fears when they enter a hospital in the USA. Alan, who always took the greatest care of me on races, was confronted with 'Show us your insurance papers or unfortunately we can't admit you.' Thankfully this was one rookie mistake I hadn't made.

I walked in the front door on my own two feet and took my helmet and kit off, and within ten minutes I was lying on a bed with tubes, wires and needles sticking out of me in all directions. They did a ton of tests and told me I had altitude sickness. The two main symptoms of severe altitude sickness are swelling of the brain and fluid in the lungs. To put it simply I was drowning. It's called pulmonary oedema and if the doctors don't get a grip on it you can be dead very quickly.

I couldn't get a breath and it started to get very frightening. They were trying to stop my lungs filling up and there was one test after another. One of the doctors freaked me out the way she was talking about my chances of survival. My saviour was a nurse who said calmly, 'Don't worry. We'll fix this for you.' She pumped one litre bag of I/V fluid into me after another. She was determined to do all she could for me and for that I'll be forever grateful. I owe her my life. She told me she grew up on a local farm and I could tell she really understood life in the Rockies and how this special place responded to anyone without respect for it.

They kept wheeling me in and out of my room for MRI scans and whatever tests they could stick on the bill, including a helicopter they put on standby. I couldn't understand why I didn't feel any pain. I couldn't get a breath but apart from that I felt fine. Then the doctor came to talk to me. Apparently the fluid on the lungs can put a terrible strain on the heart and she said I was in imminent danger of heart failure, a coronary. They couldn't treat a coronary in South Fork. I'd have to get to the hospital in Denver. And then came the catch-22 – the only way to get to Denver in time was to fly, 'and the minute we put you up in a helicopter you're going to die'. Simple as.

I couldn't fault the doctor's honesty, but she was just a tad blunt. She said they would have to get my problem turned around within four hours or I'd be in serious trouble. I looked at Alan, desperately hoping he'd come up with a plan. 'It looks like we'll be here for a while,' he said. They say your life flashes before your eyes at times like this, but I was more concerned about phoning home. I spoke to my two sons. Ross was only five years old at the time and Reuben was seven. What can you say to kids that age? I told them I was sick; that I was in the hospital and they were doing their best to fix it. I told Sinead I didn't know how it was going to end up, but I veered away from the dark thought that 'I'm not coming home.'

The nurse kept on with the treatment. She never left my bedside and she was determined to keep me ticking over. She said not to worry about what the doctor had said and that she would get me through. This terrible fear had come over me that I was so far from home and I might never see Ireland or my boys and family again.

I may be imagining this but I'm pretty sure I heard the rotor blades of the helicopter lifting off when they realised they wouldn't be needing it for me. I even said to the nurse, 'Look, I'm sorry for putting you through all this when it's all going to be a wasted effort.'

Then I blacked out. They told me later I'd been asleep for six hours. When I opened my eyes, I had a mask over my mouth, and they were putting something up my nose to help my breathing. It had this weird smell that I can still sense as I'm sitting here. And that was it. My chest had slowly cleared and I could breathe again. They'd saved my life.

I lay on the bed and within three or four hours I felt almost back to normal again. For the first time since arriving at the hospital I was able to take in my surroundings. It was almost like a hotel room. Then I sensed this figure sitting quietly in the corner. The man appeared to be a kind of orderly who was there to tend to my needs. It made sense, I suppose, since I was in no state to do anything for myself. I tried to engage the guy in conversation. He was reluctant at first, but I soon had him chatting. John was a Native American. He lived in a settlement just over the back fence of the hospital.

The company that ran the hospital had charged $15,000 to save my life, including $8,000 for the helicopter that was never used. John explained that his people, the families who lived over the fence, were not allowed to be treated in the hospital because they had no insurance. If a child got sick, they would be treated with natural remedies by the tribe's medicine people, but if the natural medicine wasn't up to the job there was a chance the child would die. I struggled to understand how this could happen in a developed country. They were US citizens, after all. I'll never forget that long conversation with John. He was the loveliest man. It took me straight back to Belfast and the many days and weeks I'd spent at Ross's hospital bedside when he was little more than a babe in arms.

Once I was feeling better, I didn't want to hang around in the hospital any longer than I had to. There was a bit of a struggle with the doctors to get me discharged. It's hard to believe it looking back but in the end I was in the hospital for just a day and a half. They sent me off with a tank of oxygen and a mask to get me down from the high mountains and onto the Kansas prairie.

Wolf Creek Fallout

There was a lot to think about as I slumped in the back of the motorhome and watched the miles spool by. The sheer physical trauma of the previous few days was just one of them. The knowledge that I had cheated death had a profound effect on me mentally. My responsibilities back home came crashing in. Even though I was only going to be away for a short time, at the back of my mind before I set off from home I knew I was being a little bit reckless. The phone call home to Sinead when I spoke with Reuben and Ross ran through my head. I shuddered about what had so nearly happened.

I simply hadn't appreciated the level of risk involved in something as extreme as Race Across America. It wasn't like my experience in Ireland, where I had been able to bully my way through. RAAM can hit you very hard, very quickly and with serious consequences. Several riders have been killed in collisions down the years. One Danish rider was in a coma for three years before he died. My lack of the correct preparation and knowledge left me in an extremely vulnerable position when I got into trouble at Wolf Creek. We didn't have the necessary equipment and while the guys were dedicated and working to the best of their ability, we didn't really have the correct skillsets on the team.

There was a sense of deflation as some of the crew drifted off to the airport to catch early flights home and the rest of us stuck to the race route to deliver the vehicles to the east coast. I was still tethered to the tank of oxygen as we descended to 5,000 feet. Each time we passed one of the other riders it was a salutary reminder of how fine the line is between triumph and disaster. No one seemed too keen on talking about what had happened so there was no proper post-mortem. Two thousand miles is a long drive to ignore the elephant in the room. Luckily, I had Alan with me. We always had something to talk about and there wasn't a moment during the whole experience when he let me be in harm's way.

There was too much time to think and I slowly started slipping down the rabbit hole into that familiar dark place. With nothing to drive me forwards and having just endured a physical and mental kicking, I was drawn back to thoughts of those painful nights on the children's ward in Belfast. It felt like all the progress I had made since Race Around Ireland, all that self-belief, had fallen away at a stroke. The feel-good factor around *No Ordinary Joe* that had buoyed me up now became a source of trepidation. There had been a lot of positive media coverage back home about my RAAM attempt and I feared there would be a backlash. 'Joe Barr has failed in his attempt …' are not words you want to hear directed at you. As I cast off the oxygen mask and we hit the Great Plains of western Kansas, I knew I had to bite the bullet and share the news of my misfortune before we landed back in Ireland. We rolled on past deserted gas stations, KFCs, grain elevators and powerlines before stopping off in a little place called Fort Scott, where I called in to BBC Radio Ulster to do an interview.

At times it felt like the journey would never end. Walmart allows people in motorhomes to park up for the night, so that's how we leapfrogged our way across the States, from one desolate supermarket parking lot to the next. I was getting kind of cheesed off with it. Late one afternoon, as we came spinning through Indiana on the lookout for yet another Walmart we came upon a perfect little bubble of Americana. St Mary's is an immaculate little hamlet with a red-brick church in the middle, a handful of houses and a pub. The lawns looked like they had been cut with nail scissors. We were through the place in the blink of an eye before I called out to the guys, 'Why can't we park up here instead of a manky Walmart for a change?' We turned around and headed back to the pub. The landlord was as laid-back as they come: 'No problem! Park her up alongside and come in for a beer, guys!'

We had a good yarn and it turned out he was not only the pub owner but the local fire chief and half a dozen other things as well. It was a bit like one of those islands off the west coast of Ireland where they run an undertaker's at the back of the Spar shop that's also a pub. I'm not sure what the villagers made of this strange group of Irishmen descending on their patch, but we were soon invited to take part in a community fundraiser for a little girl and a local woman, both with serious medical conditions. We had pretty good connections in the States by then so I made a few phone calls and managed to scrape up some donations. It wasn't exactly *Sunday Night at the London Palladium*, but that night in St Mary's was very special. Just about every person in the village seemed to have a party piece, whether it was country singing, guitar playing or reciting poetry. The lads even made a botched attempt to remember the words of 'The Irish Rover'. We made some great friends there and I am still in contact with them to this day. In fact, I even looked into getting St Mary's twinned with Eglinton. When I went back to Race Across America in 2014 the route still ran through St Mary's. I made sure to phone ahead and there was the fire chief/bartender at the side of the road to greet us, along with some of the neighbours. We stopped for five minutes for a chat.

We ran out of road at the City Dock in Annapolis, Maryland, where the race finishes, and decided to go to the big RAAM banquet. It was a bit of a non-event for me watching all the finishers being so enthused and sharing their adventures. We probably shouldn't have bothered. It's a famously fun event but there wasn't much craic to be had from me that night. I just wanted to get home. We still had a long journey ahead of us and I was getting nervous about the reaction of the sponsors. Race Across America is such a big undertaking and my backers, some of them personal friends, didn't get the result I had hoped for them.

We flew from JFK to Dublin and within hours I had walked through the front door in Eglinton and dumped my bag in the hall. This was going to be difficult. RAAM had been such a massive moment for me and for the people I had brought with me. But I was the one on the bike, the one with his face in the newspapers. The reality was that I had failed miserably. It became easy to start slipping away, telling myself I was crap and a failure. I started to believe that I had overextended myself and taken on something I wasn't capable of achieving. How could I have been so naive?

My body had taken a hell of a battering and I quickly became aware that I had some medical problems to deal with. Whether it was the altitude sickness or the strain caused by coming back to sea level, I had a pain in my diaphragm that I couldn't seem to shake off. Through it all I never gave up on riding the bike but I kept well away from the sportives and any group riding. I just wanted to be by myself in the hills with my thoughts. I needed to be kind to my body and mind. In truth, I suppose I was hiding until the dust settled. I didn't want to talk to anyone about what had happened out in Wolf Creek. There are only so many ways you can tell that story before it becomes wearing. I certainly didn't want to dwell on it because it was just destroying me. What happened over there just showed how brittle and fragile my mind had become. In the past, if I lost a race I would have picked myself up and got back into the fight the next day. Now, my resilience was shot to bits and life at home was quite painful. The lack of understanding was just too much for me. Looking back, by the end of 2012 I knew that my marriage was in trouble.

The one ray of hope that emerged around that time came from the guy I met by the side of the road when we were driving to Annapolis. Len Forkas had been the rider in front of me at the start of the race in Oceanside. I remember being impressed by the presentation of his service car. His whole team was very professionally turned out, although I could tell just by looking at him that he wasn't a cyclist. He'll kill me for saying this, but he looked like a businessman who was riding a bike. We caught up with him by the roadside shortly after I was released from the hospital in South Fork. The team was parked up at the side of the road taking a break so we pulled over and had a chat. Most of Len's team were ex-military, tank drivers and the like, and the crew chief was a senior firefighter. As you can imagine, their logistics set-up was top notch and everything was stowed in the crew car like a fire truck on inspection night. I left with Len's business card in my pocket and a promise to keep in touch after the race.

Len's background is in communications. His Washington DC-based company built many of the mobile phone masts across the eastern seaboard. In his spare time, he was an endurance athlete well before he took to cycling – climbing high mountains and running marathons on every continent. In that 2012 Race Across America he raised nearly $400,000 for his charity. Hopecam, which he founded in 2003, provides tablets, web cameras and high-speed internet connections to enable kids with cancer to stay in touch with their classmates. The idea is to combat social isolation, lower the child's anxiety and help them face the biggest challenge of their young lives. Len was on a similar path to my own. At nine years old, his son, Matt, had been diagnosed with childhood leukaemia.

I rang Len from home one day to congratulate him on winning his category in RAAM and to chat about how he had approached the race. He was happy to take the call even though I had contacted him out of the blue. We talked for quite some time and discovered this common ground of our boys' cancer journeys. To this day, I don't think Len realises quite how much he helped me to dig myself out of my black hole. We had a number of conversations during those months after I returned from RAAM and I opened up to him about how disappointed and beaten down I felt about the experience. Len is such a positive, engaging personality and as we discussed the practicalities of Race Across America it began to rub off on my view of myself. He was the first person I had a real conversation with about altitude, how to prepare for it and how to manage it. When I looked into his background, I became more and more impressed with Len and his attitude to life. He knew of my background in mainstream bike racing and encouraged me not to walk away from the sport. 'Why am I beating myself up over this?' I thought. Once again, I had convinced myself that I was useless, a failure. Len shared with me his knowledge about the equipment, training and attitude required to tame the beast. With his help, Race Across America had turned from a defeat into unfinished business.

In early 2013, I was contacted by Valerio Zamboni. The world of ultra-cycling attracts many colourful characters and Valerio has a heck of a backstory. He learned to fly gliders as a youngster in Italy and now lives in Monte Carlo where he runs a company selling business jets. Before taking up cycling he was a passionate mountaineer but smashed his pelvis in a serious fall. Valerio has completed Race Across America a number of times and is one of the most popular figures on the ultra-cycling scene. He explained that a friend of his was organising the first ever Race Across Italy and asked if I wanted to give it a try.

The new route was roughly 400km across the boot of Italy, just the right length to try out my legs. With the trouncing I'd had across the Atlantic, I didn't know how my body was going to respond, and I knew I needed to walk before I could run again. It also had the advantage of being cheap, little more than the cost of the trips to gran fondos I had done with Alan. He couldn't come this time so I was accompanied by two of the RAAM team, Killian Galligan and Garth Young. The race started and finished in a little seaside resort called Nettuno, south of Rome. They say that the Roman emperors used to escape down to Nettuno for a spot of sun, sea and sandals back in the day. As it was the inaugural race the whole affair was very low-key. The sign-in was at a little hut near the harbour between the pedalo hire and an ice cream shop. There would have been no more than a dozen riders. Even so, there were three or four top-notch entrants, including world number one Christoph Strasser and Valerio, who was world champion at the time. Strasser is ultra-cycling's megastar. He holds the record for the fastest RAAM and has won the event six times. In July 2021, Christoph did the unimaginable: he smashed the 1,000km-in-24-hours barrier by riding 1,023 km, all under the watchful eyes of World Ultra-Cycling Association adjudicators. That's how good a rider he is. Not only is he brilliant technically, he also has youth on his side. Many ultra riders come to the sport in their thirties and forties. Strasser was the youngest ultra world champion at the age of 25.

There was no real comparison between the Italian race and Race Across America. They were chalk and cheese. The route took us across the Apennine Mountains that form the backbone of Italy, hardly in the same class as the Rockies; so I could safely forget about altitude sickness and leave the oxygen tank at home. Likewise, Italy in May can be warm enough at times but it's not in the same league as Tuba City, Arizona. This was more like a mini version of Race Around Ireland, a proper old-fashioned road race. RAAM is just one big, wide road from sea to shining sea. Italy had the winding lanes I was familiar with, and when you're in between the hedges I'm as good as they come. The 400km was done and dusted in 24 hours.

Fourth place. It's always the most frustrating ending to a race. I stretched my body to its limits but I just couldn't make it back to the Italian rider, Omar Di Felice, who passed me as we neared Nettuno. He didn't beat me by much, just a handful of minutes, but I didn't have the strength on the day. So there was no podium but the mental boost the race gave me was huge. When you blow up in the spectacular way that I did in the Race Across America it's tough trying to scrabble your way back. It was like starting all over again. I'd been fighting to breathe back home and the Italian race gave me a little bit of fresh air, a hint that I could haul myself out of the black hole.

Where next? It wasn't as though I could go full tilt at another big race. I knew from my professional racing days the level of commitment that was needed. I still had work and home, and a pile of real-world stuff to deal with. That's when I discovered there was a cycling version of the Le Mans 24-hour race. The classic 24 Heures du Mans motor race is part of the Triple Crown of Motorsport, along with the Indianapolis 500 and the Monaco Grand Prix. I was intrigued and immediately fired off a request for information. The race is run on the classic Circuit de la Sarthe with the same format as the car and motorbike races. The bikes are lined up on one side of the road and the cyclists are on the other; when the flag drops you have to leg it across, clip into the pedals and tear off up the track. It starts at 3 p.m. on a Saturday and finishes at three on Sunday.

It wasn't at all what I expected. The French cycling fans are really into it and there were crowds in the grandstand right through the night. It turned out that Le Mans was a fantastic venue for a bike race. Some of the two- and three-person teams were hitting crazy speeds of 50km/h non-stop. As a solo rider there's no way you can keep up with them so you have to develop a strategy. I would try to keep up with the fast team boys for maybe six laps and then let them go. Once they came around to lap me, I'd jump on the back again for another six. The circuit is more hilly than you would expect so there's more than enough to test your legs. There's an uphill drag past the grandstand that you can't see on camera. Then you hit some big, snaking turns. There's a right, a left and another right before you come to the famous Dunlop Bridge. So you're under the bridge and cresting over the hill. Then it's 60, 70, 80km/h as you sweep down the other side through another series of bends.

The toughest thing about the race is dealing with the sheer monotony of it. The circuit is just over eight miles long so you quickly lose count of how many times you've rolled past the grandstand. I found it enormously stressful doing lap after lap after lap. It really starts to ramp up once you've made it through the night. That period from nine on Sunday morning until three in the afternoon felt like the longest six hours of my life. It's incredibly intense when you are struggling with your brain to keep awake. You almost feel like you're on the verge of hallucinating. If you have any kind of mental weakness it brings it to the fore. As for the climb up through Dunlop Bridge, for the first hour or two it's just a little rise and you can fly up and over the top of it. By sunset it becomes a major climb and it keeps getting higher through the night hours. It wasn't just me; I could see everyone else was on edge.

At times like this I have to adopt my 'eating the elephant' tactic. The way to eat an elephant is to take one small bit at a time. Usually this means I break up a race into 15-minute chunks. That way I'm thinking about getting to the end of that 15-minute block rather than drowning in the thought that I have five or six hours still to go. It's the same on a 3,000-mile race like RAAM. If I've still 600 miles to go and I'm feeling crushed I break it down into those 15-minute chunks. Otherwise, I'd probably be overcome by a wave of helplessness.

Racing at Le Mans really caught my imagination. They run endurance bike races at a number of racetracks now. You can go to Imola, Monza and Brands Hatch. They've tried it out at Silverstone. One of the most prestigious in the world of ultra-racing is at Sebring in Florida. Still, with its unrivalled place in the romantic history of speed, you couldn't beat Le Mans. Everyone wants to win there.

I didn't win. In fact, I think I rolled in 15th or 16th. I wasn't disappointed. I'd spoken to a couple of people who had done it before and they both said the same thing – you really need to experience Le Mans once before you can go back and properly race there. There's no one who can rebuild your confidence quite like yourself. Once I'd been through Race Across Italy and Le

Mans without stretching myself too far, I knew I could risk going back to RAAM. In fact, I'd pretty much decided I wanted to have another crack about a month before I went to Italy. Len had taught me a lot about feeling positive about yourself and I was starting to feel alive again. I had lost interest in pretty much everything, but the racing had sparked the life back into me.

CHAPTER 12

Little Red Corvette

I must have hit 100km/h as I leaned the bike into the long, fast descent. Back on the road again, back at RAAM again, slicing through the bends on the Glass Elevator. People go trail walking here. Why would you? There's nothing but rocks, heat and rattlesnakes. One of the main attractions is a little oasis with the delightful name of Hellhole Palms. Don't forget to pack your trunks, people. In 2012, I'd crept down this road like a learner driver on their first lesson. This time around I carved my way through the switchbacks. I'd learned from other RAAM veterans that you need to go full gas from the start in Oceanside. That's where all the real players are setting their race up and there's no escaping the descent of the Elevator at high speed. A big gust of Arizona desert air came rushing up and over the Armco barrier. I had the deep-section wheels fitted, and the entire front end of the bike was thrown up in the air. The handlebars turned sideways, and it actually felt like the bike had bent in the middle. By pure chance as the wheel thumped back down on to the tarmac, I grabbed a handful of back brake. I lost control of the steering and the bike went into a big, curving slide. The barrier loomed ahead and I gently applied both anchors, hauling up just in time and leaving a long, skinny skid mark on the road. That's what they call a bench test for the heart-rate monitor.

Once I'd dipped my toe back into the water the previous year it wasn't simply a case of filling in a form and posting off an application fee. Race Across Italy had qualified me to go back to RAAM, but I needed a serious fistful of cash to launch my latest attempt. I needed a backer. Tony Culley-Foster is a man who knows about endurance sports. In the summer of 1976, he ran across America, 2,988 miles from San Francisco to Washington DC. Four years later it was a 1,234-mile circumference of Ireland. He was also one of the torch bearers for the 2012 Olympics. Tony was born in Derry but lives in DC. As President and CEO of the World Affairs Council he became an influential figure in US–Irish affairs. He has a particular interest in promoting peace in Northern Ireland and in cross-border co-operation. I was introduced to Tony by William Allen from the company that owned the *Derry Journal*. Tony would fly over from DC every few months, visit his family and catch up on business. I spent many hours chatting with him in a hotel lobby in the Diamond in the heart of Derry. Tony is an inspirational figure who always left me feeling positive about myself. I even took him to meet my mum and the two of them nattered away over tea and her legendary scones. With his sporting background he knew where I was coming from and used his contacts in the USA to raise much of the sponsorship that I needed for 2014. My new DC friend Len's Hopecam charity was to be the beneficiary of my fundraising efforts on the 2014 RAAM. Tony took one look at it and became enthused about the possibility of setting up a cross-border Hopecam equivalent in Ireland, so we agreed part of the fundraising proceeds would go to the Irish project.

Everything appeared to be running like clockwork until we came down the steps at San Diego airport. I glanced across towards the two Dodge Caravans we had hired as crew cars. These were the perfect solution to supporting a rider through the challenges of RAAM, and all the big teams used them. My California-based sponsors BRL had arranged to have the vehicles liveried in this fantastic design incorporating the names of the sponsors and our own logo. The graphics company literally cocoons the car in a plastic wrap with the design printed on it. It was one of the aspects of Len's preparations for his 2012 RAAM that had so impressed me. The cars simply looked the dog's and a big smile spread across my face. But trust Alan to put a downer on it. 'I see the first problem,' he said. 'Would you even let me get out the front door first?' I groaned. The problem was that in 2014, Dodge removed the roof railers from the Caravan. We had no way to fit the bike racks.

We ended up pitching a lot of our flight boxes and equipment into the back of a pick-up owned by a guy called Larry Froome. Len had arranged for me to stay with the Froomes for the days before the start of the race. The Froomes were big supporters of Hopecam and they had a beautiful home in the suburbs. I stayed with Larry while the rest of the crew were staying with another family of Hopecam supporters, the O'Sullivans, out in the San Diego Valley. When the guys told me that I was invited over for dinner I was tempted to say, 'Thanks but no thanks, lads, I'm living in five-star luxury here.' It turned out Mr O'Sullivan was a former vice-president of Caterpillar, the company that makes the big diggers. The O'Sullivans' home was stunning. There was a sheer cliff-edge drop from the end of their garden with a remarkable view down the length of the valley. On a little concrete pad next to the big drop were two rocking chairs, strategically placed to catch the evening sun, perfect for a glass of fine Californian wine before bedtime. Dinner turned into one of those unforgettable nights, a perfect last supper before the agonies of Race Across America.

Down on the seafront at Oceanside those same old pelicans were still perched along the pier, but my mindset was very different this time. With hindsight I'd say that in 2012 I was hopelessly overconfident. Full of enthusiasm and self-belief, I thought there was a serious chance I could win the race. I certainly didn't envisage that it would suck me up and spit me out in the way that it did. In 2014, I was ultra-cautious. It's easy to get drawn into the excitement and razzmatazz of RAAM. At the sign-in there's a crowd of maybe a thousand riders and crews, all uber-positive and oozing excitement. They have spent maybe two or three years preparing for this moment. In that atmosphere you can easily lose touch with reality.

I didn't feel particularly apprehensive at the start line as I knew I had prepared well. I had trained hard, but I had also trained smart, working on those aspects that I had screwed up in 2012. There was also the knowledge that no matter how good you were, how good your equipment was and how well your team worked, there would come a point in the race where it would be just you and the road. And that's where you find whether you can or you can't hack it. This time around I split the race into three chunks to make it a little easier to swallow. The first thousand miles was a head down, backside in the air bike race. The second thousand was about managing your body and the damage you'd done to it in the first thousand. The final thousand was about sheer survival and who could drag their sorry ass across the line first.

Everybody talks about Wolf Creek. Just the name has that kind of legendary, brooding ring to it. For me it was personal, and it was my biggest fear ahead of the 2014 race. By then I knew I couldn't just charge ram stam into that climb. It had to be managed. If I could manage the desert furnace, the climb up to the top of Wolf Creek and the drop down below 5,000 feet, I had a chance of surviving the race. That's where the equipment came into play. In 2012, we didn't have simple tools like an oxygen saturation meter to measure the level of oxygen in my blood. In fact, we were clueless about all aspects of riding at altitude. But Len and his crew of ex-military guys knew all about altitude. On my second attempt at Race Across America, Len was able to help, and was monitoring the race from his home in Washington DC. Andy McMullan, my physio, was a keen mountaineer and had a good grasp of the challenges posed by altitude. We were able to use the metering to manage the oxygen saturation. It still dropped, but it was a managed drop. We knew when to stop and how long the breaks needed to be.

This made a major difference to how I coped with the altitude, but the furnace-like conditions of the desert required another specialist piece of gear. I had never seen an ice vest before 2012 and I kicked myself when I saw other riders using them. The vest works to lower your core temperature and the ones we use look like bulletproof vests made from long thin tubes like kids' ice pops. You steep them in water and they crystallise. We had two with us in 2014, frozen before departure and buried in big coolboxes full of ice. The vests last for two hours; they're cold when you slip them on but literally within seconds you don't even notice it. Ice vests make a big difference, but only if you're using one. In the manic charge in the opening section of the race we waited too long to start using the vests. That period was so intense, with the leaders racing so hard, that I forgot to shout for the vests and the team didn't force one on me. We got there eventually, but the vests would have been a big help earlier in the race.

Dehydration has always been a problem for me. Any cyclist will tell you how important it is to drink regularly – that's why we have bottles on the bike. Little and often is the rule. In Ireland it's not such a big deal, but in the desert not drinking enough can bring on a shedload of problems. My hydration was better than in 2012 but I still struggled to drink the sheer volume of liquid I needed to keep myself hydrated. When you sweat as you're riding in the desert you don't even feel it. It evaporates off your skin instantly. Only when you stop do you see that it's running off you like someone's running a tap over the top of your head.

I was aware that hydration was a bit of an Achilles heel for me, so I managed to wangle a lab test at Ulster University before the race. An expert from the Australian Institute of Sport had been working on secondment in Belfast. I managed to get hold of her on the day she was due to fly home and she did a sweat test on me. This determines the type of sweater you are and how much liquid you can ingest to hydrate yourself before you start to flood the system. For me, the safe limit was 600ml an hour. Out in the desert I was doing my level best to hit the 600ml but I just couldn't make it and my hydration was in deficit. My body was drying up inside and my jersey was covered in white, dusty salt.

We stopped at the top of Wolf Creek Pass and pulled over into that tourist car park with the Great Divide sign where I had bowed to the inevitable in 2012. There was no real need to stop, but it seemed symbolic. It had suddenly become one of my proudest moments. If you were being sober and rational about it, you could say I had managed my efforts efficiently. In my mind I had just beaten the damn thing and I deserved a rest. Maybe there was a bit of carelessness on my part, but I didn't think twice about climbing into the motorhome to get my head down for a bit.

When I surfaced half an hour later I detected a slightly strange atmosphere among the team. It turned out that Len had been screaming down the phone from DC to get me down off the mountain as soon as possible. Andy, on the other hand, felt that from a medical point of view, it made sense to have a rest, go at my own pace and not panic. I guess Andy won the argument because he was there on the scene. To be honest they were probably both right. I was happy to be distracted by the arrival of a woman who had helped me when I was in hospital in 2012, when she was working as a RAAM official. She had brought her little grandson with her to meet me before I set off down the mountain. I signed a T-shirt for him and I got to thank her for everything she had done for me in 2012.

I had briefly lost sight of my priorities up there on the Great Divide, but I got away with it and soon I was careering down towards South Fork though the mountain tunnels. Alan's voice came crackling through the radio: 'We're nearly at your favourite place, Joe.' I'm not sure that's how I would describe the hospital where I almost drowned in my own sputum. But it was the cue for me to perform another symbolic act, one I'd been planning for two years. When I left the hospital, weighed down with the oxygen tank and mask, a nurse had issued me with a big plastic water container with the name of the hospital printed on it. At the time I'd jokingly promised to drop it back the next time I was passing through. We fished it out of the back of the crew car, and I posed for a picture as I hung it on the sign post at the hospital gate. I was glad to get past the hospital. I had learned a life lesson there and been granted time I probably wasn't owed.

We still had a long way to go. In fact, there were still 200 miles to go before we even got below 5,000 feet. Wolf Creek is the climb that everyone talks about, but in my opinion, crunch time really comes at a place called La Veta. It's just a little bit further along the route through the Rockies. La Veta is a huge climb that seems to go on for ever up these small switchback roads. You spend the better part of a day crawling up onto the plateau. So you've come down from 11,000 feet at Wolf Creek to maybe 7,500 feet. La Veta is at 9,000 feet, but by the time you're starting the climb the damage has already been done just getting there. Every rider is ready to fall apart at that stage. You have already been on the bike for about 1,200 miles by then. I stopped several times on the way up to get in the van and recover. I took it bit by bit to get up La Veta. It's about twenty miles and the climb lasted for ever.

La Veta itself has a population of 800, and after all that struggle I was through it in about thirty seconds. Then it was across the plateau and down, down, down to a little town called Trinidad. It's a place that's been welcoming long-distance travellers for a couple of centuries. Trinidad was a stopping-off point on the Santa Fe trail, the legendary long-distance Wild West trading route that was known as the Great Prairie Highway. And that's where the pancake-flat heartland of the United States begins. The murderous climbing and threat of altitude sickness were behind me and 200 miles of utter tedium beckoned. Kansas may only be the 23rd flattest state in the USA but it certainly feels like the flattest. The roads are wide and straight, and because there are no hedgerows for 200 miles you can see a vast distance ahead of you. You could be out there for hours and hours on end just turning over the pedals and not seeing a soul. The night skies in Kansas were one of the most incredible things I'd ever seen. The Milky Way curves from one end of the black velvet heavens to the other. Seeing those uncountable pinpoints of light and knowing how far away they are kept me starstruck through the night.

Anyone who's seen *The Wizard of Oz* will know that Kansas is slap bang in the middle of Tornado Alley and when the warnings of storm force winds started coming over the radio it was more than a little unsettling. Then a massive thunderstorm appeared over the horizon to the right. Forked lightning crashed into the ground. Vast flashes flared across the night sky. It was genuinely scary, and the handlebars shook as I flinched. Meanwhile, back in the car, the guys were checking the weather apps. 'Chill out, Joe. That lightning's 200 miles away.' Warnings came over the race radio of tornadoes on the route. There were teams whose vehicles were damaged, even washed away, but when I spun through a couple of hours later it was bone dry and nothing out of the ordinary. You wouldn't have known it had happened.

The prairies are known for their extreme weather conditions and I was able to use the strong sidewinds to my advantage. The first thing most of the other riders did when confronted by a big side wind was to swap out the solid disc rear wheel. Back in my mainstream racing days I had learned a lot about crosswinds, especially from riding in the Belgian spring classics. I could ride in echelons, but I also knew how to work with and manage the wind when riding solo. So I kept the disc wheel on and used it to gain assistance from the wind. I let the wind fishtail me right across the road into the opposite gutter and then I fought it back. Each time I zig-zagged across the road I was gaining a little bit of forward motion. If you did that for a mile the difference would be little or nothing, but do it for 200 miles and it's a different story. When we crossed the state line into Kansas, my old friend Valerio Zamboni and I were almost level on the road. By the time we crossed into Missouri I was ten or twelve hours ahead. The disadvantage was that because I was wrestling with the bars for hours on end my hands became badly blistered. When I took my racing mitts off, the skin came off with them, and my hands were left completely raw in the centre. I had painful hands for the rest of the race.

As part of the fundraising effort, I followed Len's example of connecting directly with the Hopecam kids along the route. The charity put together a portfolio with the details of a dozen children who were either having treatment at home or were convalescing, and I would chat with them on the phone. It was all co-ordinated very efficiently by Len's team. The calls were scheduled for a certain time each day and the crew would give me a briefing over the radio before we stopped. Then it was hop off the bike, ten minutes on the phone and hop back on again. It came to be my favourite part of the day. With my briefing notes I was able to talk about their friends, their teacher and their pets as if I knew them personally. Some were real little characters. Their homes were dotted across the map in several states and the local media in those areas would carry the story. My only regret at the time was that I wouldn't get to meet them in person.

I wouldn't like people to get the impression that this racing business is all about me, me, me. The back-up team is vital and there are three basic roles: managing me; managing the service cars; and managing the race. Race management is key to the entire project. Back in the early days of RAAM there was no real way for riders to know where their competitors were on the route. Nowadays all the riders have GPS trackers. This makes the race highly tactical. Where are our rivals now? Have they stopped for a rest? Will they need to stop soon? There may be four or five you're keeping an eye on. Then there's the question of me. How do I feel? Do I need a rest? This is all complicated by the fact that you are in two races – the overall race and the age group race, which in my case was the 50–59 age group. The race management role was passed around as the guys were working in shifts. At any given time, someone would be sitting in the back seat of the service car with the laptop open trying to read the race. It can be a very frustrating job, not least because there is no mobile connection across large sections of the route. You have great gaps of time when there is no access to the GPS feed. A lot of the time we relied on getting a heads-up from Len sitting on his couch in DC.

We had almost reached West Virginia when we came on one of the teams parked up by the side of the road. It's not unusual to pass another rider who's taking a break, but we could tell there was something not quite right here. Rather than roll on past we pulled over to check it out. It turned out that the rider was Paride Miglio, an Italian cyclist who I was tussling with for third place at that point. He was suffering from a very nasty condition called Shermer's neck. The muscles of the neck completely collapse through fatigue and become too weak to hold up the head. The first time anyone developed this was on the second edition of Race Across America, in 1983. One of the racers, Michael Shermer, was forced to prop up his chin on his hand to stop his head flopping over as he rode. Unfortunately, it wasn't enough to get him to the finish line. Many RAAM competitors have suffered from the infamous syndrome over the years and have resorted to everything from neck braces to bizarre contraptions made of gaffer tape and plastic plumbing pipes. When a rider is in trouble in RAAM they're not playing games. We couldn't leave Paride suffering and potentially having to abandon the race. We spent quite a while there and I jumped in the motorhome while my physio, Andy, set to work. It was a matter of taking my sleep two or three hours early, no big deal. Luckily for the Italian, the neck collapse had not fully set in. If we helped him out, he might still make it to the finish but in any case he would be limping home and there was no doubt that I was going to beat him. Andy's intervention meant there would be no DNF (did not finish) for Paride at the side of the road. He managed to make it to Annapolis, and we've been great friends ever since. In fact, he's even been to some of the events I run in Ireland.

The whole race management thing became a lot easier with a serious rival out of the way, but I was about to meet one of the stiffest challenges of Race Across America. The Appalachian

Mountains are maybe 250 miles from the finish. You might think you'd be coasting home by this point, and they may be tiddlers compared to the Rockies, but the statistics show that more racers drop out in this section of the race than in any other. How disappointing must it be to drop out with exhaustion when you've got 2,800 miles under your belt and less than a tenth of that to go? You see people who just cannot go one mile further. There are something like 22 severe climbs one after the other and everybody is on their knees. It just scythes through the riders. I can climb hills till they're coming out of my ears, but this was no pushover.

RAAM takes on a completely different characteristic depending upon whether it's been dominated by tailwinds or headwinds. In 2014, I had favourable conditions the whole way across the continent. I've done it since then with headwinds dominating and it leaves you twice as knackered by the time you get to the Appalachians. These mountains are all elevation without altitude. You climb and you climb and you're waiting for the big descent but it never seems to come. It drops down a bit and you get a little bit of flat and then you're back up another brutal climb. It's a very strange type of climbing. When you get to the Appalachians you are well into that final third of RAAM where it's just a race for survival. I've seen quality riders who win ultra-races all over the world and then you look at the RAAM statistics and they have never been able to finish the big one. It takes such a toll on the human body that only a third of the rookies taking on the race for the first time make it to Annapolis.

The Appalachians take a full day. Any time I've been through there it was searing hot, and the roads in West Virginia are rough. I hit a long section of dual carriageway where the hard shoulder was covered in debris. There were trucks constantly flying by, so I was forced to ride on a rumble strip that nearly bounced the bars out of my hands if I tried to get up any speed. Despite all the terrors of the Appalachians, I was still feeling relatively strong. I was piling on the power, absolutely flying. There had been a massive chase on from back in Ohio. Len was keeping a close eye on the race feed and he reckoned I was twice as fast as anyone else in the mountains.

It was while I was up there that I made it into second place. An American rider, Dale Capewell, had been in front of me but he was struck down by exhaustion and had to stop for a sleep. We rolled passed him but I didn't see him at the time. It was in one of those GPS dead zones, so we didn't know what had happened until the tracker popped up again. The guys came straight up to me and said, 'Joe, you're in second place now whatever you do. Let's just keep this thing pinned.'

'Better not go under a school bus,' I thought. So it was down off the mountains and into Maryland, the final state of this mad journey. I could tell I had crossed the state line because there was pink stone in the roads, and they were billiard-table smooth compared to what I'd just been through.

It was a massive relief to know that the torture was almost finished, but come the final 100 miles I was really suffering. The sleep deprivation really started to kick in. When I was in fifth or sixth place, I had been happy enough to take the prescribed sleep breaks. But as I started to pick off my rivals and make an impact on the leader board I was just flat out. They call it riding on the rivet, absolutely on the limit. That's when the soles of my feet started burning. It got to the point where every pedal stroke was painful. It felt like there was a blowtorch aimed at my feet and the soles were being scorched away. You have to manage it with ice, continually changing socks and lots of foot powder. As for the sleeping, by the time I got to Maryland I'd gone the better part of 11 days and 11 nights with little or none. For the first fifty hours, when the top guys are all jockeying for position, there's no sleep at all. When you do get stopped you can have two hours but no more than that. If you go too deep you won't wake up, you'll just sleep on. I found that an hour and 30 or 40 minutes worked best for me. Then it's ten minutes to get your clothes on, get sorted and hit the road again.

The culmination of all that mind and body pummelling was actually rather uninspiring. The official finish line for Race Across America is in a big service station by the side of the main road about 25 miles from Annapolis proper. They took the timings and I got off the bike to get cleaned up. Frankly, by that stage I was stinking, and they put me into clean kit for the sake of the sponsors. Then I followed an official RAAM lead car all the way to the heart of the city. I rolled into the famous dock where we had stood around gloomily watching someone else's party two years earlier. All the guys from the team were there and Len had driven down from Washington with some of his crew. What I didn't expect to see was a whole gaggle of kids from Hopecam with their families. They presented me with all these great pictures they had drawn. One little girl called Eva had a big motto written on her picture: 'I fought, and I won.' I looked round at Alan and said: 'That's the story of our race.' We went to the big post-race banquet again, but this time Eva and her family were our guests. She got up on stage with me to receive a special award from the governor of Maryland, which declared that 23 June each year was to be a charitable day for Hopecam.

That wasn't the only fancy dinner on our agenda. Culley-Foster arranged a slap-up reception for us at the National Press Club in Washington DC. The club is a venue for many of Washington's big hitters, and the Derry man is a familiar figure in its conference rooms and restaurants. Back in the day it was the sort of place where politicians and dignitaries could kick back and relax. There's a photo from 1945 of President Harry Truman at the club battering out a tune while the film star Lauren Bacall drapes herself across the top of the upright piano showing just the right amount of leg for the photographer. Admittedly, the place is a bit more formal now, but we had a fantastic meal in one of the restaurants and felt like kings. It's a day I'll never forget. I hadn't succumbed to the failure of 2012 and with the help of my wonderful team I had turned it into my greatest success in ultra-cycling to that point.

Taken in the round, I'd say that the 2014 was probably the best RAAM I have ridden, even though it wasn't my best result. I go to every race to challenge for the overall win, and that includes RAAM. If I performed well in the overall race, which includes riders of all ages, the likelihood was that I could either win or come close to winning the 50–59 age category. At least that was my thinking in 2014. I was already in my fifties when I first came to Race Across America, so I had to be realistic when it came to the overall. Strasser won it in 2014 in an incredible seven days and 15 hours. My friend from Race Around Ireland, Mark Pattinson, finished second. I finished tenth in the overall and was beaten to the top spot in the 50–59 category by a Swiss rider, Hans 'Hansi' Nyfeler, on his first RAAM. It's quite an achievement for a rookie. Hansi is renowned as being one of the best in the world so the result shouldn't have rankled as much as it did. I knew when I counted the stupid little mistakes I had made along the way, the stopping when I shouldn't have and the drinks not drunk, that I probably could have finished fifth or sixth in the overall rankings. That's the way my head works; I'm never happy with 'close but no cigar'.

Race Across America is a massive operation. Never mind the number of people involved; the amount of stuff that builds up in the crew vehicles – bikes, tools, communications gear, clothes, food and drink, and good old-fashioned trash – must be sorted out somehow. You have three vehicles and a motorhome that have been driven non-stop across America. Frankly, it looks like a bomb went off. Most teams book into the Sheraton Hotel in Annapolis, which has a big car park that allows for plenty of space around the vehicles. Then the big clear-out begins. It looks like a massive car boot sale. Everything gets put into piles. There's the stuff that's coming home with you and the stuff that's going in the bins. The RAAM organisers also take a lot of useful gear that you just couldn't take home and recycle it to charities – things like the big cooler boxes all the teams have. The business of unloading the van can take a couple of days. Then the fancy graphic wraps that I got so excited about back at the airport in San Diego had to be torn off the cars and binned. So you were left with the boring-looking white vehicles that had to be dropped back to the hire company. It was all a bit deflating.

I plonked myself down on the hotel steps to feel the Maryland sun on my face before we headed back to Ireland, where it would inevitably be grey and drizzling, even in June. The guys had all headed off to a mall in town to buy gifts to take home. I cast my eyes across the tidied-up car park and noticed the most gorgeous red Chevy Corvette. A middle-aged man in a business suit stepped through the revolving door, yawned and loosened his tie.

'Are you with the race?' he asked. I nodded. 'Those guys are fucking incredible. You must be one of the crew, right?'

'No, I'm one of those incredible guys,' I smiled.

He was in no hurry to get back into the accountancy conference he'd escaped from so we got talking about cycling and Ireland and how great that Corvette looked.

'Well, if you like it so much, what say we go for a drive?' He reached into his pocket and shook the keys in the air.

That long drive took us through the streets of historic Annapolis and out onto the coastline of Chesapeake Bay in the afternoon sunshine. The chat flowed easily. He told me he had a stable of six or seven Corvettes and that he and his sons raced them at tracks all over the States.

'How come you're not out celebrating with your buddies?' he asked. That's when it all poured out. The truth was I'd been sitting on the hotel steps holding back the tears.

'It's a long story,' I said, 'but when I get home I'm about to start divorce proceedings and leave the two boys I love.'

I had bottled up the truth and not a single person on the team knew about it, not even Alan. Here was someone I thought I'd never see again, so why not tell him? It was eating me up inside. Right from the moment we landed at San Diego, through my time with the Froomes and all through the deserts, the mountains and the plains I had this hard knot my stomach. You get too much time to think on an 11-day bike ride and my own two boys were rarely far from my mind. And here I was spilling it out to a stranger, a man I'd met an hour before. I believed that it was the best thing for me and for the boys, and probably for Sinead as well. I would always be looking over my shoulder to the time when we almost lost Ross, but I was equally aware that Reuben had suffered from a lack of personal attention. To some extent he'd been thrown under the bus during the drama of his little brother's illness. I tried to keep a special bond between us; I would read to him at bedtime or make up silly stories. His birthday falls during RAAM so we had had to celebrate before I set off for California. I was dreading getting back to Ireland now because I had told Sinead I would be moving out of the family home. Every turn of the pedals took me closer to that moment.

The thought of moving to a strange house and spending the days on my own was frightening. It's all those little things woven into the day, picking the boys up from school, the hug at bedtime. All of that would be gone.

I know now that I'm a good dad but I'm not sure how good a parent I've been. As I see it, being a dad is about the relationship with your kids, and being a parent is about how you bring them up. Everyone parents their kids in a different way. I'm just not that good at the day-to-day parenting. To be fair, I'd have to say that Sinead is a better parent. I don't remember any time when I didn't tell my sons I love them every day. They don't live with me now but when we meet up it's like we've never been apart.

No one goes into a marriage intending to have kids and then for the family to fall apart. Financially it made no sense for me to move out of the family home, but these things never do. I'd be working flat out to keep two households, so the chances of ever going on a crazy adventure like Race Across America again seemed virtually non-existent.

CHAPTER 13

Jackals Howling in the Night

When I arrived back in Ireland, I arranged to take Reuben and Ross up to Daisy Lodge for a few days, just to kick back and make up for the time when I'd been in America. When we got back home to Eglinton, Sinead told the boys that their dad was leaving home. It all moved quite quickly after that. Some day, when they're older, I hope I'll be able to sit down with Reuben and Ross and talk everything through properly. Was I right to think my moving out was better for everyone? The boys will have their own opinions.

To be as discreet and as protective as possible, I packed a few things into the car each day while the boys were at school. It was difficult; one of the saddest times of my life. I had arranged to rent a house near Limavady, a pristine white cottage down a winding Irish lane. It's a beautiful part of the country, where the River Roe flows under Binevenagh Mountain to the sea and I could see Donegal across the water. I took very little with me, just my workshop tools and my clothes. When the time came, I closed the door of the new house behind me and sat among the boxes in the semi-darkness with the blinds drawn. I didn't open those blinds again for months. There didn't seem to be any point.

I chose to live there because it was only ten minutes from the boys. I could pick them up from school but it was far enough away to take me out of that village community, a place where people would have judged me. It was a new environment where no one knew me and it was also close to Alan's house. That's when the whole recluse thing began. I just disappeared from the face of the earth. I put the hours in for my job with the logistics company and I went to my mum's; otherwise I just shut down. It was the easiest coping strategy, but at what cost? I spent entire days on my bike rolling over those familiar Derry and Donegal hills and not speaking to anyone.

At the outset, it worked well with the boys. I'd pick them up from school a couple of days a week and they'd come back to my place. We did their homework together. We had fun and relaxed in each other's company and I had them every second weekend.

The saving grace for me was that I spent more time with my mum in Newtowncunningham. The stress I'd been under meant I had started to drop a lot of weight. Cyclists tend to be skinny enough, so when I began losing pounds, I became positively skeletal. My mum was making serious efforts to feed me up. It was a 45-minute journey over there in the car and 45 minutes back. It became a regular thing. I would drive over, and my mum would have the dinner ready. After dinner we would talk. I didn't realise at the time how important that family time was in keeping me the right side up. There was no judgement. As far as my mum was concerned Joe was the Golden Boy. She worried about her children all her life. When I was racing she worried about me getting injured or badly hurt. After the break-up from Sinead she could see what was happening and she knew I was in trouble. I thought I was a bad person, a bad dad. And I was struggling with the pressure of paying for the two homes. People see you putting in an outstanding physical performance as an athlete and they don't see the dark place you are in in your life and in your head. I kept it well hidden, but it was all smoke and mirrors. It almost broke me.

In April 2015, I was in the seaside town of Pescara on the Adriatic coast for my second crack at the Race Across Italy. This was my first big event since things fell apart back at home. I was still feeling vulnerable, so there was a lot hanging on it. It felt like I needed to prove myself all over again. The race was a different event now, having doubled in distance. Riders set off from the east coast and crossed the Apennine Mountains to Nettuno, where they did a U-turn and headed back to Pescara. We checked into a neat little hotel at Silvi Marina on the edge of the Adriatic next to the start and finish. We were a small team. I had Alan, Ian Struthers, Andy McMullan and a driver called Mark Beggs with me. We also had my friend from Rimini, Valentina Giubielli, who was familiar with the strange ways of cycling. She was the ex-partner of my old friend Jamie Burrow of Nove Colli fame. Vali was on her own at this point but she very kindly came to help me. Most important of all, I had brought Reuben along for the ride.

The start was like a seaside party. Big crowds, live bands, sun, sea and sand. And that kind of overexcited, hyperventilating announcer you get at Italian sports events. Race Across Italy is the most popular of the European races. It has its own kind of charisma and attracts a big entry, many of them top racers. The country oozes cycling and the landscape the race runs through is stunning. The riders set off from a big square, open to the sea. Then it was along a road parallel to the beach and up and away towards the mountains.

It was early enough in the year for the mountain roads to be lined with the deep snowbanks that had formed over the winter. Reuben was blown away by this. It's not the sort of thing a ten-year-old kid comes across in County Derry. He stretched out of the passenger window of the service car and ran his hand through the snow. Ian took a great picture of this little arm reaching out and the snowbank towering over the car. Later, we passed through a ski resort, and Reuben shouted out in astonishment – there was a man in his Speedos sunbathing in the snow. His delight at the mountain snow was one of the highlights of the race. He still talks about the snowbanks and it's one of those shared memories that has brought us closer together.

The big race favourite that year was Omar Di Felice, who had pipped me for third place the first time I did Race Across Italy. He was directly behind me at the start and set off at a hell of a lick. Within five miles he had caught and passed me. I was a little bit wary of the race as the route was completely new to me, but as time passed it was clear I was in a good position to make the podium. The problems started on the return leg. We had two cars but not enough crew. Ian and Mark became so exhausted in the middle of the night that they had to stop for a rest. We lost touch, so I was left with Alan and Valentina in the service car. There's a very strict rule that riders must not be left alone after dark. The service car must follow behind with its roof lights flashing. In the Italian mountains you can see the orange lights flicker along the winding road ahead of you. If you can see three or four sets of lights, you know it's maybe ten minutes in front. I paced myself to keep up and the GPS clicked over at a steady 20mph right through the mountains. In Italy the speed is unrelenting through the night, and the descents are extremely cold. My whole body trembled, and the bike shook as I struggled to grasp the handlebars. Try keeping this up through hairpin bends at speed and in the dark.

Around 200km from the finish I felt in my back pockets for something to eat. The cupboard was bare, so I dropped back to the car and told Alan I needed some food. 'I'm sorry, Joe, we're completely out. We have nothing left.' I took up my position in the headlight beams again, my legs pumping on the pedals. Up until that moment it seemed that I was on target for a great result, possibly even in the top three. Suddenly my only hope was that Ian and Mark would show up and would have supplies in their car. I was screwed if I couldn't get the carbs I needed to keep going. In a few kilometres I could have been down off the mountains and spinning along on the flat, past a beautiful lake, and on to Pescara and the podium. But that's when it hit me. With 180km to go, the energy drained out of my legs and my body hung heavy over the bike. I had exploded, bonked, drained the tank. Just like all those years ago on my little Raleigh Chopper on the Letterkenny Road. I pulled over to the side of the ride and swore. I was full of anger with myself for this elementary mistake and shouted back to the car: 'Stuff it! This whole thing's over!'

Chucking it in was a bad move and one that I later regretted. If you look at the results of the 2015 Race Across Italy, I'm on the top of the DNF list. There were things I could have done – I could have hung on for Ian and Mark or waited for the sun to come up. The 2015 Race Across Italy fundamentally changed the way I approached racing. There is always a solution and it is never getting off the bike. It was a hard one to take on the chin because it was another 2012 RAAM – another failure. I didn't want to talk about it in public because it looked like I had bombed through stupidity, but I'm not stupid and the team isn't stupid either. We just didn't have the cash to take the number of people we needed to compete at this level. Before I start on any race now I say to the team, 'Whatever happens we are going to finish.'

Omar Di Felice rolled home first in a time of just over thirty hours. We parked up at the hotel as the party was about to kick off around us. Sitting in the pasta restaurant across the street, the guys were keen to join the fun, but I sat and glowered, lost in my thoughts. Valentina understood what was going through my mind. She had been partner to a pro-level mainstream bike racer herself and knew the disappointment of the DNF. Nobody died that day but it still had a big impact on me.

Italy 2015 changed my approach to racing, but it was another event that shook my life to the core, raised me up from the dark rabbit hole where I'd been lurking for many months and brought me blinking into the sunlight. Jill contacted me from Canada. It was a bit of a jolt, to say the least. We hadn't exchanged a word in twenty-five years and yet she had rarely been far from my thoughts. Our first attempt to hook up over Skype was a technical nightmare but when we did get to speak it was a revelation. There were two decades of life to catch up on. I had expected her to tell me about kids and a husband but that wasn't the path she had followed. She was an independent woman with a successful career in the biotech industry, specialising in infertility products. We talked, and talked, and talked. And laughed, and laughed, and laughed.

Shortly after my Italian misadventure, Jill announced that she would be flying to Europe for a conference, stopping off at home to visit her mum and dad for a week. I quickly asked if I could meet her at Dublin Airport and drive her north. Standing by the sliding doors in Arrivals, next to the limo drivers with their name cards, and the anxious grandparents, was a bit unnerving. Would I recognise her? Then she stepped through the door, in a long, elegant winter coat. There was that same unmistakable smile. It was Jill, and when we spoke, she hadn't changed a bit. As we walked to the car it was almost as though we were picking up a conversation from last week.

The three-hour drive disappeared in no time. We kicked around those funny old memories that everyone has of past relationships and some of the not-so funny ones as well. There was the overwhelming sense of having a conversation with someone who understands you deeply and instantly. As I dropped her off at her parents' house, I felt calm and happy. I drove home through the hills to Limavady and left her to her family time. I ran Jill back to Dublin at the end of her trip and we stopped off for a picnic. It was time for a proper opening up. I wanted to let her know exactly how things stood with me. I'd made such a bollocks of our relationship the first time around. When we got to the airport and she was going into security, she looked back and waved – and I knew we were not finished. From then on I was determined do whatever it took to be with Jill, even if it meant going to Canada. I had finally started to change within myself. Jill was the light at the end of the tunnel I had been in for so long. With her I had been able to articulate and be understood. And I was beginning to think about the future in a way that I had not been able to for a long, long time.

I decided to go back to Le Mans, to rebuild my confidence after Italy and to sort out the problems I had with nutrition. The best nutritionist I knew was Jill, so I invited her to accompany me and the boys. I hadn't been sleeping, and I wasn't recovering properly. 'You're super scrawny and you've been living on toast and cheese. Time to sort you out, Joe,' she said. Since then, she's been as good as her word. Together we built up my nutritional resilience. That's how I can race so much and then recover and race again.

Ian Struthers made up the rest of the Le Mans team. This was the beginning of a big adventure for Reuben and Ross as we hitched up my big caravan and headed for the Rosslare to Roscoff ferry. The idea was to drop off the caravan at Le Mans and swing back to pick up Jill from Paris Charles de Gaulle. Things got off to a bad start when Ian and I underestimated how long it would take to get to the airport. We were already running late when we ran into gridlock on the Périphérique ring road. We arrived two hours after Jill's flight from Canada landed. It took a bit of the shine off the reunion.

We set up shop in the garage in the Le Mans pit lane. We were in the same concrete bunker as two years earlier but the atmosphere was entirely different. Reuben was in his element; he's a massive car racing fan and we were in the end garage right under the iconic Le Mans clock. You could see up the hill to Dunlop Bridge. The grandstand is directly above you and the fans were making a racket right through the night. We had a big air mattress at the back of the garage with a duvet so the boys could chill out when the excitement became too much. Before the race, the organisers open up the track to allow crew members to try their hand at riding on the track. So Reuben and Ross and Jill and Ian got on their bikes and joined me out on the circuit. This was an important moment for me. When Ross was being treated for cancer, his consultant, Dr McCarthy, told me he would be fine but he would never be able to ride a bike. And I remember thinking to myself, 'Okay then, if it's the last thing I do I will teach my boy to ride a bike.' I spent months on end with him on a balance bike. I made sure that Ian got some video of him wobbling along on his little Batman bike so that I could send it to the doctor. He took up almost the full width of the track, weaving from side to side. For me that was the best part of the trip. It's hard to put into words how I felt seeing him fight through all the riders on the track. I still have the photo as my screensaver – the two boys with Jill and Ian on their bikes. My wee Ross, from lying flat on his back in a cancer ward to his first road race, at Le Mans.

The fun side completed, Jill set up her laptop in the garage and prepared to collect the data she needed to calculate my nutritional needs. Le Mans is a great venue for this because the bikes spin past the pits so often. She was able to collect all the information on my average heart rate, calorie burn and power output. Jill has the knowledge to gather all the data together, work out the nutrition required for maximum performance and prepare the food. We had access to the caravan through a tunnel at the back of the garages, so she was able to nip through there and use the little kitchen. I don't know of any other sports nutritionist who has Jill's skills; she's uniquely talented.

My race strategy was going well until after night fell. Le Mans is infamous for having heavy downpours in the night. At two or three in the morning a storm broke over the circuit. It was pelting down. There were rivers forming across the track and you could barely see a couple of yards in front of your face. That wasn't the worst of it. All the oil and rubber laid down by the cars and motorcyclists formed a slick and slippery sheen on top of the tarmac. When I leaned ever so slightly, I could feel the edge of the tyres beginning to slip. It was frightening. Sweeping down from the bridge through the S-bends, you could be going 45 or 50 miles per hour. There was no way I could back off because I was in the middle of a pack and I knew there would be another cyclist almost touching my back wheel.

As soon as the deluge began, my instinct was to pull the plug and ride back to the garages to wait for it to blow over. On the other hand, the rain might be gone in a couple of minutes. I decided to hang in there and see what developed. Two bends later I had my answer. Someone at the front hit the deck and the whole line went down like dominoes. I only had time to feather the brake, and the front wheel went sideways. Before I had time to think, I was sliding along the asphalt into the gravel trap. It took the skin off my side, hip and elbow. Skin abrasion, or gravel rash, as they call it, is an occupational hazard for bike racers. Everyone comes off the bike at speed from time to time, but it still hurts like hell no matter how many times it happens. I gave the bike the once-over before jumping back on and cruising back to the pits.

The pit lane was congested with bikes and crews as I wobbled my way through. No one was prepared to go out again until the rain cleared. It was just too dangerous. Back at the garage we cleaned my wounds and I got patched up and changed into clean kit. The bike was sorted, the rain finally started to clear and I was back out on the track for another 12 hours of punishment.

The only way to win the overall category at Le Mans is to go there with two or three teammates who have registered as solo riders. Their only job is to pace you and to fetch your food and drink. That way you never have to leave the track. I noticed several of the serious French contenders were essentially being supported by a back-up team. Some of the guys getting the food and the bottles would only ride for six hours and then retire from the race. They didn't care if they DNF'd. The job was to get their man the result.

I managed 148 laps and 619km in the course of the 24 hours. That put me in 14th position overall and I won the over-50 category. It was a pleasing result and the nutrition data-crunching that Jill had carried out was a great success.

We decided to stop over at a hotel for a couple of days with the boys before heading home, just relaxing by the pool. It had been Jill's first experience at an endurance race. For me and for Ian the insanity of ultra-racing had become second nature, but it isn't a fun experience for everyone, so it was cool to see Jill fit so easily into the groove. At the hotel we stayed up all night chatting as the boys slept. I made a proposal to Jill. Would she like to come to the Texas desert in a month's time and join me on my toughest race yet? She said yes, and I came home from Le Mans buzzing.

Brewster County in West Texas is the biggest in the state. It covers over 6,000 square miles and is home to just 9,000 people. The landscape is mostly hot, arid desert. A perfect spot for a bicycle race. In 2012, veteran ultra-cyclist Dex Tooke began organising a race he christened No Country for Old Men. The race runs almost entirely through the Big Bend National Park, which borders Mexico along the Rio Grande. The original NCOM ran for less than 400 miles. In 2015, I took on the classic 1,000-mile route.

Once again, finances were a problem so I could only take the trusted old hands Alan and Ian to crew for me. There are no direct flights from City of Derry Airport to West Texas, strangely enough, so it was a bit of a hike to get there. Jill, on the other hand, was able to fly direct from her home in Calgary to Midland, both hubs of the oil industry. We picked up the hire cars and set off on the three-hour drive to the little town of Alpine, where the race was starting. We drove through a massive electrical storm on the way from the airport. I'd seen storms like this in Kansas, but this time the lightning bolts were striking the ground far too close for comfort. Texans like to believe everything they have is the biggest, and sure enough the storm went on for three days and it was still raining when I set off on the race.

We checked into a little hotel close to Kokernot Park where the start and finish were held. Alpine sits on a plateau in the Chihuahuan Desert, surrounded by high mountains. It's one of those tiny American cities of 5,000 people that still manages to have a university and a professional baseball team. Being a country boy myself, I took an instant liking to the place. At the sign-in in the park the night before the race, I had a chance to size up the other contenders. I reckon I have a pretty good eye for this. You can tell if someone is going to be a threat just by their demeanour and the way they hold themselves. Colin Stokes stood out like a sore thumb among the other riders. I'd never raced against him before, but I could see instantly that I'd have to keep an eye on him. He's English, but he's based in California, and he has a thing for red dragons on his kit.

It was still dark when we set off from the city park. I noticed that Stokes's flashing rear light had a pattern to it and I made a mental note of it so I could keep him in view. It was a bit chaotic at the start as we thousand-milers were mixed in with people riding shorter distances. I didn't sit directly on Stokes's wheel, but I kept a close watch on his light and stayed within one hundred metres of him. The race timer started as soon as a rider passed the speed limit sign on the edge of town. It's also where the biggest desert in North America starts – endless vistas of dust, creosote bushes and distant hills. Stokes put the hammer down big time as soon as he tripped the timer. I saw what he was at and set off in pursuit.

I thought to myself, 'I'll give him a hundred and fifty yards and not one more until we see how long he can keep this up.' Boy, did he keep it up: five miles … ten miles … twenty miles. That was his game. He wasn't going to ease off; he just kept going full gas. Thirty miles in and dawn had broken. I looked back and the road was empty. The speed was phenomenal, but I knew he must sense me on his tail the whole time. The pressure was all on him. The first 100 miles was all on a slight downhill. He's a big guy, over six feet, so he must have thought he would have the advantage over me on the way down. It made sense for him to try to make a clean break before we reached the Chisos Mountains and the climb up to 6,000 feet. Once the sun came up, a brutal heat was reflected up off the road. I've rarely come across a worse road surface: large stones roughly mixed into tar.

Down the years, I've developed certain routines with Ian and Alan: the same bad jokes and rough edges that develop when men hang out for too long together in a confined space. This time was different. Jill brought a whole new air to the proceedings. I had been a little bit concerned about how she would adapt to the whole business of being cooped up in the car for three-and-a-half days. I needn't have worried. She knew instinctively what she should be doing, and she didn't flinch at having to go to the toilet in the desert while we looked in the other direction.

'You know, this is the first time I've found myself in a real team,' she told me later. 'It was totally authentic: one common goal and everyone working together. You don't get that in other walks of life.' It was great to hear this from Jill. She had worked for many years in the corporate world, where they do all those team-building exercises and it's all a bit forced and fake. Many corporate teams say the same thing: in practice there are often too many egos pulling in different directions. In endurance racing, performance declines in proportion to the egos involved. Listen to Jill talking about 'pulling an all-nighter' in the crew car and you'd think she was a teenager again.

But if Jill was taking things in her stride, I had a distinct problem in the digestive area. We were using a kind of food preparation called Ensure. It comes in a liquid and is mostly used by cancer patients when they lose their appetite. It was dark and we were in the middle of a downpour when Jill handed me a small bottle of the stuff and told me to take half of it. I was freezing cold and my hands were shaking on the handlebars. Rather than hand it back, I necked the whole bottle. It's highly concentrated stuff and it completely upset my gut. I had a bad stomach ache and couldn't eat for the better part of a day. The problem finally cleared in dramatic fashion, and in the video we made of the race you'll see me sprinting off into the desert in search of a creosote bush to crouch behind.

I'd expected to dish out some punishment to Colin when we turned right and headed up into the Chisos Mountains but I was maddened when a race marshal pulled us over and said the road up there had been deemed too dangerous due to the storm. So now it was straight ahead in the direction of the Mexican border. At one point, the route drops down from the plateau for about 25 miles and runs directly into a chain-link fence the height of a two-storey house. It was hot as hell down there, forty-plus degrees. The Rio Grande runs along the other side of the fence. I say 'runs', but it was actually bone dry when we were there.

There's a lot of border guard activity around the area because of the drug smuggling. It's an eerie sort of place. I turned around to begin the sweltering 25-mile ascent in the opposite direction. Later, the route crossed over the border into Mexico for about thirty miles. The guys had gone on ahead and waited for me on the other side. They parked up by the side of the road for a couple of hours, growing increasingly worried when I didn't appear over the hill. I'd been held up at the border post while the Mexican guards went through every conceivable check. The only thing they didn't do was X-ray the bike. You do hear stories about the extraordinary lengths people will go to in order to smuggle narcotics, some of them quite painful, but dressing up in Lycra and riding a bike for a thousand miles seems a bit extreme.

Eight thousand feet up on top of Mount Locke is the McDonald Observatory, a massive silver golf ball in the desolate landscape. There was a full moon as I crested the mountain road by the observatory. It was a magical place. A little earlier on we came across a vehicle by the side of the road. It was Colin Stokes taking 40 winks. I purred silently past and surged into the lead. We would only have been about 250 miles into the race at that point. Later, he dropped off the tracker completely and the guys were able to work out that he'd been taken to a hotel for a sleep. I rode on and we passed through the little town of Fort Stockton with its giant statue of a roadrunner bird called Paisano Pete. I hauled over for half an hour, had a wash and a change of clothes and ploughed on.

I don't know how I managed it because my body was taking a hell of a battering, but I felt driven forward: on, on, on through the pain. It was a beautiful night in the desert. Jill spent a lot of the night hours leaning out of the window of the service car. She was looking for the flashing light of Colin Stokes's car, but it never appeared. So we were just talking and being in the moment in this strange place. Suddenly, there was a rattle of hooves and hot breath and a family of deer appeared out of the blackness. They were galloping alongside the road, like dolphins diving alongside a boat. We were far from alone out there. A pack of coyotes let off a demented howling in the distance, and a bloody enormous snake hissed across the road so close I nearly ran over the damn thing.

If Dex Tooke intended to lay on the full Wild West experience for his competitors, he had succeeded. In the eerie ghost town of Dryden, curtains flapped from the broken windows. A rusting fifties pick-up sat on bricks next to a dusty gas station. James Dean filmed *Giant* out here and if he'd stepped around the corner of the post office in his big white cowboy hat, I'd have been spooked but not surprised.

I had been dreading the final hundred miles. The route was a kind of clover leaf, which meant I'd be headed up the same road to the finish in Alpine but this time it would be uphill all the way. Then we were stopped by the race marshals at that same junction at the bottom of the Chisos Mountains climb. It was getting dark again. Guess what? Now that the weather had cleared, the climb was back on again. Whose insane idea was this? After 900 miles on the bike, I was directed up a vicious climb to 6,000 feet. Oh, and by the way, they said, there are mountain lions up there. One of the first hazards I'd learned to avoid as a kid in County Donegal was the occasional crazed sheepdog sprinting out of a concealed farmyard gate. Dogs are one thing; Simba the freaking Lion King is something else. There's only one lonely road up to the peak and it was freezing cold. Ian followed me up. At the top we made a dead turn in the road and headed straight back down. Close to the bottom, Jill and Alan were cooking up some food in a little clearing next to some woods. You could smell the food from up the road. And you can bet the lions could smell it too.

The final section of the race was even worse than I had expected. Colin Stokes had long since disappeared and I knew if I could finish I had the race won. I had never ridden anything like this far without stopping for a kip. Three days without sleep and I was on the verge of hallucinating. The heat haze rippled across the blacktop in the distance, and I dropped back to ask for a drink. We were rapidly running out of water and there was nothing to eat but a Hershey bar and a can of chicken noodle soup. The shops were all closed in the last little town we'd been through. My legs and back felt completely broken, but it was the dehydration that was killing me. For the final fifty miles I was running on empty. Crazy thoughts ran through my head. The last thing you want after riding 1,000 miles non-stop is to have the whole effort shot to bits in the last twenty or thirty miles. It's depressingly easy for that to happen and I've seen it with other riders. We were in such a desolate place that even if we knew what the solution was, we couldn't get to it because there was nothing for miles and miles.

It wasn't until the last three to five miles that I became confident that I would win. That last part was downhill, and I literally freewheeled into Alpine, my body close to collapse. God alone knows what I looked like as I rattled through the park and peeled myself from the bike. I had gone 80 hours without sleep and won the overall category in the toughest ultra-race in America outside of RAAM. Dex Tooke came over and held me in his arms. A white cloud of pure salt rose from my cycling jersey. As an ultra veteran, Dex knew the enormity of what I'd just done and he was so proud that it had been achieved in his race. I could barely walk from the bike to the showers. The guys helped me off with my cycling shoes and I teetered over to the shower block looking like an elderly drunk. I flopped onto the floor in the shower and let the water massage my torn muscles. Alan and Jill passed in bottles of chilled water and I chugged them down.

The elation didn't set in until after my body stopped screaming. That evening we relaxed over the usual post-race pizza and it occurred to me how immensely proud I was of the crew. The three of them had sat in the car for three days and nights non-stop in the baking heat and I was the one getting all the glory. Would I have made it without Jill? I don't know, but her being there made the torture much more bearable. Being with her is a tremendous motivation for me. Even now, in quiet moments, we sometimes talk about that warm night in the desert and the deer galloping alongside the car.

I knew that after my exploits at NCOM the ultra world would have to take notice. It was an extraordinary thing to have done. I won because I took the lead relatively early on and fought like a dog to hold on to it. Not sleeping for 80 hours was just part of that. When I sat down and thought it through, I realised that it wasn't a strategy that was transferable to RAAM. It's three times as long as NCOM and if you rode for 80 hours non-stop from the west coast to the Rockies, you'd take a hell of a long time to recover.

There wasn't a lot to keep us in West Texas, so once I'd licked my wounds it was time to head for the airport at Midland and go our separate ways. Jill and I travelled in her little hire car, while Ian and Alan were in the crew vehicle. We talked about where our relationship was heading. Jill had a successful life and home in Canada and a job that had her travelling around the country. We'd been living our lives on Facetime in different time zones. You can only keep up a relationship for so long that way.

This wasn't easy for me. Sitting in the airport lounge I drew a line in the sand. Jill was about to board a plane to Canada, and I was headed thousands of miles in the opposite direction. I couldn't let this happen again. The years had just fallen away while we were together, and I knew I wanted to be with her.

'I'm in trouble here,' I said to Alan, 'I don't want to go home.'

Alan's a very level-headed guy and he gave me the most sensible advice he could: 'Calm down, Joe. Get yourself home and the pair of you can think it through later.'

Then, if I still wanted to go to Canada I could jump on a plane. That would have been the sensible thing to do, but I was hell-bent on being with Jill. I said to her: 'How would it be if I just threw in the towel and caught the plane to Calgary?' It was an unfair question, really.

She tilted her head to one side, and smiled gently: 'Joe, you know that's a crazy idea.'

It was the most difficult point that we'd had during the reconciliation process. I think I'd been so intent on the pleasure of being together in the moment I wasn't seeing clearly. In the end, Jill boarded the plane to Canada without me. That was October and we didn't see each other again until Christmas.

CHAPTER 14

'Just Keep It Pinned, Joe'

was up early and out on the roads before breakfast; fast empty roads with endless climbs up through the snow-capped Selkirk Mountains and switchback descents through the pines with distant views of glittering Kootenay Lake below. There's a special beauty about British Columbia that exists nowhere else. Jill and I were staying in a lovely forest lodge built into the mountain like an eagle's nest near the lakeside town of Nelson.

It's a little gem of a place in an impossibly beautiful location. Sadly, we weren't there on holiday. Jill's sister Fiona lived in Nelson. She had ovarian cancer and was nearing the end of her life. They had been especially close as sisters when they were growing up and had shared their Canadian adventures. Jill had been with Fiona through all her surgery in previous years and now was with her in the final weeks as a primary care giver. She wanted to be there for Fiona in her moment of need. It was a difficult time for the family and I did whatever I could in terms of fetching and carrying and being there for Jill.

That year, 2016, cycling was put on the back burner. It was an unsettling time. Fiona passed away in May, which was a major blow for Jill. We flew back and forth between Calgary and Ireland a number of times. There were big questions to be resolved. Was I finally going to up sticks and move to Canada? Could I really cope with being thousands of miles from Reuben and Ross if I did?

I had a lot of time to think about these things during those hours in the saddle around Lake Kootenay. At the same time, I was mulling over my exploits in Texas the previous year. The ability to ride for 80 hours non-stop was of little use in the context of Race Across America, but if I could truly master the skill of riding 50 hours without depleting my strength, I would have seriously added to the weapons in my armoury. It would be fair to say that working on the 50-hour benchmark became something of an obsession. The key to this was dealing with sleep deprivation and its effects on both the body and the mind.

The training regime I adopted was more subtle than simply jumping on the bike and riding for 50 hours on a regular basis. Alongside the normal road mileage, I was doing a considerable amount of training at night. I also did a lot of reading about the effects of sleep deprivation in different contexts. Nurses and doctors, truck drivers and factory shift workers all suffer from this problem, and it can bring about catastrophic results. I was interested in the period immediately before the sleep deprivation strikes. In the past, when I'd been riding all day and hit 10 or 11 p.m. I started to get wound up, almost as though I was about to get into a fight. I was full of bravado, convincing myself that I could bully myself through to sunrise.

The truth was that I really suffered at night and was more times off the bike than on it. When it's three o'clock in the morning and your body is determined to pull down the shutters it's damned hard to convince it otherwise. All I could do was pull over because the drive for sleep was so intense. At the same time, I tried to hide the fact from the crew, sometimes making up all sorts of excuses for stopping. I was scared that they would lose confidence in my capability.

My training regime was initially aimed at identifying the little trigger points where my body and mind were changing as the darkness approached. They could start as early as 8 p.m. or as late as midnight. I would ride out into the night, keeping fairly close to home and not clocking up huge mileages. I did lots and lots of repetitions of these small efforts. It's probably different for other people, but I found that for me the effects of sleep deprivation kicked in at around one or one-fifteen in the morning. I then started to experiment with my sleep patterns and even to gauge the effects when I wasn't on the bike. I tried staying awake much longer without any physical activity at all to see if there was any correlation with what happened on the bike.

In a race situation, such as the Race Across America, a heap of other factors come into play. Have you ever been in the baking heat of the desert, fighting with the effects of altitude or suffering in cold and wet conditions? Nutrition, hydration and the distance already travelled all have a role to play. Ensuring that you're drinking enough and keeping an eye on your hourly calorie intake can help you to cope with the dreaded arrival of the darkness. All my training and research showed that you can't beat sleep deprivation but you can learn to manage it a lot better.

One of the things I discovered was the importance of easing back on my average speed. My coping mechanism when facing the night had always been to wrestle with it. I had tried to keep up the same sort of speeds I was churning out in the daytime. But you simply cannot do that; it will always defeat you. Easing off on the intensity of effort required to keep up those daytime speeds lowers your mental stress significantly and lifts the sense of fighting the darkness.

I had been forcing my mind into a tunnel where the only thing I could see was that fight to keep up the average speed. Ironically, easing off on the speed meant I spent less time off the bike and kept my average higher. A clear mind allowed me to think more clearly and that opened up a lot more options. When I came to apply these lessons in night riding in a race situation, I found myself dropping back to speak to the crew a lot more. Ultimately, I found I was able to navigate my way through that crippling period in the middle of the night without having to stop at all. It was an invaluable resource.

I did most of the work on the night riding when I was at home in Limavady, but I also spent a considerable chunk of that year in Canada. Fiona's illness had a big bearing on this, but Jill and I were also trying to make a final decision on whether or not I would move to Calgary. I was desperate to be sure that our relationship didn't fall apart through circumstance, the way it had done the first time around. She had a beautiful apartment in a heritage block next to the Bow River. There was more than enough room for both of us. I suppose it was inevitable that Ireland would win out. The needs of Reuben and Ross came before anything. They were just too young, and I would have struggled with being so far from home. Not seeing them every day was incredibly difficult. Another argument against Canada, although it was far from being the clincher, was the climate. I simply wouldn't have been able to train outside on the roads for a large chunk of the year.

There was a lot of to-ing and fro-ing while Jill wrapped up her life in Canada and prepared to move back across the Atlantic; practical stuff like organising the sale of the apartment and car, and arranging for the removals company to transport her possessions. Jill had built a successful life and career in Calgary, a life that would be the envy of many young women. It was a big emotional investment and one that she didn't walk away from easily. Looking back on that time, it was such an enormous shift for her and to have come so soon after the loss of Fiona made it doubly difficult. In an ideal world we could have made the transition slower and perhaps easier.

We found ourselves living in my rented house in Limavady and I had the slightly surreal sense of being back in the early 90s, before I stupidly let our relationship drift apart. Every morning I awoke thinking: 'This is real. We are here. Jill is in Ireland and living with me.' This was my second chance to be with the woman I fell in love with so many years ago. Not many people get a chance like that. It's hardly surprising that everything to do with cycling took a back seat for a while. There had been a fundamental shift in my life and a massive change to Jill's. We needed time to adjust.

When eventually the time did come to pick up the reins and think about the 2017 season, we decided to take a tilt at the 500-mile world championship. This would allow me to build on my 50-hour training. My previous experience at the RAAM distance proved that because I had failed to cope with the first night-time section my performance went on a downward spiral. My thinking was that most of the top 500-mile races are won in a time of 28 hours or 28 and a half. This would give me plenty of practice at racing through the night and would serve as a stepping stone to another crack at RAAM further down the line.

In the past, my time for a flat 500-miler would have been well above 33 hours, so there was plenty of room for improvement. The rules for the 500 world championship at the time required that you take part in two qualifying races. One of these could be a solo world record. We decided to target two races in particular, the Race Across Italy and the Silver State 508, held in Reno, Nevada.

Italy came first and we set about it like a military campaign. I was determined that there would be no embarrassing cock-ups this time and definitely no DNF. We had a stronger crew and better resources, food and cars. Having Jill with me was a major boost. Most of the team flew into Rome but Ian Struthers and Mark Beggs took the ferry and drove down. This meant we could have all the equipment we needed without the colossal expense of flying it over. The two lads took their time on the drive over. They are both history buffs so they stopped off at the Normandy landing beaches and a few other spots to break up the journey. There was no point in having them arrive completely exhausted when we had an endurance race to take on. My intention was to make everything as simple and stress-free as possible. We stayed at the hotel used by the race organisers, right next to the starting line, and the weather was kind.

I'd calculated that my biggest rival in my category would be the Italian rider Martin Bergmeister. I had raced against Martin before and I knew he was a very smart operator. I made two decisions: attack from the start; and concentrate on winning the age category. Once I knew I had the category under control I could concentrate on the overall race. Having been there before I knew that the start of Race Across Italy is super-fast. If you lose time it's very hard to make it up before the mountains. The race starts at noon, so it isn't very long before you hit the night time.

I set off at the back of the field along with the really top guys, about fifth or sixth from last. The cyclists starting behind me were the cream of the crop. Sixty to 80 miles in, the route makes its way up through tunnels in the foothills of the mountains. Rainer Steinberger, the German, caught me around that point and just motored past. I was giving it full gas but he must have been doing 2–3 mph faster. What I didn't know was that I had missed one of the riders out of my calculations. Ian To is an English rider and

I'd never even heard of him before that race. When I got to know Ian I discovered he was a lovely guy with a first-class team behind him but that first time out I didn't pay him enough attention. He passed me and so did Omar Di Felice, the Italian guy who won the year I blew up and DNF'd.

Quite a few passed me as the race progressed but I stuck to my plan to secure the age category in the first instance and kept a close eye on Martin Bergmeister. He had started behind me and was gradually catching up, but by keeping my speed high I was able to ensure that his efforts to overhaul me were gradually wearing him out. There's a point along the route, about 140 miles in, where you have to check in and sign a book. I took this as an opportunity to play a little game with his head. There's a tendency with a stop like that to drop your tools for a moment, a sense of relief that you've reached that milestone.

I made sure that I was still at the check-in when he arrived and that I had put on my warm clothing ready for the night ride ahead. Then I threw my leg over the bike and battered off up the road at a hell of a lick. Martin had expended a huge amount of effort to catch me up. I kept the pressure on and the speed up as darkness fell and that imaginary elastic between us began to stretch. It stretched until it snapped and I found myself riding away from him like I was on the back of a fast train.

A couple of other factors then fell into my lap. Omar Di Felice made a big mistake. He and his team took a wrong turn and finished up way off course, miles from the official route. Omar was furious with his crew. He threw his toys out of the pram, jumped in the car and DNF'd. Another rider made an even more spectacular exit. My crew communicate with me through a radio earpiece, but this guy was operating with loudspeakers on the roof of his crew car, barking out information and playing loud rock music. I was riding past in the darkness when I noticed a kerfuffle at the side of the road. I glanced over and there was a police vehicle with flashing lights parked up next to that crew car. It seems there's a law that you can't play loud music outdoors in the hours of darkness in that part of Italy, so here were the Carabinieri giving me a leg-up. 'Opportunity knocks!' I said to the guys, and I slammed the hammer down.

With Di Felice out, there appeared to be only three men faster than me. They were Ian To, Steinberger and an Italian, Giuseppe Francesco De Giacomo. A Swiss woman, Isabelle Pulver, was also putting in a great performance, but I eventually caught her. Another rider came into play when we were coming down from the mountains towards the end of the race. Mads Frank is a young Danish rider with a background in pro road racing. He's an established ultra contender now but showed his inexperience by riding extremely fast and then repeatedly stopping to take a rest.

The high-speed descent followed a cliff edge with a steep rock wall on one side and a sheer drop on the other. Every so often the road would disappear into a tunnel. These tunnels are badly lit and the road surface is broken by ridges that are part of the drainage system. I've learned to be ultra-cautious in them. You fly in there from the daylight glare into pitch darkness and you've no idea what could be lying in the road. I switched the gas off and slowed right down as I entered one particular tunnel. There was no lighting and the bike rattled over the ridged surface. All of a sudden, I heard a bike belting up behind me and I knew it was Mads. I yelled to let him know I was there and a split second later there was a shower of sparks as his wheel caught on a ridge and threw him into the air. He screamed as he hit the road and the ridges tore into him. On a smooth road you'll just slide to a halt but if you hit anything with an edge it will throw you up into the air.

I got off the bike. I couldn't see him but I knew from the groans that he was badly hurt. Then a car appeared from the far end of the tunnel. I frantically waved my arms as I ran to the dim shape slumped on the ground. Mads was conscious and trying to get back on his feet. I had to keep him down and I held his head straight. He was moaning about his leg but I was more concerned that he could have broken his neck. When my crew car pulled up they took over and I was able to continue with the race. I met Mads again a couple of days later when he was plastered and bandaged up. He thanked me and I've remained friends with him and his family ever since. It was a salutary reminder of how a moment's carelessness can put your life in danger.

I started to gain a lot of confidence in that Race Across Italy. Since I hadn't set out to target the overall win I didn't feel that I had to engage in a damaging all-out war with the favourites. I wasn't worried about food or running out of energy because Jill was taking care of that, and I thought: 'You know what, let's just keep going flat out.'

I can honestly say that it was one of the few races where I went full gas to the finish with no let-up in the final 100km. I caught up with De Giacomo with about 50km to go, beating him by a handful of minutes. I won the over-50 age category and came third overall, finishing in just over 30 hours. Steinberger won in just over 27 hours, but I was much closer to him than I'd been in the past. Ian To was second.

I was really pleased with the result. I'd only stopped twice, once after the check-in where I'd put on the warm night-time clothing and the second time to help Mads in the tunnel. And as the sun came up, we'd paused briefly for Alan to pull the extra layers off me. In the past, I would probably have made four or five stops. The whole strategy of working on my sleep deprivation, winding back to 500-mile races and choosing Italy as the first outing had gone really smoothly. With Jill alongside me and the entire team better co-ordinated, it felt like the start of a big step up. It wasn't a perfect performance but it wasn't far off.

When we came away from Italy there was a feeling that the team had really arrived on the world scene. I was getting to know a lot of the other riders on a personal level and there was a growing sense of mutual recognition. I was bouncing when I left Italy, feeling I was in with a real shout for the world championship. The psychological boost allowed me to train harder and plan better for the next big challenge – the Silver State 508.

Under the rules of the world championship, you had to race on two separate continents. I chose to go to Nevada because there was lots of desert and plenty of heat. It's a very tough race with brutally hard climbs, and in places the conditions mirror pretty closely the first 1,000 miles of Race Across America. The first six miles of the race lull you into a false sense of security. You spin through the wealthy suburbs of Reno before the race kicks off in earnest. There's a T-junction where you swing to the left and you're immediately on this killer climb up to 9,000 feet. Whoever planned this route clearly had a cruel streak. It ramps up through three platforms before dropping down into Virginia City. If this old silver-mining boomtown looks like something from a Hollywood backlot it's hardly surprising: Errol Flynn and Humphrey Bogart starred in a corny old gold-smuggling yarn set in the town. We took some time out before the race and spent a day there doing the tourist thing. The crew even rented cowboy outfits and we had our photo taken. It's my dearest hope that no one ever finds that photo and publishes it.

The race rolls through Main Street past the Red Dog Saloon before taking an abrupt left turn and dropping like a bomb down into a canyon. The road was so steep that I was hitting speeds of over 60mph. It was frightening but I didn't let up. As you know, I'm pretty handy on the climbs so I wanted to be sure to make the most of the advantage I had built up on the ascent. I went down that canyon road flat out before it emerged into the desert. I found myself bowling along this wide, flat, long road through the most bizarre lunar landscape. It appeared to be pockmarked with craters. Suddenly, a military jet tore through the sky immediately above my head, then another and another. The US naval air station at Fallon is nearby. This weird lunar landscape is where they shot the flight sequences for the Tom Cruise film *Top Gun*. There was nothing alive that I could see; not even a cactus. Farther on you hit the most iconic part of the route. It's called Route 50, also known as the loneliest highway in North America. It's flat and straight and disappears into the base of the Sierra Nevada mountains 84 miles away. The road surface is concrete and it felt like my tyres were sticking to it. I have a photo that shows me as a tiny speck disappearing up the road. Needless to say, it was baking hot. The race itself is one of the oldest in the USA. It originally ran through Death Valley but the government later refused the organisers a permit because of the danger posed by the heat

The race didn't follow a big loop. After a killer climb, you rolled into a little village, there was a dead turn and you headed all the way back to Reno. Do not pass Go. Do not collect £200. There was a little restaurant and a marshal with a flag directing you to the opposite side of the road to begin your journey homeward. It was deadly, mile after mile of windblown dusty nothing, with tumbleweed rolling across the road. As we headed in towards the turn, I was in the lead. What I wasn't counting on was a young firefighter called Charles Bell from Santa Rosa, California. I had never met Charles before the race but I noticed him at the start with his time trial bike and thought: 'That's a crazy bike to start a race like this.' The climb up to Virginia City must have almost wiped him out, but once he got out into the desert and onto the flat, he was super fast.

Charles was part of a different long-distance cycling scene. In California they have numerous 200-mile races. They call them double-centuries. The races are fast and run through the Californian deserts. If I was stepping down from the longer-distance races to do the 500, Charles was stepping up from the 200-milers. There was no reason why we should have been aware of each other. In planning for the Silver State I would have been considering the threat from riders capable of riding a thousand miles or more.

The guys in the team car picked up Charles on the tracker. 'You've got company, Joe,' I was told. 'Better get a move on!' But no matter how hard I tried he kept gaining on me. Silver State is a mass start race; there isn't the staggered start you would get in a time trial. So once he caught me, we would be on equal time. I took a gamble that he was laying down the speed in order to intimidate me and that he couldn't keep it up for long. I decided to let him pass, give him 60 seconds and suss the situation from behind. I was convinced he would have to shut off the gas, but it didn't happen. Then I started to get a bit panicky. Darkness was about to fall. I felt the need to stop, sort my clothes and have some food. The timing of this stop was to prove a huge mistake. To be fair to them, Alan and Jill both tried to convince me to keep going. I didn't and I have to own that mistake.

The Sierra Nevada mountains can be bloody cold at night. I was keeping it steady and paying attention to my heart rate. Jill handed me a bottle of lukewarm water. I took a few sips and slipped it back into the bottle cage on the bike frame. The climb was a bit of a brute, with steep hairpin bends. When I reached for the bottle again the water was frozen solid. I had put on all my warmest layers but I was still shivering. One of the crew passed me a North Face puffa jacket and I slipped it on top of all my cycling gear. It was the sort of thing you'd wear to a football match in February. I was already dreading the descent before I'd even reached the top of the mountain. As the road dropped downwards my entire body began to shake. The handlebars were vibrating and I almost came off the bike. I had to stop and take my gloves off while Jill poured warm water over my hands. We had to repeat this numerous times. My fingers were so numb that I couldn't operate the gears or brakes.

What I didn't know at the time was that Charles Bell had also struggled with the vicious conditions on the mountain; plus, he had the added disadvantage of the time trial bike. I used three different bikes on the race: my climbing bike, a time trial bike and my usual road bike. Even on the climbing bike the ride up the canyon to Virginia City was almost impossible. In places the gradient hit 28 to 30 per cent. The final step up into Main Street was at a bizarrely steep angle – the pedals were almost hitting the road at the top.

There's no doubt that Charles deserved to win. He was the better rider on the day. I pretty much freewheeled the last part of the race from Virginia City down into Reno. I knew I'd blown it and finished about 2.5 hours back. Speaking to him after the race I discovered that he had almost folded on the climb. If only I hadn't stopped where I did I could have overhauled him on the way up. But that didn't happen and I have to take it on the chin. It's still a sore spot with me. I'd love to go back for another crack at the race. The fact is that I threw away the Silver State 508. It was totally down to me.

With the result in the Silver State I won the 50–59 age category in the world 500-mile championship. I was also lying second in the overall competition. This was deeply frustrating as I felt it could be my last chance to win a big overall title. There was only one way I could still win the 500-mile championship and that was to take on a world record attempt. Under World Ultracycling Association rules you are allowed to substitute a world record attempt for one of the races as long as the record is 500 miles or greater. Alan, Jill and I discussed it on the plane on the way back across the Atlantic. That's when the idea began to form of cracking the Ireland end-to-end Malin–Mizen–Malin record. I had already done the ride in 2015 but that had been in June. It's brutal enough in reasonable weather with only four or five hours of darkness. This time it would be November with half the distance in complete blackout. I only had a week or so to make the decision and, to be honest, I was almost afraid to talk about it in case I was laughed out of the room.

I would have to break my own record for the distance, but how could I go quicker when it would probably be pissing rain and blowing a gale? And I would have to persuade the team into backing me up in what looked like a futile last throw of the dice. But it was the thought of that last throw of the dice that convinced me that I had to go for it. If I didn't try it, I would always regret it. And the reason I would regret it would not be because I tried and failed but because I hadn't tried at all. I sat up late into the night for two or three days, drawing up schedules and calculating average speeds. I didn't need to break the record by much; I just needed to break it.

I already knew the route, but the big change from the last time

I'd gone for the record was that I had cracked most of my night riding problems. My strategy was to stay on the bike for longer. Once I had made all the calculations, I could see that maybe, just maybe, I could pull this off. Once I managed to convince Jill and Alan that I had a fighting chance, the hunt was on for finance. It was the end of the season and the cupboard was pretty much bare. There would be no fancy, logoed team vehicles this time. Ian Struthers would have to do the job in his own car.

We drove up to Malin on the morning of the record attempt. As predicted, heavy rain was blowing sideways off the North Atlantic. I glanced out at the waves, white horses tearing in from Iceland. Water was streaming across the road in rivers. There was some nervous laughter among the team – 'Lovely weather for ducks,' all that kind of thing. Inside I was thinking, 'Holy shit, there's eight hundred miles of this.' I threw the leg over the bike at midday and carefully rolled away. Four hours later the dark was coming on and I could barely see through the incessant rain and the headlights of the approaching cars. It was still pelting down as I crossed the border near Enniskillen into Cavan. I couldn't see the potholes under the puddles. One false move and I would have been picking myself up off the road with a broken collarbone.

The entire crew was stressed out. We knew there was going to be a headwind the whole way down the coast. It makes every effort twice as hard but the hope was that once we got to Mizen I'd have a tailwind the whole way home and I could maybe still make a fist of it. Deep down I had a vision of arriving somewhere about Lifford on the Derry–Donegal border with around 50 or 60 miles to the finish and the time would have run out. I would have thrashed the life out of myself for nothing.

The rain cleared in the middle of the night and a big, bright full moon appeared. My spirits lifted as we left Mizen Head and turned for the run up north. We hadn't gone four miles down the road from Mizen when a torrential hailstorm broke, setting my helmet rattling. That part of the route is brutally hard, with lots of small, tough climbs. The road swings in and out of numerous little bays and the wind direction distorts all over the shop. By the time we reached the little town of Dunmanway, any hope of a tailwind was lost.

I battered on through the back roads of County Cork with stiff gusts buffeting my left shoulder. No harm to Millstreet, it may have hosted the 1993 Eurovision Song Contest, but to me it will always be the place where I almost blew the WUCA 500-mile world championship. I was beginning to drift well behind on time and my head started to tell me I couldn't do it. Then I started to say it out loud, repeating it to myself: 'Forget it, you're not good enough.' My thinking was utterly negative and I found myself actively searching for reasons to quit. I stopped by the side of the road feeling busted open. The crew car window rolled down.

'Jill, I can't do this,' I said.

Jill's a remarkable person in those kinds of tight situations. She may not be a sports psychologist but she knows all the right questions to ask.

'Joe, I'm not going to ask you to believe you can beat this record. I'm going to ask you to suspend your disbelief. Neither believe nor disbelieve. Just keep the bike going forward.'

It says a lot about our relationship that she could read my thinking. She wanted to take me out of the pressure cooker of the world championship and keep my legs turning the pedals. Once I stopped stressing about not being world champion my performance began to pick up. Within a couple of hours, I had got my mojo back. The guys in the back seat crunched the numbers on the laptop and said, 'Joe, you don't need to do a lot more to be back on schedule.' If the wind changed or I started feeling better, I would be back in the game. But the wind didn't change: it got worse, and the torrential rain came back again during the night.

As we reached Swanlinbar on the Cavan side of the border

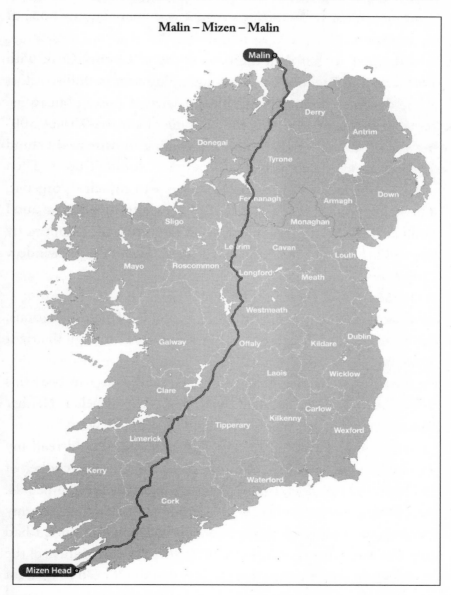

Malin – Mizen – Malin

it became a full-on storm. Branches were blowing off the trees onto the road. Then the service car developed an electrical fault that affected the lights. You can't race at night without a car with the specified lights. These little problems were starting to build up and as the timing yo-yoed I was becoming more and more agitated. I was so close to the wire. A big hill would put me behind schedule, but then there would be a fast descent on the other side and I would be ahead again. We finally emerged out of the darkness around Enniskillen. There's a corny old saying about Lough Erne that half the time it's in County Fermanagh and the other half of the time Fermanagh is in the lough. This time it was definitely the latter.

It's only about 14 miles from Ederney to Castlederg, but the route takes you up over a place called Scraghy Mountain, a hard climb at the best of times but twice as bad in these conditions. I was still behind, but the timing was going up and down between 20 minutes and 12 minutes. I came down off Scraghy devil take the hindmost and made up a chunk of time. Jill leaned out of the window of the car and said, 'Right, Joe, you need to grab yourself by the scruff now because you can break this thing.' I thought that couldn't be right but I had no option but to go with the numbers they were giving me and I piled on the pressure.

The last few miles to Malin were desperately hard. The road takes you up through high bogland with no hedges and no respite from the wind. At Five Fingers Strand the gusts careering off the sea almost blew the bike on its side. The timings were still tight and I only became confident about the result right at the end. The road passes by the Malin Head weather station that you hear about on the radio shipping forecast, but there's still a fair way to go to the finish line by the old signal tower. The service car rolled up alongside and Jill said, 'Just keep it pinned, Joe'. Then it was all uphill. The tower appeared around a bend but there was still a mile and a half of steep hairpin bends. You wouldn't believe the amount of time you lose just climbing that final section.

As I rolled into the car park, I was 23 minutes ahead of the previous record. Not much, but it didn't matter. I stood over the bike and dropped my head. I was a world champion over 500 miles. There was a crowd of people in the car park cheering and sounding their horns. They had been following me on social media. It was lunchtime but strangely dark as the rainstorm continued to blow.

The team wanted to shout about our victory from the rooftops but the record attempt still had to be authenticated by the World Ultracycling Association. The officials who travelled with us had to submit a report. Everyone in the sport knew we had won, but we couldn't do any media and go public until it was confirmed. It wasn't just that I was world champion; it was the brutal route I had to take to get there. Life would have been so much easier if only I hadn't made that mistake out in the desert in Nevada.

In the end it came down to a congratulatory email from Larry Oslund, the records keeper at WUCA. A trophy plaque arrived later in the post. It wasn't exactly like standing on a podium spraying champagne into the crowd but it would have to do.

I felt immensely proud of becoming world champion. My life had changed so much since I won the Race Around Ireland in 2009. I had gone back into competitive cycling at the age of 50 in an entirely different discipline. There's no doubt that I took a hell of a kicking along the way in some of those races as I dragged myself up to the top level of the sport. I had chased after sponsorship – an essential part of the enterprise that still takes up almost as much effort as the training. And I had built the team, a team of good comrades and best buddies. When we came home from Reno we could have thrown the tools in the box and said, 'We're done and we didn't do too badly.' But getting the band back together for that final assault on the end-to-end record proved once again that we were a force to be reckoned with.

CHAPTER 15

Up! Up! Up!

Summer 2018 was the hottest on record in Ireland. The fields of the Emerald Isle were toasted to a light tan and holidaymakers looking for a light tan were boiled like lobsters. Temperatures soared to over 30°C and over 16 hours of sunshine was recorded at the weather station on Malin Head.

Jill and I decided it was time to go back to Race Around Ireland. I grew up on the roads of this island, tearing through its country lanes on two wheels as I learned my trade, and I was super motivated to come back to race on my home turf. It's my homeplace and I never tire of telling foreign riders they need to come and experience it for themselves.

Nine years had passed since my introduction to ultra-racing and the Irish race had changed considerably. It was now a respected fixture on the world ultra calendar and was guaranteed to attract a strong international field. My credentials in the sport had grown enormously and I was a much better rider than I had been in 2009. I had learned more about nutrition and strategy, and most important of all, I was able to ride through the night without sleep. No matter whether I won or lost I knew I could make a fantastic race. This year's entrants included the Czech Svat'a Božák and Stefan Schrenk from Switzerland. They were both class acts and I knew there was no point in starting the race and going off at half cock or thinking it would be an easy victory just because I was on home turf.

Social media had become a big thing for the sport, with fans across the world following the riders' progress through the GPS tracker. I had barely raced in Ireland since 2009 and I was putting my head on the block in order to prove I could win my home race again.

We set out to prepare as I had never done before. Jill and I spent weeks, at the end of June and through the whole of July, touring the length and breadth of the island. She was sweltering in the car and I was on the bike. We took detailed notes of each mountain climb and turn of the road, the potholes and the crosswinds. Back home we collated all the data and worked on our strategy. This meant going through the whole race mile by mile.

My sleep patterns had to be calculated. How far was I going to ride before sleeping? Where would we stop, and for how long? We wrote a strategy for me and one for the crew. In 2009, I'd had a cavalcade of vehicles longer than the Lord Mayor's Show. This time, we decided to do without a motorhome. One of the crew, Andy Campbell, had a converted VW Transporter van fitted out with all the electrics we needed for cooking and recharging all the equipment.

We booked rooms in two hotels along the route. The crews swapped over at the hotels, with the second crew jumping into the beds vacated by the first crew. We also hooked up with the charity Cycle Against Suicide. We provided publicity for them, and their network of supporters helped us out along the way.

The strategy was brutally simple. I was going to take the race to my competitors from the very start. It's not a route where people hang around and wait for you. Rather than have someone else set the pace I was going to map the game plan and they were going to have to react to my every move.

The starting line was in Trim, County Meath, less than ten miles from Navan, where the 2009 race had started. Božák and Schrenk both left the start before me. I set off like a greyhound out of the traps. My first target was to get them in view. When they saw me coming, and they would have clocked me on the tracker, they would know I was motoring. I caught them in Moira, County Down, about 75 miles into the race. It was time for a rest. I shut the gas off and just sat on their tails. I was in control and they would have to wait for my next move.

Night was coming on and I stopped by the side of the road in Ballyclare to get my warm clothes on. We were headed up into the bleak Antrim hills towards the Causeway coast and it would be cold. This was familiar territory, one of the roads where Morris had held his seemingly endless trials for the Commonwealth Games squad 32 years earlier. It was near Coleraine where I passed Božák. I spun past him in the darkness, my speed unwavering, and without so much as a 'hello'. I went flat out through the remainder of the Northern Ireland section, up past the distillery in Bushmills and through Coleraine in the direction of Derry.

A knot of spectators had gathered by the side of the road in Greysteel, just outside Derry. It must have been all of one a.m. In the midst of my deep concentration, I picked out a wee voice shouting 'Daddy!' It was Reuben. He'd come out on the road with his aunt and uncle to cheer me on. I stopped and lifted him for a big hug. It was only 30 seconds, but it gave me a hell of a boost and I held on to that moment in the hours to come.

Over the bridge in Derry City, across the border and I was into the most familiar territory of all: Raleigh Chopper territory. The inevitable loop over Malin Head led to the first decent climb of Race Around Ireland. I've ridden bikes over Mamore Gap more times than most people have eaten a hot breakfast. A few miles from the start of the climb I finally caught up with Stefan. Every serious cyclist in Ireland has heard of Mamore Gap and some have spent half a lifetime avoiding it. I had been training for eight hours a day in the weeks leading up to the race and must have been up and over Mamore 24 times.

I picked out Schrenk's light among the hedges just as he reached the foot of the climb. I was already on his tail so there was no need to go flat out; Mamore is too steep for that and I was happy to sit where I was. I kept going at my own pace up through the bleak bogland and bare rockfaces. Not knowing the climb, Schrenk struggled to pace himself as I slowly pulled away. Once over the top, I powered my way down into Buncrana, where the crew had a time trial bike waiting for me for the flatter roads that lay ahead. Božák was in it for the long haul, though. He was definitely the stronger of the two and had finished fifth in RAAM the year before. When you come off Mamore you have hardly started Race Around Ireland. It was a question of whether or not I could use all my preparation and native knowledge to outsmart him.

The Czech remained stubbornly visible on the tracker and I pressed on full throttle through the little town of Castlefin, down through the borderlands of Donegal and Tyrone, Fermanagh, Leitrim, Sligo. It sounds easy when you rhyme them off like that. Let me tell you, when I stopped for a proper rest at Castlebar in Mayo I had only paused briefly for the clothes change in Ballyclare and to hug Reuben. That was 500 miles and 28 hours into the race. I had my full hour's break at Castlebar and Božák passed me on the road. The chess game was developing nicely. Most important, I was now one sleep ahead of my rival. As soon as I got back on the bike, I was up to full speed again within two miles.

We were well on to the Wild Atlantic Way now, headed for Connemara. There's a long, steep climb just out of Castlebar. You can see no distance ahead of you but then it opens out into a wide horseshoe shape and the road is dug into the side of a cliff face. Jill and I had spent half a day on this section of climb alone. I went up two or three times finding the right gear and getting a feel for the steepness of the road. I went belting down the far side of the hill, flying past Božák. He immediately stopped. Was he stopping for a team discussion? He had some hard decisions to make. I was one sleep ahead of him and he needed to take a sleep before he went much farther. If he didn't, he would never recover. I had him in check.

By the time I stopped in Spiddal near Galway City I was one sleep plus an hour and a half in the lead, but there was still a third dog in the fight. Schrenk had by no means given up. It's always a good policy to hang loose and see if the two ahead of you burn each other out. It's not unusual in a sport like ultra-cycling where you're pushing your body to the limit for days on end. It was just south of Galway that the other guys stopped and I really started to win Race Around Ireland. I kept pumping the pedals, on past the Cliffs of Moher, through Spanish Point and down to Ennis, where I stopped for the usual routine of 15 minutes for food and 45 minutes of sleep.

Jill had prepared a homemade mix of creamed potatoes with salted butter and other goodies. This produces a huge sugar spike and then a big drop. When the drop came, I could put my head down and within 30 seconds I was asleep. It's a very deep, REM sleep, the sort where you have vivid dreams. There's no lag. The 45 minutes of sleep is a genuine 45 minutes. I have to be woken up to get out of it.

We had been relatively lucky with the weather so far, but this being Ireland, even in the driest year for decades, the heavens opened just south of Limerick. I put on all the clothes I had but within ten miles I was wet through and chilled to the bone.

The crew arranged for a stop in Tralee. I got out of my freezing clothes and changed into some dry kit. When you come out of the town, the race route takes you up a narrow, tree-lined road that's ferociously steep. It's called the Short Mountain and they've used it a few times for the National Hill Climb. At times the gradient hits 15%, like some of the famous cobbled climbs in Belgium. It feels twice as steep as Mamore and twice as long. The back wheel had no traction when I stood on the pedals and it spun around uselessly. Meanwhile, the water was running down the road in streams and I had to descend very carefully. Even a dog would have had more sense than to be out on the road on a night like that.

The situation wasn't much better when I reached the Gap of Dunloe. Foreign tourists flock there in the summer for an overpriced ride in a jaunting car so the narrow road was covered in horse crap and pitted by horseshoes. This is where the route drops steeply into the Black Valley as if you've fallen off the edge of the world. It's a spooky kind of place when you ride through it in the dark along a narrow country lane with grass growing up the middle and barely a farmhouse to be seen. The most surreal sight is farther along the road at Moll's Gap. In the dead centre of nowhere an enormous Avoca shop flogs fancy woollen blankets and serves posh cream teas to well-heeled visitors.

Božák and Schrenk hadn't dropped off the radar. They were still chasing from behind but I had opened up the gap to nearly 90 minutes. We stopped at the little village of Sneem and I took the third of my planned one-hour breaks, then set off again, onwards to Kenmare and Bantry. I reached Mizen Head at the southern tip of the island still ahead of the others and with the advantage of one sleep. Mizen's an interesting section, with a loop down to the head and back. I passed Božák on the road around Goleen as he was heading into the loop. We looked across and raised our hands, an acknowledgement that we were both riding on the limit. We were two warriors, each saluting the other.

If Short Mountain had been a leg-buster, goodness knows how you'd describe St Patrick's Hill in Cork City. I aimed to hit this 23% monster in daylight and was greeted by crowds cheering me on, or perhaps they were just there to see me suffer. There were some odd interactions with the public along the way. I was struggling up a killer climb at Mount Melleray in the Knockmealdown Mountains close to Cappoquin. It was about half past two in the morning and we were passing through a pine forest in the pitch dark when a character swinging a hurley stick burst out of a hedge shouting and screaming: 'Keep her going, fella!' He frightened the life out of me and the guys in the crew car were splitting their sides. My greatest fan ran the whole way to the top of the hill with me, swinging the stick above his head. Like one of the fairy folk, he disappeared as abruptly as he had arrived.

Strange things happen in the dark when you've been riding for days on end with almost no sleep. Your mind can play tricks on you, as though you were hallucinating. We dropped down into the Suir Valley Drive between Clonmel and Carrick. The placenames around here are quite a mouthful: Toberagattabrack, Tikincor and Kilroughtaun. I turned into a section of road that runs through a kind of forest of ancient trees. Big old tree roots the thickness of your arm had grown under the surface and pushed up through the tarmac. A thick canopy of branches and summer leaves overhung the road.

This section was about seven or eight miles long and as I was riding in the dark with the car lights illuminating the road ahead there was a kind of optical illusion. I felt like I was riding through a tunnel. I couldn't shake it off and it was beyond disconcerting. I actually began to feel like I was upside down, utterly disoriented because the top and the bottom looked the same. The roots were so big they could have easily knocked me off the bike. Trying to navigate my way through them was just brutally hard. I got about three-quarters of the way through it when I was overcome by a kind of tidal wave of exhaustion.

I said to Alan: 'This is no joke. I don't know how I'm going to get out of this frickin' place.' I stopped and took a ten-minute micro-sleep, then got back on the bike and slogged the hell out of there. Dropping back to the crew car, I told them to keep an eye on the tracker. Božák was still one sleep behind me and I wanted to see how he coped with the disenchanted forest. Sure enough, he got stuck in the middle of it and lost another big chunk of time. He had kept up with me pretty well and was probably an hour behind, but the cracks were starting to appear. Schrenk was also still hanging in there but he was about two and a half hours back, lurking in case one or both of us hit the buffers.

Somewhere near Waterford, the guys wanted me to eat and I wanted to press on. It's not good to have friction in the team so I eventually pulled over and sat on a jacket, warming myself by the car radiator and eating my food. An elderly lady emerged from a house across the road, thinking that the flashing lights meant there had been an accident and I had been injured. She was in a bit of a tizz but the guys calmed her down. Alan explained that I was in a race and once she had disentangled his County Derry accent the woman invited me in to use her shower. The warm water eased my tired muscles and I emerged to be greeted by a massive fry-up breakfast that I couldn't possibly eat. The lady threw another load of bacon and sausages in the pan and the crew greedily horsed down their full Irish by the side of the road while I prepared for another backbreaking session on the bike.

I kept pushing on, over the top of Mount Leinster, an old favourite from the Rás and Tour of Ireland days. It's a seven-mile climb with a maximum gradient of over 16 per cent. Even so, this was only a hint of what lay ahead in Wicklow. Drumgoff, Glenmalure, Aughavanna and my old nemesis from 2009, the Sally Gap. These are serious climbs. With a big mileage in your legs, they become a major challenge and they come literally one after the other. I was determined to get to the Sally Gap and down off the mountain again before nightfall. The thought of my chilling experience up there in 2009 had never left me.

As we reached the foot of Glenmalure there was a cyclist in Lycra who looked as if he had a problem with his bike, which was lying upside down at the side of the road. Normally, if you were out on a training ride you'd ask if they needed a hand, but I had a job to do so I just nodded and said hello. He glanced up at me and said: 'I'll be with you in a minute and give you a hand to the top of the hill.' The poor man obviously didn't realise quite how fast I was going. The team could see him struggling up the gradient behind us before he blew up and stopped. As usual, the bunch of cynics in the crew car found this utterly hilarious.

I managed to get down off the Sally Gap by the skin of my teeth. There was a marshal by the side of the road at the bottom who had evidently been watching the tracker app: 'It's in the bag; all the hard stuff's over! Just coast her to the line now. You're an hour and a half in front of the guy and he's stopped again. You'll have two hours before this is all over; just keep her lit!'

Sure enough, I was only a mile up the road when Alan came on the radio and warned me there was a right turn ahead: 'Mind, now, it looks like it ramps up straight away. Make sure you're in the right gear, Joe!' This was the one serious climb Jill and I had missed during our recce. It's called Cupidstown Hill and it's the highest spot in County Kildare. Almost immediately I ran out of gears and ground to a halt. There was nothing for it; I had to stop and switch to one of my climbing bikes. I glanced up and the road just lifted up into the sky. We must have gone miles up this thing in the pitch black. Up! Up! Up!

Just then I started to hear bells ringing. I pulled my earpiece out thinking it must be a problem with the radio. It got louder as I rode up. Then out of the darkness I saw a group of people lining both sides of the road shaking cowbells, cheering and waving lights on their mobile phones: 'It's really steep – be careful! You've got five hundred metres to the top.' I crawled past them with a big grin on my face, struggling in the low gear. There were two people at the top of the climb: 'Two hours and nine minutes and he's still stopped.' Even as I passed, I heard them shout to the crew car: 'Keep her going! He's going to get it!'

The route circled high up above the back of Dublin and I could see the city lights twinkling below. I ploughed on and got a shock when I looked up and saw a road sign saying 12km to Trim. My mind and body were utterly battered but I was nearly there. I dropped back and asked how things were looking. Alan leaned out of the window: 'He's still stopped.' I knew then that Božák had thrown in the towel. He knew he couldn't win and was taking a long sleep. The Czech rider had been caught at the top of Sally Gap as I had been in 2009. Schrenk was clever enough not to venture up there. He'd stopped between the climbs and was taking a break before heading for the finish.

'Why don't you take a break?' Alan said.

I wiped my mouth on the back of my sleeve. 'No. Let's get this thing done and dusted before the sleep deprivation hits me again.'

Inevitably, my eyelids started to close, and I began to wobble. I had to pull over and rest again. I remember seeing the road sign on the edge of Trim and thinking, 'I could walk to the finish line from here.' In truth, I couldn't have walked the length of myself.

There was a long driveway down into the GAA grounds with a welcoming party of media and well-wishers at the end of it. It was around one in the morning after a 1,400-mile (or 2,200km) hard slog. I had completed the race in 104 hours, 12 hours faster than in 2009. All that on three hours' sleep.

We hung on until four or five in the morning, when Božák finally arrived and they did the medal presentations for the two of us together. He's a really ballsy guy and gave everything he had to give. It was my strategy that did for him rather than any great physical capability on my part. Between the two of us we had created quite a race. I had done my homework and was a little bit smarter. Stefan Schrenk didn't arrive until daylight, by which time I was semi-comatose in a Navan hotel bed catching up on four days' worth of sleep.

There was a great satisfaction in how the team had pulled together. The crew was rock solid and it was one of the few races where we made an absolute minimum of mistakes. There are times during a race when I feel I've been stripped back to the bare metal. That's when I need to have complete trust in the people around me and for them to have belief in me. Mile for mile, the 2018 Race Around Ireland was probably the best planned and executed race I ever did.

I've raced across deserts and through vast mountain ranges, but I would argue that the Race Around Ireland is one of the top three most difficult races in the world. It's half the length of the Race Across America, but the intensity of it is just brutal. All the top racers have done it, including the king of Race Across America, Christoph Strasser. Pierre Bischoff, the only cyclist to have won both RAAM and the Trans-Siberian Extreme, won Race Around Ireland in 2019, the year after me.

I'm a proud Irishman and what makes the race special for me is that I am the only Irish guy who has ever won it, and won it twice. I'm determined to have another crack at it and go for the hat trick. Once I've been around the island for the third time, win or lose, I could happily walk away from Race Around Ireland. But the career I have built in ultra-cycling, which has brought so much meaning to my life for the past decade, would never have got off the ground without Race Around Ireland.

CHAPTER 16

She Never Judged Me

My mum died in 2018. Suddenly she wasn't there any more. It left me stunned. In my world, almost every time someone interviews me they ask me who my greatest inspiration was. They expect me to say Eddy Merckx or someone like that. In truth, the one person who inspired me was my mum. I used to look at the tough life she had, the eight kids she had to raise, the endless work she did around the home. She wasn't lonely: my sisters Sylvia and Georgina still live in the house and another sister lived next door. The whole tribe would meet up on a Sunday and I would sometimes drop by to catch up. When mum passed away, the Sunday meet-up came to an end. It shows how much of an anchor she was for us.

She deserved a much better husband. My dad had no respect for her and he was no help with the family. Life dealt her a dud set of cards in many ways and yet she went on giving so much of her life to others. Mum always gave the impression that she didn't need a lot. Other than going to church on a Saturday night or trips to the shops, you would rarely have seen her away from the house. I was different. I wanted more. I wanted to do more.

I think of the times when I came back from races in the very early days. She would have sat and washed my clothes until midnight. For her it was unconditional; it just was. We had this relationship that ran like a thread through my life. We could sit and talk about anything and move on. We never had a cross word. When things were bad, especially when Ross was sick and, later, when my marriage was in difficulty, I used to go over and we would sit by the fire and talk about anything, silly things, the weather. We were both content with that. I haven't always been the best person in the world. I've done some stupid things in my life, I know that, but she was the only person who never judged me.

In later years, I would go to see her before every big ultra-race. It was important for me to be with her in the home place in Donegal before going out into the world. She lit a candle the moment I left and placed it in the kitchen window looking out over the back fields. It was her way of protecting me and guiding me home. When things got bad out on the road, I thought of her and the light shining in the darkness.

It was typical of her not to have told anyone she had cancer. I still feel bad about it to this day. All through the last part of her life I was living in Limavady and going to see her regularly. I never dropped that ball, always visited her when I could. I remember getting into the car sometimes and thinking, 'Mum was odd tonight,' but not for one second did I think she could be seriously ill. When I look back on it, I can see that my mum knew she was dying. It was something that encapsulated her way of thinking about life, and about death: 'Just stay silent, get on with it yourself. I'll not tell him because he has enough troubles of his own.'

After we found out how seriously ill she was, she was taken to hospital and she passed away a short time later. Jill was with me when my mum died. There was silence in the house. I couldn't believe she was gone. I just couldn't fathom it. For the first time in my life there wasn't this safe place that I could go. I realised the true meaning of home for the first time. I was like that for a couple of years. Sometimes Jill would ask me: 'Do you ever think about your mum?'

'I don't want to think about that,' I'd say. I had pushed it from my mind. Only recently have I been able to tell Jill, 'I was thinking about my mum last night,' or that something had reminded me of her. She was my last real link to Newtowncunningham and Donegal.

I haven't had the courage to go to her graveside since the day she was buried. I'm not proud of that. Sometime soon I'll have the strength to go there. I just need to work on it.

CHAPTER 17

Mr Boone's Plastic Contraption

I turned 60 in 2019. A lot of guys my age spend their days walking the dog or buying bedding plants at the local garden centre, not shredding their bodies to the absolute limit on some far-flung killer mountain pass. I had been racing pushbikes for 45 years. 'Kung Fu Fighting' was in the charts when I first threw my leg over a racing bike in the backwoods of Donegal. Jill and I had talked a little bit about me retiring. This was after Race Around Ireland. It wasn't a serious decision-making heart-to-heart but I was very clear that I didn't want to jeopardise our future together. We couldn't keep on racing around the world and be building a home together at the same time.

Hitting 60 would be a big milestone but it also crystallised my plans for 2019. It would put me in a different age category; the perfect excuse to return to Race Across America. And if I was going to RAAM it would make sense to take a crack at the overall World Cup. In fact, it would be silly not to. Jill and I sat down at the end of 2018 and talked through the next season in detail. She's 50 per cent of everything I do. We make all the big decisions together. The process is slower than when I was operating on my own but you only have to look at how my results have improved since 2015 to see how important Jill's input is.

The criteria for the overall World Cup were simple. You had to do a 12-hour event, a 24-hour event and a 1,000-mile event. You could also insert an optional record attempt, like we did with the Ireland end-to-end in 2017. The winner is decided by who completes the races with the highest average speed. It can come down to as little as 0.1 or 0.2mph. You have to be good at all the disciplines, the relatively flat and hot 12- and 24-hour races, and be able to sustain the big 1,000 plus.

We chose to start the season with the 24-hour race at Sebring Raceway in Florida. Sebring is a legendary track that hosts the 12 Hours of Sebring car race. From the 1950s through to the 70s the race was a mecca for American sports fans. Film stars like Steve McQueen, Paul Newman and Gene Hackman took the wheel for the 12 Hours. Marilyn Monroe draped herself across the machinery on the start line and posed for publicity photos. The cycle race differs from Le Mans in that while in the French race the emphasis is very much on team competition, at Sebring it's all about the solo riders. For Americans who haven't raced abroad Sebring is very much top of the pile as far as endurance track racing is concerned. For those of us who have raced on both, Le Mans wins every time.

There are very few super-fast 24-hour events around the world where you can pretty much guarantee good weather. I could have raced in England or Slovenia, but what were the chances of getting ideal conditions? As for Le Mans, I had already experienced the horrors of crashing in a thunderstorm there. So Sebring it was to be. It was going to be an expensive year, with RAAM sucking up almost all of our resources, so Jill and I decided that I would go on my own. Even as a one-man band it would be three or four thousand quid. Take two or three crew members and you would soon be into five figures. I set off with two bikes in boxes on a holiday flight from Dublin to Orlando full of overexcited kids on their way to Disney World.

If this sounds a bit crazy, I should explain that I had arranged some help Stateside. I'd been on quite a few podiums by that stage and had won the 500 championship, so my name was getting around. Through a series of very fortunate events I became acquainted with Marc Poland, and he offered to be on hand if I ever needed help in the States. Marc had been a vice-president at Sikorski Helicopters before he retired. He was a trained engineer and had been a bike nut all his life. We were a great fit. He met me at the airport and it was almost like meeting your body double. We're both about the same age, small in stature, with similar faces, and people often mistake us for brothers.

Marc drove 700 miles from his home in North Carolina down to Florida with his amazing truck. It's basically a big workshop on wheels, with sleeping accommodation, that he converted himself. We were able to park it up in the pit area and have access to everything I needed. The race track belongs to NASCAR but it's not one of the banked ovals they're known for. Sebring is based at an old World War II airfield. It's about three-and-a-half miles long, which means you're lapping really quickly through the night. This being Florida there are rumours that the occasional alligator has to be removed from the track.

The race starts at 6 a.m. at a set of tollbooths at the entrance to the racetrack. There's a 100-mile loop out into the orange groves along public roads. That's 50 miles out followed by a dead turn in the road and 50 miles back. You really need to be doing well under four hours over the first 100 miles to stand any chance of winning. I made it back to the racetrack in 3.57 and was lying in third. There were a number of big hitters in the race. A French rider, Evens Stievenart, was in the lead. He's a fascinating character, the only person to have won both the car and cycle racing versions of the Le Mans 24 Hour. Racing cars on ice is another of his specialities. World champion Marko Baloh from Slovenia was lying in second. That was the race set-up; there was a good chance one of the three of us was going to win.

I didn't really think I was in with a great chance of snatching it. Stievenart had managed 593 miles in 24 hours at Le Mans in 2017. My main aim was to make a solid start to my World Cup campaign. If I could come home with a place on the podium, I would be more than happy. And at the back of my mind was the thought that I could finally break the elusive 500-mile mark myself. Only a small number of people have managed to beat the 500 miles in 24 hours barrier at Sebring, so it's a pretty exclusive club. The only way to achieve these two aims was to be in the fight right from the get-go. If I wasn't there after the first 100 miles there was no point in thinking I could ride myself back into contention. The very idea was laughable.

There was no let-up from the leaders. Stievenart went off at a phenomenal speed. He was throwing down the gauntlet to Marko, and Marko was responding. It left me with no other choice than to hang on to their coattails. I found myself in the same position as Stefan Schrenk in the Race Around Ireland. If they kept up this crazy speed there was a possibility one of them would blow up and I would be there to pick up the pieces. Marko is renowned at Sebring. He was the one I was expecting trouble from; Evens came as a bit of a surprise. From what I'd seen of him at Sebring and later in the year at RAAM, where he won the two-man team category, I would say he is a shoo-in for a solo RAAM win in the future.

Every race has its own characteristics. Unlike Le Mans, where the road surface is perfect, much of the Sebring track is cracked and pitted concrete. I did a lot of recce work before the race memorising where the big cracks were. If the wheel falls into one of those at speed, it's game over. I spoke to Marko before the race and he advised me to keep to the front at the mass start. Sure enough, I could hear the bikes clattering to the ground behind me as we set off. There were hundreds of cyclists on every type of machine. There were the normal road bikes, recumbent bikes that you lie back on and human-powered bikes. These look like little spacecraft with a pilot inside. Recumbents are fast, but the human-powered UFOs were hitting 50 or 60mph and they disappeared over the horizon in the blink of an eye.

What with the road surface and the high average speed I made a little mistake by taking too many pit stops through the night. I was also concerned about hydration and food, something that wouldn't have bothered me if Jill had been on hand to take care of it. I was still lying third with an hour to go when I took my eye off the ball. I was so concerned with the guys in front that I hadn't been concentrating on what was going on behind me. An American rider, Chris Miller, slipped past me straight into third place. I hadn't bargained for this and with nothing left in the tank I had to let him go. I was able to keep going but I couldn't lift the speed to match what he was laying down.

In a split second I had lost my place on the podium. Fair play to Chris; he had ridden a great race and absolutely deserved to be where he was. What was more disheartening than missing the podium was that I'd missed the 500-mile mark yet again. Stievenart rode 535 miles in the 24 hours, Marko Baloh rode 517, Chris Miller was on 497 and I managed 482. I could have kicked myself. I had been so close to the 500 and to the podium. There are very few people who have been on the podium at both Le Mans and Sebring. I still haven't broken 500 and I know it's possible for me to do it at Sebring.

The result was frustrating but far from devastating. As a small climber I'm not built like the kind of beefy time triallist who wins major 24-hour races on the flat. The big success to come out of Sebring was the relationship I built with Marc Poland. We had literally spent only three or four days together and I felt like I'd known him all my life. When I got home, Jill and I ran through all the lessons to be learned from Sebring and how I should prepare for the forthcoming Race Across America. Sebring was in January and we set off for RAAM in May.

One aspect of my effort from 2014 that could clearly be improved on was how I coped with altitude. Marc had invited me to use his home in North Carolina as a training base. His house stands at 3,000 feet, but once you ride out of the driveway you're soon up to 7,000 feet on the stunning Blue Ridge Parkway. It was ideal for training and Jill and I spent some idyllic weeks there with Marc and his wife. They live in a very special rural community called High Cove in the Southern Appalachian Mountains. The people who live there describe it as 'a green community for the incurably curious'. Marc and his wife, Carol, built their home in the woodland, where you can lie in bed and hear the coyotes howling in the night. If you stand on the balcony you are almost level with the mountain ranges, which seem to stretch on for ever.

The traffic-free roads up there are perfect for cycling and Marc is the local bike guru. A lot of people in the area use bikes but they maybe don't know how to fix their gears or do basic maintenance. Marc is the go-to guy for bike repairs. He fixes them up for free and goes riding with anyone who will come with him. Marc's life there centred on his big barn-cum-workshop, which was filled with bikes, tools and equipment. I've done all the work on my own bikes since I was a kid in Donegal, so this place was a paradise for me, When I wasn't out training, we would be tinkering in the barn or messing about on every type of bike imaginable. My favourite was the big-wheel fat bike, a cartoon-like mountain bike with enormous tyres. I'd never ridden one of those and was soon raking up and down muddy paths on the lookout for bears.

Also parked up on the property is Marc's race van, the one he brought down to Florida for Sebring. He agreed to let us use it for RAAM and it really was a perfect fit. Apart from the sleeping accommodation and the workshop gear, there was also a kitchen where Jill could prepare my food and we could charge up all the radios and lights. The thing I liked most about it was that it was based on an old-school Ford van. It looked really cool alongside the latest Challengers and Dodge Caravans in the race paddock at Oceanside. It was the sort of van they used at RAAM back in the 80s, so it attracted quite a crowd.

Another of the people we met at High Cove was a guy called Chris Boone. He was a descendant of the famous American frontiersman Daniel Boone. His family were athletes and his son competed for the USA at international level. Chris had some expertise in coping with altitude. He also had an oxygen tent that I borrowed. It was a see-through plastic contraption that draped over the bed and connected to an oxygen cylinder. I found it quite claustrophobic but got used to it and slept in it while I was at Marc's house.

There was no physical difficulty in using the oxygen tent but I couldn't get over the feeling that I was doing something wrong. I was quite directly doing something to my body to increase my performance. In fact, it's perfectly legal in the sport and there was no reason to feel guilty about it. It's second nature in America because you race in so many mountainous places and you have to learn how to cope with high altitudes.

The days we spent with Marc and Carol in the Blue Ridge were so relaxed and enjoyable that it quite took my mind off the enormity of the task that lay ahead. It really felt like a home from home and we made some special friends among the folks at High Cove.

I had wanted to take Jill to RAAM ever since we got back together and now we were about to set off on a big adventure. The next stage of the plan was to do RAAM in reverse in the van. We set off from North Carolina in the Ford headed for Colorado and the Rocky Mountains; next stop Wolf Creek Pass. After checking into an Airbnb in Pagosa Springs, I spent a few days training at 11,000 feet on Wolf Creek with Marc. Each morning the three of us would have a leisurely breakfast, then Marc and I would ride up the pass. On some days we did it twice. Marc was doing more training than me, but it wasn't the number of times I rode the climb that really mattered. That's not why I was there. I was acclimatising my body to operating at 11,000 feet. We had the oxygen tent with us and I was following a lot of Chris Boone's advice. Pagosa Springs is popular with backwoods tourists, people who enjoy hiking or kayaking on the local rivers. I mostly chilled in the apartment when I wasn't training. My body felt in great form but I was conscious that it had been a very busy time. We had done a lot of driving and the admin was reaching fever pitch with emails firing hither and yon.

There was one more task to be completed before we left Pagosa. I had a RAAM haircut at a place called Gabe's Barbers. You can't have hair hanging in your face when you're slogging through the desert. It was a US Marine Corps-style buzz cut and it felt like I was getting my warpaint on.

After the week at altitude we upped sticks and headed for Arizona. I wanted to get some time in the heat. Jill drove the van while Marc and I rode through the arid wilderness for four or five hours. It was cooking hot and the place is fit for nothing but rattlesnakes. That was a bit of a wake-up call: 'Remember, this is RAAM Arizona. This is the real deal.'

We hit the coast in time to meet the rest of the team, who were flying into LAX from Dublin. Aside from Jill and Marc, that meant Alan, my physio Andy McMullan, Ian Struthers, Mark Beggs, Eamonn Diver, Noel Cusack and Andy Campbell. I had been to hell and back with most of these guys many times in the past and they each knew their job perfectly. Eamonn and Noel were rookies, however – or new to us, anyway. But we invited them because we trusted that they would fit, and we were right. There was a heap of stuff to be done: bikes to be built, food to be bought, equipment to be checked. Then there were the endless meetings. I let the guys get on with organising all the logistical side of things.

We had three vehicles: Mark's van, which was now adorned with an amazing graphic wrap; and two Dodge Caravans. Ian and Mark were in their usual media role, taking photographs, streaming video and running all the social media. They were also the gofers, doing the runs to buy food or stock up on ice. We used one vehicle as a crew shuttle to get people to a motel up the road to grab some sleep. The RAAM timing stations are usually at big Walmarts. It's a good place to pick up provisions and there's usually a motel we can use. We operated the same system we used at Race Around Ireland. The guys organised a motel every 300 or 400 miles. They made the bookings via the internet as the race progressed. So you had one crew driving ahead and getting their heads down for a few hours. Then, when we caught up, the crews swapped over and the second lot had a sleep. It's simply the most efficient way to do it.

As I sat on the bike at the seafront in Oceanside, my mindset was pretty confident. I went there feeling on top of my game.

I had delivered the goods at a very tough edition of the Race Around Ireland. There was not a single piece of non-belief in my head. What I did have was an enormous respect for what lay ahead out on the road. In 2014, I was still in the dark about much of the race because I had DNF'd on my first attempt. Now I understood what lay ahead. I didn't have to look at the route; the navigation was already stored in my head and I could tick off the markers as I passed by – a strange rock formation here, an abandoned gas station there. I was concerned about the heat in the desert; the brief Arizona recce had brought it all back to me. But I still felt confident about it. There would be a fight, that much I knew, but I was going to bring the fight to the road, not vice versa. It was as simple as that.

One thing I've learned about the Race Across America is that you don't focus on the other riders for the first 1,000 miles. You must concentrate on your own race, the strategy you have set and how well you execute it. Developing trust with the team is also important at this stage. The opening part of the race is all about looking after your own shop. Once you get over the Rockies you can start to keep a close eye on the opposition, where they are and what their strategy is. Unless you can survive the first 1,000 miles you are on a road to nowhere and you might as well book the first flight home.

I had three priorities for RAAM in 2019: to finish in the top six overall, to win the over-60 category and to break the course record for that category. I set a blistering pace from the start right through the Mojave Desert and into Arizona. I was fourth on the road. This was a huge confidence boost. I felt I had a right to keep up with the big boys. We reached the Glass Elevator, dropping 3,500 feet steeply down towards Borrego Springs. Christoph Strasser caught me and I swooped down through the bends behind him. We were flat out but Strasser wasn't riding away from me. A German rider, Stefan Schlegel, had suffered a spectacular crash in 2014 descending the Elevator behind Strasser. The level of concentration required is immense. As I sped down the hill, Marko Baloh slid in behind me.

Marko punctured near Borrego Springs and I cramped quite badly at the bottom of the descent. The sheer level of heat in the Mojave Desert had affected me. We were powering on so fast that I had become dehydrated. I stopped and sorted the problem with Jill. By then, the three in front of me were Strasser, Baloh and Mark Pattinson. I knew that I wouldn't be able to keep up with Strasser's relentless pace for 3,000 miles but right then I was pretty much in the sweet spot for where I wanted to be in the race.

Wolf Creek was no serious barrier this time. Given the number of occasions I'd been up it with Marc in recent weeks I pretty much knew every crack in the tarmac. It was a far cry from my near-death experience seven years earlier. Where the altitude really started to kick in was between Wolf Creek and La Veta and on to Trinidad. That section is my nemesis. When I got down to South Fork, where the hospital is, I felt I needed to take a break, but the crew wanted me to push on. Wolf Creek is about 900 miles into the race. It wasn't my first stop but it was my first proper two-hour sleep. There was no major disagreement with the crew but we had rubbed up against each other. When you've been going flat out for that distance the crew are under stress too and people can get a little bit antsy. There were a few feathers being ruffled. Let's say it just felt a little uncomfortable.

Coming off Wolf Creek you're dropping from 11,000 feet down to 7,000 and then back up again to La Veta at 9,500. It's incredibly hard, as I had discovered in 2014. You go out onto a plateau and then there's a big descent. At one point you turn off the main road and it turns into what I would describe as a little Irish lane, all twisty and up and down. Then there's a turn on to a mountain road and it just goes frickin' straight up. It's a brutal climb with hairpin bends right to the top. The guys hadn't wanted me to stop at South Fork because they knew I needed to get to the top of La Veta and down to Trinidad, which lies at 6,000 feet. It's a distance of about 200 miles from the top of La Veta down to the level of 5,000 feet. Then your altitude problems are over.

And then I hit the usual problem. Literally within 500 metres of where I was forced to stop and rest in 2014, I was floored by the effects of the altitude. I just ran out of power. Because we have all the equipment and meters now you can see that the oxygen saturation in your blood just drops off a cliff. I could barely pedal and was sweating buckets and feeling dizzy. Trying to push the bike along was close to impossible. I couldn't put my heart rate up because the minute I did the oxygen dropped even more. I had fallen into a classic trap. Same thing, same place. My mind was swamped by the feeling that 'here comes failure again'. The only way to fix it was to stop, but I ran the risk that if I stopped, I wouldn't be able to get started again. I was at 9,000 feet and the hardest part of the climb was yet to come. I was very fortunate in the end. Eamonn Diver kept me company both from the crew car and on the road, talking in my ear the whole way up. 'Don't stop, Joe! Keep her going, you can do it if you just stay on the bike!' I was just staring at the stones on the tarmac in front of me, totally zombified. I was in the lowest gear on the bike. All I could do was to try to keep it moving forward.

I knew I was in trouble but I was never going to get off. That was a dead cert. I would get to the top. I had to get there. Eamonn and Alan got me into the car and told me to rest for a few minutes and let my body settle down. They put a lot of water over my head and we watched as another rider, an Australian, Alan Bradley, crested the climb. He prepared himself for the descent and quickly pushed on. That's where I made a big mistake. I should have followed him on the descent, using him as a guide through the switchbacks, but there were sinister black storm clouds approaching. If there was hail I would be soaked and freezing. I felt I wouldn't have been able to cope with that. In my battered and exhausted condition, it would have been very easy to misjudge a bend and come a cropper.

I stayed in the car and we passed Bradley on the road as we drove down to Trinidad. Even in the crew car it took an hour and a half to get to the hotel. I collapsed into bed but I knew that by the time that I awoke my position in the overall was gone and more than likely I'd also blown whatever chance I had with the course record. I know now that I could have made it down the mountain – it would have been slow and painful, but I should have tried. We were at the hotel for three hours and those were two out of my three targets missed.

You're allowed to get in the car and drive elsewhere as long as you check in with the race HQ and restart from where you left off. The guys rang in and informed the authorities that they were taking me out of the race to go to a hotel, giving all the details. We had to notify them again when we were leaving the hotel to go back to the point where I stopped. They check your GPS when you get back to the original point and then ring you to say you can restart. It sounds complicated but it happens quite often with riders. My problem was that I had wasted a huge amount of time getting down off the mountain and back up again. Now I was going to have to set off on the descent several hours after we'd watched Alan Bradley disappear down the side of the mountain. It was daylight when we arrived at the hotel but midnight when I set off from the top of the mountain on the bike. The whole thing was a royal fuck-up.

Looking back at what happened in RAAM 2019, I firmly believe that I rode too much before the race. That period of time in North Carolina, lovely though it was; the big drive across the entire country. If I were to do it again, I wouldn't be so bothered about the altitude training. I should have spent the time in the heat. I was going at a hell of a lick through the desert in order to defend my place in the overall but I just wasn't sufficiently acclimatised to the searing temperature. In the end, it was the heat that did more damage to me than the altitude.

By the time I had got my act together after the Rockies I was lying in ninth or tenth position overall. I was still in the fight for the age category so I kept pressing forward.

Next on the agenda was Kansas. Unlike 2014, there was no sidewind or tailwind. Instead, we had a headwind right across the prairie state. It was utterly soul-destroying. My body still hadn't recovered from the high mountains. I fought it the whole way across and it left me exhausted. Once we got into the daylight after Trinidad it was time to start sizing up the opposition and checking how they had fared in the hellish first thousand miles. The guys fired up the tracker and had a look for my old friend Valerio Zamboni and the other guys who were my main rivals for the age category. Your category is based on your age when you finish the race. I actually turned 60 while I was battling the heat in the desert, so there was no jelly and ice cream for me that year.

The course record was probably the top of those three initial aims because if I broke it I would almost certainly have won the age category too. As it appeared to slip from my grasp, I became a bit demoralised. I was really struggling to keep up my enthusiasm for the fight, and in a race like RAAM you need all the steely resolve you can get. I'm not a quitter but I couldn't help feeling it had all gone to shit again.

In Kansas there's nothing to look at but the two-lane blacktop and the horizon. I started to think to myself, 'You know, fuck it, I got the whole lead-up to this race wrong.' Then I started listing all the things I'd screwed up. There's an awful lot that goes through your mind when your focus is 80 or 90 miles ahead, and I was slipping into a very dark place. Jill could see that I was in trouble and she was magnificent. So were the rest of the crew. But I could see that they had lost a little bit of faith in me. They knew the task ahead was monumental.

I was edging closer to the eastern seaboard but I was fighting a war with exhaustion. I dreaded reaching Missouri, not because of the landscape or the weather but because the road surfaces were terrible. There is a big section of the RAAM route in Missouri that takes you along a dual carriageway. The tarmac is broken and potholed and some of the truck drivers seem determined to knock your shoulder off as they pass. The roads roller-coaster along, up and down all day in the searing heat.

I hit the buffers hard at a place called Grafton in West Virginia, just before the route loops into Pennsylvania. It was after dark and the cold was brutal. I had emptied the tank to make up time after my Trinidad misadventure and the effort caught up with me big time. I had a discussion with the crew. They wanted me to go on but I knew I couldn't.

'It's craziness,' I told Jill. 'If I try to go on it's all going to fall apart in the Appalachians.' We found a motel and I slept for a couple of hours. Getting back on the bike was rough after that. It was the middle of the night and freezing cold. I felt beaten up, both mentally and physically. Even talking was an effort. There were only two-and-a-half days to go but I needed to get up to 20mph, and there was an entire mountain range to get over. Sometimes 50 hours can seem an impossibly long time.

You can see why so many riders drop out in the last couple of days of RAAM. The only way to deal with this is to cut the efforts up into chunks. 'Let's get another ten miles up the road and see how I feel then.' On a really steep climb a chunk can be more like a hundred yards than ten miles. When you reach the end of your tether your body can suddenly turn on you, with disastrous consequences. This effect is multiplied during the hours of darkness, and as I rode into the daylight, things started to ease off. I felt a little bit more energy come into my body and the team kept talking me through it. They somehow convinced me that this torture would soon be over.

One of my favourite sections of the route is through Indiana and West Virginia. The roads were good and the weather held. It started me thinking that if I made it to the Appalachians with some power left in my legs, I could still make it to the finish in good order. The temperature was steadily rising until it became uncomfortably hot. Not Arizona hot but enough to cause serious problems when you've been riding a bike across a continent for days. I kept pounding on the pedals and, emerging from a bend in a forest, I came across the German rider Markus Brandl stretched out on the road beside his crew car. His top was off and the straps of his bib shorts hung at his waist. The team were working to bring him round and they had the situation in hand. It's not the sort of thing you like to see happen to anyone but it gave me a little bit of reassurance that I wasn't the only rider who was in trouble.

I was in the lead in the age category by the time I reached the Appalachians. My body had reached some kind of equilibrium and I was able to make it through the twenty-odd climbs in fairly good order. A lot of riders make the mistake of using too high a gear in these mountains and burn themselves out. I wasn't flying like I did in 2014, but considering the condition I'd been in back in Grafton this was major progress.

There was still some drama to come before the finish. We had come out of the darkness into a Maryland dawn. I had about thirty miles to go as we approached a right-hand turn. I was utterly burnt out and my reactions were shot to bits. Alan called it a little bit late and I didn't have time to make the turn safely. I let the bike spin on past the junction and prepared to turn around and go back. I was unsure how close the service car was behind me. I made a really tight turn and fell over, smacking the point of my elbow heavily onto the road.

It sounds like nothing, zero mph and all that, but it hurt like hell and I thought I had broken a bone in my arm. I didn't want to alarm anyone so I gritted my teeth and rode on. We stopped at a McDonald's at about 5 a.m. and Jill came with me to the bathroom to examine the damage. It seemed to be okay, just a massive bruise, but the pain was off the scale. I had a quick wash, changed my clothes, walked out and threw my leg over the bike. A tidal wave of exhaustion hit me out of the blue. I just couldn't get going. I started and stopped, and started and stopped again, three or four times. It was impossible. I stood with the bike between my legs. Alan came over: 'Are you okay, Joe?' He was fiddling with the GPS on the handlebars and I slumped over on top of him. I was spark out, dead to the world. I'm told I was asleep for five or ten minutes. Our social media jokers made sure it was streaming live on the internet, of course. They took a photo of the two of us and then woke me up. The catnap somehow did the trick and I made it to the finish.

Those last 30 miles of Race Across America in 2019 were very emotional for me. My head was all over the place and my body was beaten to a pulp, yet people were almost dragging me by the collar along the road. The crew were passing on messages from well-wishers who were watching my progress on the web. It made a big difference when I was fighting off the exhaustion. Jill was incredible. She hardly slept during the entire race. When I was awake, she was awake. The whole crew was great but Jill had a special place. You have to know me really well to know when I'm in trouble, because it doesn't register. Jill always says I have my race face on and I'll do anything to keep from showing my cards. I know it tears her up inside to see me struggle.

'The noises that come out of you, Joe, when you're suffering ...' she began to tell me, weeks later. I knew how nervous she was for me, that it was physically hard to watch me on the road sometimes – struggling to stay awake but determined to go forward. I'd seen her trying to hide her tears in the back of the crew car. It all brought us closer together.

By now I was well used to the big Race Across America finish. I rolled into the dock at Annapolis in the sunshine to be greeted by a crowd of well-wishers and was welcomed on stage for an interview before the media swept me away. I loved the experience and I especially treasure the photographs taken with the team that day. Those were hard-earned pictures. I was presented with my trophy for the RAAM over-60 category at the banquet the following evening: a big plaque shaped like a map of the United States. Just for the record, I had ridden 3,000 miles across three deserts and three mountain ranges, and completed 170,000 feet of climbing in 11 days, 16 hours and 23 minutes.

It was a massive achievement, probably my greatest so far, but there was a sense of disappointment and regret at my failure to beat the course record. I should have concentrated on the category and the record. My hunt for a high overall place had led me to burn too many of my bridges in the desert. Those first couple of days were not a true indication of my fitness level. I had peaked too early, probably ten to fourteen days before the race. I think it's in the nature of the competitor to be constantly unsatisfied. It's what drives you forward. But it can also damage your chances if you start to fixate on the negative side.

RAAM 2019 was an unusual race for me. I feel I made a rare mistake in judgement when I got the preparation wrong. But those were the choices I made and I have to take responsibility for them. I also allowed myself to become very mentally stressed, reaching fever pitch on the mountain at La Veta. I'm usually calm and precise in my thinking during a race, but this time I was so wound up I found it difficult to make rational decisions.

My Hopecam buddy Len Forkas invited the whole team to come to his place in Virginia to kick back for a few days and enjoy the summer weather. It was a great opportunity to spend time with the guys and reflect on what RAAM has done for me. I've learned a huge amount about myself and made a lot of friends along the way. If I wanted to go and race in the States tomorrow, I know I could just turn up at the airport with my passport and there would be people to help me on the other side. Goodness knows, I was a late starter at RAAM, but I've had three cracks at it now and I still feel there is some unfinished business. And I've always said that unfinished business is one of the most powerful motivators there is.

CHAPTER 18

Toast by Christmas

arrived back in Ireland to a splash of media coverage. The journos all seemed to be fixated on my age, and the word 'inspirational' was being bandied around. I was flattered and only too happy to do the interviews and have my photo taken on the bike with my tough-guy, Arizona desert stare. In the meantime, there was the little matter of the World Cup to be dealt with. I was lying second to Marko Baloh in the overall and topped the table in the over-60s category. I had one more event left to complete the list – a 12-hour race.

Marko had finished second overall in RAAM and it was a good second; his average speed was very high. He had been ahead of me in the World Cup standings since Sebring at the beginning of the year. My chances had been severely dented at Race Across America but I wasn't dead in the water just yet. It gets harder to find suitable races towards the end of the season. Marko was going to race in Borrego Springs in November. I decided to go for the Mid-Atlantic 12/24, at a little town called Washington on the Atlantic coast of North Carolina.

The race was relatively close to Marc Poland's home, so I was able to stay with him for a few days. I'd had a really cool time that year hanging out with Marc at Sebring, RAAM and now the Mid-Atlantic. I was still recovering from RAAM, so mountains were out of the question. The Mid-Atlantic was pancake flat, running through an area of seaside marshland. The start and finish were in a big car park in town and the route looped out through a point about ten miles away as the crow flies. They were small country roads with little or no traffic on them. Marc had raced there before so he knew all the ins and outs of the place. We also had local back-up in the form of Rich and Carol Beliveau. They were keen cyclists and friends of Marc and later became good friends of mine and Jill's. Rich did the crewing at the Mid-Atlantic while Carol rode the 12-hour and Marc rode the six-hour event.

I made my way to the start line through a maze of service cars and prepared myself mentally. I'm a great believer in the saying 'It's never over till it's over.' I've been caught out so many times when the battle was only part won, or lost. There was always the possibility that I could do something extraordinary, or that Marko would have a bad day and DNF. The final result was largely out of my hands. All I could do was the best ride I was capable of. And that's precisely what I did.

We set off in the pre-dawn darkness, a warm Carolinas night. The field was congested and very fast, 27–30mph or more. I decided to go with the flow and keep it high. When no one else appeared at the front to keep up the pace, I slipped through and filled the gap. Keeping it at that pace meant the weaker riders were falling away like flies. And that's how the race unfolded for the first 100 miles. It also meant I was able to help out Marc as he was riding in the six-hour race. The reality was that there were quite a few decent riders in the field but they all seemed to reach their limit around the 100-mile mark.

By mid-morning, as the sun rose in a clear blue sky, it was becoming seriously hot. I could feel the dehydration coming over me. There was no feed zone or handing out of bottles allowed on the course. Instead, the route swung through the start and finish area where the team service cars were parked up. It was a case of trying to remember where Marc's famous van was parked up – it still had my graphics from RAAM plastered all over it. If I needed to pick up two bottles of water from Rich it meant I had to come to a complete stop, losing momentum and precious seconds.

I was spinning around the same course for hours on end, so my mind wandered. I started to notice things: gas stations, advertising hoardings, fast food outlets, the streets of pretty clapboard houses with long lawns sweeping down to the street, each with its own Stars and Stripes hanging limply from the porch. One couple I noticed seemed to spend half the day taking it in turns to cut the lawn of their big house on a sit-on lawnmower. One mowed while the other sat in the shade watching the race pass by with a cool drink. By the end of the 12 hours there were dozens of people out on their lawns cheering on the cyclists.

Out on the course, with about a hundred miles in the bag, I noticed that there was still one cyclist hanging on my tail who refused to be shaken off. Then I saw my chance. Up ahead was a guy on a recumbent, one of those bikes where the rider reclines on a seat. They're not so popular in Europe – we tend to think they look a bit silly. The UCI has banned them from professional competition. But they go like the clappers, much faster than a conventional bike. I nearly bust a gut bridging over to the recumbent, realising part way that the rider was Larry Oslund. He's one of the world's top recumbent riders. I hadn't recognised him lying on his back with his legs in the air. Once I'd caught up and started drafting behind him, I was suddenly a couple of miles an hour faster than I would have been if I'd been travelling at my own pace. I should point out that this was a race where drafting was legal. It can be considered bad form, though, and Larry eventually decided I'd overstayed my welcome and waved his elbow to call on me to come through and do some of the work.

I managed to get a lap or so with Larry before he punctured. It was a pity because the 12-hour was always about racking up more distance covered. Never mind, those valuable minutes in the wake of the recumbent had left me in a very solid position at the front of the race. From then on it was only a matter of keeping going for the next 150 miles. Dead easy, says you.

So I rolled home in first place and we had a very pleasant evening in Washington. The locals were genuinely interested that someone should have come from Ireland to take part in their race. There was a big crowd for the prize presentation and I did one of my longest ever podium interviews, about my days as a professional and how I became involved with ultra. We set off to enjoy some of Rich and Carol's fine hospitality in their home by the sea. I was fascinated by their lifestyle. They tend to a superyacht for an extremely wealthy client. When the yacht's needed they'll sail it down to the Caribbean and the owner and his guests arrive by helicopter.

It was in the van on the way back to Rich and Carol's house that I discovered how well I'd done in the race. I had to use two GPS dashboards on the bike because the batteries are only good for nine hours. But when I matched up the data I realised that it was the fastest 12 hours I had ever ridden. I managed 253 miles. You could say it was the ride of my life. I had taken the fight back to Marko and all that remained now was to see how he fared at Borrego Springs.

I don't usually suffer from disturbed sleep, but the night of the Borrego Springs race I kept nipping out of bed like an elderly gent with suspect waterworks. I had the laptop set up on the kitchen table in Limavady. While the Irish countryside slept around me, I kept a beady eye on the internet feed. I wasn't wishing Marko bad luck or anything. That's not what it was about. There was still a slim possibility that I could be eating breakfast as an overall World Cup winner. I lived in hope that something, anything, could happen. It didn't. Marko won the race. I slipped back between the sheets thinking Jill was asleep. 'Never mind,' she whispered.

I was comfortable with the result. Going to the Mid-Atlantic and giving it everything I had was a long shot, but I would never have forgiven myself if I hadn't given my all. Marko's a good friend and he deserved the overall title. The difference between us came down to about one mph overall. A few weeks later, a delayed Christmas present arrived from the States. It was a heavy package containing yet another plaque, this one declaring me the 60–69 age group World Cup winner.

That year, 2019, had been a great year for me. I rode my fastest ever 12-hour and 24-hour races. I won the category at RAAM and finished second in the world championships. Not bad for an old lad of 60. Aside from the performances, it was the relationships that were fostered that made it a special year. I'm thinking of the friendships with the likes of Rich and Carol, and the time we spent with Marc Poland and the community at High Cove in the beautiful Blue Ridge.

It's hard to remember now that there was ever a normal chunk of 2020; those first few weeks of the year before the entire world fell off the edge of a Covid cliff. We all had our plans. Some had already booked holidays of a lifetime. Others were feeling on edge about important exams coming in the summer. I had one plan – to pick up precisely where I left off the year before and give Marko a serious run for his money. As soon as he finished at Borrego Springs I started training for Sebring. I can't tell you how many hours I spent working on every last detail of my time-trial bike, from the aerodynamics to the tyre pressures. I've never had a bike prepared to that level ahead of a race.

I was busting to get going on the new season, and top of the list was to break the 500-mile barrier in Florida. The plan for the rest of the year's World Cup was to go back to Italy for the 500-miler, to do the Race Around Ireland for the 1,000-plus and to do either Borrego Springs or the Mid-Atlantic for the 12-hour. There was just enough room to shoehorn in a record attempt at the end of the season. We were going to be busy. If I couldn't beat Marko on the road, I would have to find a strategy to outsmart him.

Everything was ticked off on the list for Sebring. What could possibly go wrong? We were due to arrive at Florida with plenty of time to spare and had booked a classy Airbnb close to the track. The idea was that Marc would drive down from North Carolina and we would be helped out by Jill's nephew and his girlfriend, who had travelled from Chicago. Then fate threw a wobbly. Jill got sick just before we left home and became progressively worse with a raging sore throat and a temperature. She made it to Florida only to spend four or five days on her back in the bedroom. She barred me from going into the room in case I caught the dreaded whatever-it-was. I didn't go in at first but I felt it was important for me to help her recuperate. The inevitable happened. When I woke up the day before the race, my throat was burning and my temperature was tearing up and down. I told Marc, but didn't say anything to Jill. We decided I would try and race anyway, desperately hoping that my adrenaline would kick in once I reached the start line.

I started the race and rode the initial 50 miles out and back at full race pace. I was racing on pure belief and tried to put my fever and sore throat out of my mind as best I could, but my body just couldn't sustain the effort.

I had to stop. I sat with my head in my hands and said to Marc: 'This twenty-four hours is not going to happen. My body's in bits.' We agreed that he should go and speak to the race organisers and see if they would allow me to switch to the 12-hour race. At least I would have a 12-hour under my belt and I could look for a 24-hour race later in the year. I didn't hold out much hope with the organisers, so I was surprised when Marc reappeared with the go-ahead. It was very decent of them as they were under no obligation to let me swap. They told Marc to give them some time to exchange the timing chips, and I then was lined up for one of the most miserable experiences of my cycling career.

I managed 237 miles in the 12 hours, well down on the 253 I'd managed at the Mid-Atlantic but I had a temperature of 103 and it wasn't like I was swinging the lead. When I stumbled off the bike at the end, they could have zipped me into a body bag and had done with it.

Shortly after returning home, Jill and I upped sticks and moved to her mum's house near Strabane in County Tyrone. It's called Fox Lodge and has beautiful gardens that her dad planted. We were due to start building our own house there in the spring. 'A small cottage for small people,' Jill calls it. I was out on the roads as usual but struggling to regain my fitness after whatever that virus was that both Jill and I got. My recovery wasn't helped by the usual crappy Irish weather. In early March, we agreed that I should go to Majorca for a couple of weeks to build my fitness in the sunshine and on the high mountain passes. Flights were booked and I arranged a house to stay in. It was a bit of a hermit's existence: up early and out on the roads for seven or eight hours every day. I had little contact with the outside world apart from the corner shop and my daily espresso from the village café. The night before I was due to come home, Jill rang and warned me not to miss my flight and that I should wear a face covering. I was up at 5 a.m. and down to Palma airport. It took the best part of the day to get home via Gatwick. The next day, easyJet closed the whole thing down.

At that point the dominoes started to fall. First it was the Race Across Italy that was axed; then the Race Around Ireland bit the dust a couple of days later. Within two weeks we had no season. My entire plans for 2020 were torn up and tossed aside. Jill and I had serious financial concerns about the future. It was important to us to deliver value to the sponsors who had shown so much faith in us. We came up with an innovative plan with our title sponsor, White's Oats. Jill provided video content on performance nutrition and I came up with basic bike knowledge for kids. White's then popped it on their TV channel. It was the first time we'd done something like this. I'm no David Attenborough but I thought I did okay.

Meanwhile, with the roads during lockdown as empty as the racing calendar, I was able to get in huge training days of seven, eight, even nine hours. Even though we were right on the border near Strabane I wasn't allowed across the bridge in the town to train in Donegal. Instead, I developed a 165-mile loop through the Sperrin Mountains down as far as Lough Neagh, then up along the River Bann to the north coast and back home via Derry. I was fit for anything, but there was nothing to be fit for. Then Jill came up with an idea. There would be no world championship in 2020, so why not set up a head-to-head ultra-race in Ireland with

Marko? It would be a real Clash of the Titans. I had my doubts. Why would Marko want to race in my backyard?

When we contacted him, Marko said he was in a similar position to me as a sponsored rider with next to no races. He had some initial doubts but, with the sponsors on board, the route was chosen and the flights were booked. Marko and his wife, Irma, were going to stay with us and enjoy some County Tyrone hospitality. Then Marko went to a 24-hour race in Zürich and crashed and broke his collarbone. Plan A for saving the season was in the bin.

This was immensely frustrating. Jill and I were back to the edge of a financial abyss. Our options were rapidly diminishing so we decided to try to get an Ireland north–south–north record attempt sanctioned by WUCA. There's a huge amount of paperwork involved in record-breaking and I sent the application in, more in hope than expectation. The last time I did the end-to-end record was in 2017. Back then, it seemed crazy to be doing it in November, but here we were, proposing to do it again in the middle of a worldwide pandemic. Luckily, the Covid restrictions had eased off a bit, so it was just possible. All I needed was a window of 48 hours.

I think we all remember the beautiful weather in the first period of lockdown. But it turned dramatically in the first few days of July. That's how I came to be sitting on my bike in the familiar surroundings of the Malin Head car park on the third of July in a torrential downpour. I had woken up that morning to the sound of the rain beating against the bedroom window, but there was no going back; we had to show up. We needed to pull something out of the bag.

My aim was to break the 48-hour barrier. My own world record from 2017 stood at 48 hours 38 minutes. How I would ever manage it in this weather was highly debatable. The roads through Derry City were flooded and I hit a massive pothole where the road was broken under the water. It tore the side out of an expensive slick tyre. I was riding a new type of bike, a Spiegel Diablo, the most comfortable ultra bike I'd ever ridden and very fast. I'd chosen the slicks to go with a set of high-performance five-spoke carbon wheels, but they were the wrong sort of tyres for this weather – they're made from cotton or silk with no thread pattern for speed, but the trade-off is no grip. I could feel them slipping and sliding on the bends.

Under the circumstances I should have been feeling stressed to hell, but somewhere within the first hundred miles I was overcome by this incredible feeling of pure mental clarity. The downpour continued but I had such an easy feeling and I knew that this was going to be a good ride. I've had that feeling before, three or four times in my career. The day we got the medal at the Commonwealth Games half a lifetime ago was one of them. Some people might call it Zen. I call it a float day. And that's when I decided to take as few stops as possible. Just keep it in the groove. Don't lose this feeling.

What made this ride unique was the sheer number of people who appeared by the roadside cheering me on. I've never seen the like of it, even in my mainstream cycling days. There was a big crowd at Malin to see me off, and then the whole way down the island and back up, people appeared in their gardens or at the side of the road. For the first time, we were using a live GPS tracker that allowed people at home to follow my progress along the road. Live streaming from inside the crew car brought people right into the heart of the action. They could join in the conversation and send me encouraging messages. Lockdown meant that people were stuck in the house with nothing to do and kids to entertain. This crazy dude riding 735 miles on his bike got people out of the house. There were whole families by the side of the road with posters made by the kids. It's the sort of thing that really lifts you.

I had a vicious headwind most of the way down to Mizen, but that Zen mental state and the fact that I didn't get off the bike meant I managed it in around 21.5 hours and beat the previous north–south record. What usually happens then is that you pick up a south-westerly tailwind on the way back but you're too exhausted to make it work for you. The wind coming out of Mizen had been swirling and shifting. It was a hell of a storm, with debris blowing everywhere.

Then it shifted direction to a sidewind, and with a little shelter from the hedges, I was making good time. Once I'd hit the border and on to Enniskillen it had turned into a steady tailwind. Those five-spoke wheels really make a difference when they get some help from behind. We passed the house where we're living now and Jill's mum was out on the road cheering us on. By that stage I was flying. It felt like I had just started out on the ride and in no time I was back at the island's most northerly point with its high view across the North Atlantic. My overall time for the Malin–Mizen–Malin was 44 hours and 15 minutes. I had smashed my world record by over four hours.

We'd pulled a magnificent rabbit out of the hat but there was still a ton of work to be done if we were to save the season.

We've been running our own Race Joe Barr endurance series since I won the 500-mile world championship in 2017. It allows Irish riders to make the step up from riding long sportives to doing proper ultra distances. To that end we now have 200-, 330- and 500-mile versions. The 500 is recognised as a world championship race and it's a RAAM qualifier. It's been growing year on year on year and was due to be held in May 2020. The event looked to be dead in the water, but with a massive effort we managed to find a window between lockdowns and put on a cut-down version in late September. The team did a great job and it worked better than I could have imagined.

Still marooned on the island of Ireland, it turned out Team Joe Barr had one more trick up our sleeves. The west–east–west record runs from Slea Head in the Dingle Peninsula to Wicklow Head lighthouse in the east and back. They are the most westerly and easterly points in the 26 counties. The road from Slea Head is stunningly beautiful; then it's a long diagonal sweep across the country. At the other side you turn up through a hole in the hedge, along a bumpy concrete road, and pose for a photo at the gate next to the lighthouse. I set off on World Porridge Day, 10 October, and set a new world record, completing the 778km in 28 hours and 24 minutes. The second wave of Covid was coming and we had really cut it fine. The hotel we stayed in the night before the ride had closed when we returned. We stayed one more night in another heavily sanitised and socially distanced hotel in Tralee before hitting the road north. And that was the west–east–west. I currently hold the world records for riding up, down, sideways and around Ireland.

It was a struggle, 2020, but it was more than just making the best of a bad job. In fact, I would regard it as a success. It underlined the resilience Jill and I brought to all our work. There were many challenges: the race calendar falling apart; the huge effort put into the Marko head-to-head. Even the motivational speaking I do for companies dried up. I managed to keep focused on the training while Jill was brainstorming ideas with the sponsors and doing some really creative work. It was exhausting and by the time we got to Christmas we were toast.

I sometimes wonder what my old geography teacher, Mr

Dowds, would have thought of my ultra-cycling career. Would he have been impressed by my intimate knowledge of the mountains and deserts of North America, or would he still regard cycling as a complete waste of time? My life has been turned around by the sport. In 2019, I was elected onto the board of the world governing body. It's been a real eye-opener. I've been able to work with WUCA on some really interesting projects and I have my own pet interests. I want to see the World Cup regulations changed to suit a wider range of riders. I also want to see our sport opened up to younger competitors. One of the reasons why the ultra-cycling scene has been dominated by older athletes is the sheer amount of money required to compete in the big races. If there was a mechanism that would allow 23- or 24-year-olds to make their mark, that would be a big plus.

Epilogue

Pushbikes have been my constant companion on a lifetime of adventure – from the little fat tyres on the Sunbeam in my granny's garden to the ultra-lightweight carbon fibre racing machine that took me hurtling down a sand-blown mountainside in the Chihuahuan Desert. I was asked recently what I would have done with my life if I hadn't been a cyclist. I was stumped. There was simply no answer. For all that I've changed as a person, those hundreds of bikes I've ridden have remained essentially the same – two triangles with a wheel at either end. At heart I'm a practical person; there's nothing I enjoy more than an afternoon in the kitchen taking a bike apart and rebuilding it. And by teatime I can guarantee that the bike will be running more sweetly than a sewing machine.

As a sportsman, I prefer to look ahead in life. What does the upcoming season promise, and the season after that? Forging ahead has always been my coping mechanism, and there have been casualties along the way as a result. Looking back is a more difficult thing. There were choices I made, for good or ill. There were opportunities that fell in my lap and some kicks in the teeth along the way. Those heavy blows started early when my dad beat me with his fists, and told me I was worthless and would come to nothing. I've never really recovered from that lack of a father figure and I've spent a lot of my life trying to make up for it. At times I retreated into that dark, depressive rabbit hole but mostly I've been able to turn the scorn to my advantage. If anyone doubts my ability, I can lift my chin and say: 'Just watch me.'

What strikes me most clearly, looking back, is the role other people have played in making me what I am today. I've been inspired, advised, rescued and loved, maybe more than I've deserved. It makes me shudder to think where I would be today without my mum and Jill, the two women who have understood and forgiven me all my faults. The other day we were having a quiet moment and I said to Jill, 'You know, Jill, you're my compass. You're my compass on the road and my compass in life.' She turned her head to me and smiled.

As for Reuben and Ross, they've taught me more than they'll ever know and made me a better person. Those sleepless nights on the floor of the children's hospital marked me for life. They tested me to breaking point but they ultimately introduced me to the sport that made sense of my life. I'm looking forward to spending time with those two fine young men as they grow.

One thing's for sure: this story is far from over. Jill says it's not in me to stop racing. 'It's in your head – it's in every fibre of your being,' she said recently. And she was right. In twenty years' time, when you see a man in his 80s in pristine white Lycra powering his way up Mamore Gap, be sure to give me a wave.